SOCIAL ACCOUNTING AND ECONOMIC MODELLING FOR DEVELOPING COUNTRIES

To Flora Abdel Nabi Ani
Whose contributions have not gone unnoticed

Social Accounting and Economic Modelling for Developing Countries

Analysis, policy and planning applications

S. I. COHEN

Faculty of Economics, Erasmus University, Rotterdam

Routledge
Taylor & Francis Group

LONDON AND NEW YORK

First published 2002 by Ashgate Publishing

Reissued 2018 by Routledge
2 Park Square, Milton Park, Abingdon, Oxon OX14 4RN
711 Third Avenue, New York, NY 10017, USA

Routledge is an imprint of the Taylor & Francis Group, an informa business

Publisher's Note
The publisher has gone to great lengths to ensure the quality of this reprint but points out that some imperfections in the original copies may be apparent.

Disclaimer
The publisher has made every effort to trace copyright holders and welcomes correspondence from those they have been unable to contact.

A Library of Congress record exists under LC control number: 2002101566

ISBN 13: 978-1-138-71973-6 (hbk)
ISBN 13: 978-1-138-71970-5 (pbk)
ISBN 13: 978-1-315-19531-5 (ebk)

Contents

Preface

In the past two decades, there has been a noticeable shift of interest from the basic input-output table to the social accounting matrix (SAM), as evident from the increased momentum in the design, construction and use of social accounting matrices in developing countries.

There are several causes behind this shift. In particular, policy makers, economists and statisticians turned attention to broader statistical frameworks which relate economic structures, distribution aspects, social adjustment, and the like to the economic growth process. Besides, the efforts to integrate the 'social' with the 'economic' were greatly enhanced by the appearance in the eighties of the social accounting matrix, SAM, as a framework for organising multi-dimensional data of the economy. The SAM simultaneously integrated disaggregated data on production, income and expenditure, thereby allowing a systematic recording of diversified economic transactions for the study of growth and its distribution in a particular country.

Many SAM applications for developing countries were conducted at government agencies and academic institutes with the objective of advising governments on development policy. While some economists working on, or using, SAMs have regularly published their thoughts and findings in economic journals or in conference proceedings, as yet there has been practically no attempt to treat SAMs and their uses comprehensively in research monographs or supplementary textbooks.

It is not surprising that there is a felt need by policy makers, policy advisers, academia and students for a volume that introduces and consolidates research insights and results in the areas of social accounting matrices and related economic. This volume is intended to meet this need. The book draws on published and unpublished contributions by the author. Although several chapters of the book are reworkings of previously published articles, we have seen to it that appropriate revisions and additions are incorporated. The material has been effectively reorganised so as to fit in a consistent and gradually extendable approach towards applying social accounting methods and models in the development context.

The result is a volume of eight chapters reporting on applications in some 20 developing countries. We cover a wide range of topics starting from the simple and proceeding to the more complex applications. The topics include the construction and structural analysis of the SAM, study of SAM multipliers of growth and distribution, decompositions of multiplier effects, cross-country and inter-temporal comparative analysis of changing economic structures, SAM-corresponding policy models, SAM-based computable general equilibrium models and SAM implications for convergence tendencies.

In general, the eight chapters fall in two parts. The first part consists of chapters 1 to 4; these chapters deal with cross-country and inter-temporal applications and refinements of the SAM as a self-contained model of the economy. The focus here is on SAM multipliers and their decomposition. The applications relate to ten developing countries, with more elaborate treatments for some of them. The second part consists of chapters 5 to 8; these chapters go beyond the accounts and variables of the SAM and enter into economic modelling of development issues. These chapters look at the SAM as a modular framework and a database, which can be flexibly used in modelling the economy.

In chapter 1 the emphasis will be on introducing the SAM and elaborating on its analytical use in addressing growth and equity issues in the context of economic development. Chapter 1 makes use of one of the first SAMs constructed and published namely that for Colombia 1970.

Handling the problem of evaluating different structural patterns and performances among different countries is greatly simplified by resorting to comparable social accounting matrices. Comparative analysis of SAM multipliers, and their decomposition, allow also for the investigation of economic mechanisms behind superior performances, and can direct attention to the mechanisms that need to be strengthened to push the economy closer to its potential. These analytical applications will be the main concern of chapters 2, 3 and 4.

The SAM presents a modular structure of the economy, which can be flexibly modelled to address important aspects of fixing consistent planning targets and the monitoring of performance towards achieving these targets. A case study in this area for Pakistan will be the subject of chapter 5.

Computable general equilibrium (CGE) modelling and calibration have been facilitated by the availability of consistently constructed social accounting matrices. In chapter 6, the SAM of Indonesia is employed as a database to quantify a CGE model for the country, and demonstrate the impact of supply impulses to economic growth and income distribution. The static CGE model is extended further to a dynamic supply of labour and capital over more time periods, and the policy analysis repeated.

Elements of social accounting can be combined with elements of demographic accounting to treat more aspects of the relationship between economic growth and social welfare. Examples of such aspects are policy making with regard to income allotment by population groups, welfare consequences for vulnerable groups of adjustment policies, and the relative efficiency of direct transfers versus in-kind transfers. Chapter 7 reflects on the modelling use of SAMs, in combination with other modelling tools, in a broader framework for the modelling and analysis of social-economic development policies.

Investigation of whether the gap in the income per capita between rich and poor countries is widening or diminishing has relied mainly on supply side models of economic growth, appropriately adapted to include elements of endogenous growth. SAM models, which represent the demand side models of economic growth, predict higher economic growth at lower levels of income per capita, and therefore indicate the presence of a convergence tendency. Chapter 8 reflects on the main causes behind the convergence tendencies that characterise SAM results for 16 poor and rich countries.

It was only a matter of some time lag before SAM applications were extended to industrial economies. In the context of a transition from a planning-oriented economy towards a more market-oriented economy to which the industrial economies of Eastern Europe are subjected, SAM models are extremely useful in identifying the content and direction of, and reaction to, foundational changes. SAM models have been also successfully applied to the analysis of issues of growth and development in individual countries in Western European. Past and current works by the author on SAM analysis for industrial economies in Eastern and Western Europe are consolidated in an accompanying volume to the current volume.

Words of thanks and appreciation are due to many persons who have closely worked with me in various contexts at obtaining the results in the current volume. I wish to mention G. Abbink, M.C. Braber, I. Havinga, T. Jellema, A. Jollink, B. Kuijpers, E. Salamons, M. de Zeeuw, and last but not least S.N.H. Naqvi, W. Kim, M. Sudarsono, K.A. Krishnamurti, A. Sarmiento and W. Obungo. Typing and retyping have gone through many hands, and specially those of Jayne van der Padt, Jane Dolgova, Els van Hemert and Lydia Terheijden.

As was stated above, I have drawn in part on some of my published articles in journals and bundles. Appreciation goes to the following journals for the granted permission to employ the material: Industry and Development, International Economic Journal, Pakistan Development Review, Journal of Policy Modelling, and Quantitative Methods. The same appreciation applies with respect to parts of chapters 2 and 7 that have drawn on own contributions in bundles published by Oxford University Press.

Chapter 1

Social Accounting
for Development Analysis

1. Introduction

Until two or three decades ago, most economic development analysts and
practitioners interpreted socio-economic progress and development solely
as a GNP growth process. A superficial view, which was especially
prevalent, was that heavy investment, export promotion and the balancing
of inputs and outputs are necessary and sufficient to induce such economic
growth. Accordingly, development policies, planning methods, and
statistical frameworks at the time were developed within that narrow
perspective.

To the surprise of many observers, economic performance in a large
number of developing countries have shown that, in spite of reasonable
growth rates achieved in the sixties and seventies, income inequality,
disguised unemployment, poverty and conflict continued to be major
obstacles to sustainable economic growth and social welfare. Such
information and insights stimulated economists and statisticians in the past
two decades to work with broader statistical frameworks which relate
economic structures, distribution aspects, social adjustment, and the like to
the economic growth process.

The efforts to integrate the 'social' with the 'economic' were greatly
enhanced by the appearance in the eighties of the social accounting matrix,
SAM, as a framework for organising multi-dimensional data of the
economy. The SAM simultaneously integrated disaggregated data on
production, income and expenditure, thereby allowing a systematic
recording of diversified economic transactions for the study of growth and
its distribution in a particular country.

Since the mid-seventies, there has been a significant shift of interest
from the basic input-output table to the social accounting matrix (SAM), as
evident from the increased momentum in the design, construction and use
of social accounting matrices in developing countries, see for example,
Cohen et al. (1984), and Pyatt and Round (1985). The argument in favour
of working with the SAM, or as some like to call it an extended

input-output model, is the increasingly prevalent requirement by policy-makers and the larger public in developing and developed countries alike, to appraise development in terms of distribution, in addition to production objectives.

The idea of a social accounting matrix, SAM, can be traced back to Quesnay's Tableau Economique in 1758. The idea was revived only 200 years later. The term social accounting was coined by Hicks in 1942, and the formalisation of the SAM was the work of Stone in 1947. It was associates of Stone, working in the context of developing countries, who presented the first comprehensive publication of a SAM, cf. Pyatt and Roe (1977), where Sri Lanka was taken as a case study.

The SAM itself is nothing more or less than the transformation of the circular flow of the national economy into a matrix of transactions between the various agents, as will be shown in figure 1.1 and tables 1.1 and 1.2 in the next section. The construction of the SAM falls into two phases. In a first phase, the aggregate SAM is set up entirely from published data of the national accounts, corresponding with the circular flow; so that the SAM is no more than a presentation of available national statistics in a matrix form. In a second phase, the disaggregation of the SAM takes place depending on the purpose of the analysis and on available data sources.

SAMs are compiled according to the same accounting principles as input-output tables, each transaction being recorded twice so that any ingoing in one account must be balanced by an outgoing of another account. However, the SAM contains a complete list of transactions describing income, expenditure and production flows among sectors, factors of production and groups of households. These transactions are usually grouped into several sets of accounts belonging to various economic agents, as will be indicated below.

We review in this introductory chapter several uses of the SAM as implemented in this and later chapters. The social accounting matrix is primarily seen as that of a helpful tool in (1) the setting-up of statistical accounts, (2) the initialisation of corresponding models, (3) the conduct of diagnostic studies, and (4) the analysis of relationships between growth and distribution and the formulation of related policies. First, the advantage of forcing national statistics into a social accounting framework is that the statistician can discover inconsistencies and gaps that went unnoticed before. Second, for the purpose of building a model and initialising its base values, the discipline of building an explicit SAM assures that the initial values of the variables in the modelled system are internally consistent. Third, once a SAM is available it can be used to give a quantitative diagnosis of the structure of the whole economy, which is hardly feasible in the conventional presentation of national statistics. These three uses are highlighted throughout the book. There are other more analytical uses of the SAM, which will be the specific concern of each chapter in this book. Fourth, by appropriate manipulations, the matrix can be rearranged so as to give sets of endogenous and exogenous variables, and a coefficient matrix that can be inverted and subjected to a useful multiplier analysis. Especially in the context of developing countries, the SAM has demonstrated its ability to analyse the underlying growth and equity properties of these economies.

In chapter 1 the emphasis will be on introducing the SAM and elaborating on its analytical use in addressing growth and equity issues in the context of economic development.

With the availability of SAMs for different countries and for more years, fruitful cross-country and inter-temporal comparisons have been made on the structure and performance of economic systems. Such comparisons will be shown also to be helpful in investigating the economic mechanisms behind superior and inferior performances, and in directing attention to mechanisms that need to be strengthened to push the economy closer to its potential. These analytical and policy applications will be the main concern of chapters 2, 3 and 4.

The SAM presents a modular structure of the economy, which can be flexibly modelled to address important aspects of fixing consistent planning targets and the monitoring of performance towards achieving these targets. A case study in this area for Pakistan will be the subject of chapter 5.

Computable general equilibrium modelling (CGE) and calibration has been facilitated by the availability of consistently constructed social accounting matrices. The SAM of Indonesia will be employed as a database to quantify a CGE model for the country, and demonstrate the impact of supply impulses to economic growth and income distribution; in chapter 6.

Elements of social accounting can be combined with elements of demographic accounting to treat more aspects of the relationship between economic growth and social welfare in a broader framework. Such aspects include policy making with regard to income allotment by population groups, welfare consequences for vulnerable groups of adjustment policies, and the relative efficiency of direct transfers versus in kind transfers. Chapter 7 reflects on the use of SAMs, in combination with other modelling tools, in this broader framework.

Investigation of whether the gap in the income per capita between rich and poor countries is widening or diminishing has relied mainly on supply side models of economic growth, appropriately adapted to include elements of endogenous growth. SAM models, which represent the demand side models of economic growth, predict higher economic growth at lower levels of income per capita, and therefore indicate the presence of a convergence tendency. Chapter 8 reflects on the main causes behind the convergence tendencies, which characterise SAM results for 16 poor and rich countries.

The purpose of the current chapter will be to introduce the main features of the SAM and reflect on several of its uses, specially the use of the SAM in its capacity as a solid framework for gaining insight into development policy on issues of growth and distribution. For purposes of exposition, we shall make use of a case study of Colombia. First, the SAM for Colombia is introduced. Second, the matrix is transformed into a model, which generates multipliers that can be used as an aid, though limited, in predicting the course of the economy. Third, multipliers and their decomposition into transfer, open-, and closed-loop effects are analysed. Fourth, results of the SAM are compared with those of the input-output.

2. The Construction of a SAM

As was stated above, the SAM itself is nothing more or less than the transformation of the circular flow of figure 1.1 into a matrix of transactions between the various agents, as in tables 1.1 and 1.2, which will be shortly reviewed. In the lower bound of figure 1.1, households supply labour and capital to firms who are organizers of production activities; households are paid back in return for the use of their labour and capital factors. In the upper bound, households spend their incomes on products that are delivered by the firms/activities. In the centre there is the government, which is involved in transfers to and from households and firms/activities. Furthermore, there are the economic relations between the country and the rest of the world.

Social accounting matrices are compiled according to the same accounting principles used for input-output tables; each transaction is recorded twice so that any inflow to one account must be balanced by an outflow of another account. SAMs contain four types of accounts:

- Wants accounts; indexed as 1.
- Factors of production accounts; indexed as 2.
- Institutions accounts; indexed as 3. A distinction is made between current and capital transactions. Current transactions are disaggregated by whether they belong to households, firms, and government. Capital transactions are aggregated in one national capital account.

- Activities accounts, and rest of the world accounts, indexed as 4.

The content of the SAM may be introduced further by means of table 1.1. The first set of accounts represents the wants account. It is not obligatory to include these accounts in the SAM, but by incorporating the wants accounts, we increase focus on a whole range of goods and services which are representative of levels of well being. These will usually include expenditure on food, housing, clothing, health, education, transport and other goods and services. It is informative to know, for instance, how much each specific household group spends on food and how this expenditure flows to agriculture and the non-agricultural sectors.

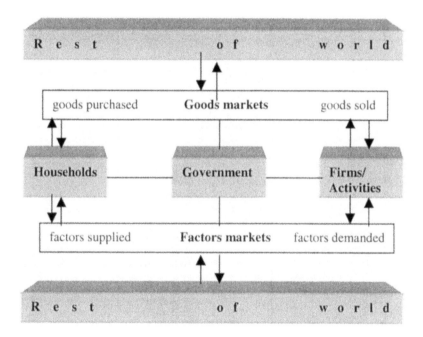

Figure 1.1. Circular Flow

The factors of production accounts are meant to show how the value added generated in the various production activities are allocated over the production factors, and subsequently how these factor incomes are distributed to the current institutions. The SAMs constructed here make a distinction between the two major factors of production, namely labour and capital; either may be disaggregated further.

Table 1.1. Entries in the Aggregate SAM

	(1) Wants	(2) Factors	(3) Institutions				(4) Activities		Totals
			Households	Firms	Government	Capital	Production sectors	Rest of world	
Wants			Household spending						Wants expenditure
Factors							Domestic value added	Foreign factor payments	Factors income
Institutions									
Households					Public transfer to households			Transfers	Households income
Firms					Public debt servicing				
Government		Public enterprise profit	Households direct taxes	Firms direct taxes			Indirect taxes	Transfers	Government income
National capital			Household saving	Firm saving	Public saving		Depreciation	Deficit balance of payment	Gross capital formation
Activities									
Production sectors	Private consumption				Public consumption	Investment goods	Intermediate goods	Exports	Gross production
Rest of World			Transfers		Transfers		Imports		Outgoings
Totals	Wants receipts	Factors income	Households income	Firms income	Public income	Gross capital formation	Gross production	Receipt Rest of world	Grand total

The institutions current accounts are split up into accounts for households, firms and government. For any institution, by adding different sources of incomes in the rows, we find the total incomings of that institution. In the columns we see how the institutions pay out some of their incomings as direct taxes and transfer payments, spend on consumer goods, and transfer their savings to the combined national capital account.

The capital transfers between the separate institutions - flow of funds - are netted and can therefore be left out from the SAM. It follows that domestic and foreign savings should be spent on capital goods. As a result, the national capital account shows that total savings equal total investment.

The activities accounts show rowwise the money receipts of the producing sectors from the sale of private and public consumption goods, investment goods, intermediate goods and exports. Columnwise, the sales revenue of the producing sectors go in part as value added to factors of production, indirect taxes, depreciation costs, and purchase of intermediate goods and imports.

Finally, in the rest of the world account, imports and exports are matched with incoming and outgoing foreign transfers.

Quantification of table 1.1 for Colombia for 1970 gives the results we see in table 1.2. The account aggregates and their subdivisions in table 1.2 are those found in the Colombia national accounts statistics, as published by the Banco de la Republica (BR). To emphasise the correspondence between tables 1.2 and 1.1, note that the largest item in the inner matrix, 109688 mp, is that of the domestic value added. Most of this goes to the second largest item, 98830 mp, which is the households factor income. Most of this goes, in turn, into the third largest item, 9386 mp, which is private consumption. Note also that, in consistency with national accounts, the total of intermediate goods deliveries, row 4 by column 4, is not as yet specified in table 1.2. This is elaborated further in the disaggregation of the SAM as in table 1.3.

A crucial step in terms of expanding the analysis, is the disaggregation of the SAM into more sub-divisions of the four sets of aggregate accounts. In the case of Colombia, the aggregate accounts have been disaggregated to give a 31 x 31 matrix as in table 1.3. The first set of accounts is the wants accounts, consisting of rows 1 to 6. The second set of accounts subdivides the factors of production into the three categories of urban labour, rural labour and profits, rows 7 to 9. As regards the third set of accounts, a disaggregation of households into household groups is more useful if the groups to be distinguished benefit in distinctly different ways from growth of the economy, and spend differently.

There are several options for disaggregating the households; namely by the characteristics of the household head (age, occupation, socioeconomic status etc.), size or location of the household, income level of the household, or by income decile. In the context of Colombia, we shall opt for a distinction between urban and rural, and within each, opt for five socio-economic groups pertaining to different levels of skills, financial and/or land assets.

Table 1.2.   An Aggregate SAM of Colombia 1970 (In million pesos (mp))

	(1) Wants	(2) Factors	(3) Institutions		(4) Activities		Totals
			Firms	Govern -ment	Prod sectors	Rest of world	
Wants							93863
Factors					109688	-3592	106096
Instit- utes							
House- holds		98830		2639		267	101736
Firms		5384		1284			6668
Govern -ment		1882	3249		10565	729	16425
Capital				7661	10109	5229	26418
Activity sectors			3419	9962	(a)	18516	122341
Rest of world	93863			59	20640		20699
Totals	93863	106096	6668	21605	151002	21149	494246

(a) total intermediate goods deliveries unspecified as yet in table 1.2. These are fully considered in table 1.3.

As a result, ten household groups are distinguished, in rows 10 to 19, each with its own income and expenditure patterns, in rows. The other accounts of institutions are those of government, firms and capital; these undergo no disaggregation. They occupy rows 20, 21, and 22, respectively. Finally, the fourth account distinguishes between eight production activities in rows 23 to 30, and the rest of the world in row 31.

If the rows and columns of table 1.3 are now examined, the following can be stated. Rows 1 through 6 contain one large block of entries on the intersections with columns 10 through 19, giving the breakdown of final consumer demand over the six wants categories and over the ten household groups. The outflows of the wants account, columns 1 through 6, are entered as inflows to the activities account, rows 23 through 30. This block of entries converts the broad categories of consumer goods into production activities making use of a product-sectoral classification. The next set of accounts is the factor account, showing, for instance, that the largest part of urban labour income originates in the services sectors, while the largest source of rural labour income is agriculture. Next are the institutional current and capital accounts. The receipts of the different institutions can be read directly from their respective rows, while the expenditures are found in their respective columns, and so forth. Finally, the SAM is completed with the inclusion of the activities accounts and the rest of world account.

In constructing table 1.3, three main types of additional data sources were used. The first type of data used is the input-output table based on the manufacturing survey, and published by Departamento Administrativo Nacional de Estadistica (DANE), for 1970. This gives slightly higher final demand and factor cost, about 2% more than the BR national accounts, although BR and DANE show differences in certain categories of final demand of between plus and minus 6%.

The second type of data used is the Household Income and Expenditure Survey of DANE, for 1970. This source overestimates total household income and expenditure by margins of 6% and 14%, respectively. The survey estimates have been downscaled accordingly. For details, see Cohen and Jellema (1987).

Finally, the submatrix that converts private consumption categories in the wants account to final demand categories in the activities account has been made consistent by applying the RAS method to a converter matrix obtained from DANE and the predetermined column, row totals of private consumption and final demand categories, respectively.

Table 1.3. Disaggregated SAM, Colombia 1970 (in million pesos (mp))

		Wants						Factors			Institutions							
		1	2	3	4	5	6	7	8	9	10	11	12	13	14	15	16	17
1	Food										1141	11280	3462	10680	4822	609	1037	3831
2	Non-food										779	6434	1624	5444	2240	230	473	1172
3	Housing										568	4838	954	3866	2456	97	171	354
4	Health										178	746	305	683	427	47	60	172
5	Education										223	1388	238	1122	367	30	65	90
6	Social services										711	2543	299	2170	751	173	169	226
	Factors																	
7	Urban wages																	
8	Rural wages																	
9	Gross profits																	
	Institutions																	
10	U proprietors							1392		2695								
11	U high skilled							13259		16626								
12	U low skilled							6866		16419								
13	U selfempl / fw							9305		6502								
14	U inactive							4529										
15	R latifundists								481	1179								
16	RuR mdm/sml owners								1209	958								
17	R farm workers								5527	4304								
18	R nonfarm hshlds								5486	822								
19	R inactive								1271									
20	Firms									15492								
21	Government									1882	491	1768	148	1317	642	262	64	64
22	National capital										20	1130	-109	583	857	211	137	-328
	Activities																	
23	Agriculture	13662	24	425			149											
24	Mining		4	68			54											
25	Processed coffee	854																
26	Industry	29886	12034	43	1064		1628											
27	Electricity/gas/water			13627			934											
28	Modern services		752			3632	3379											
29	Personal services		7740		1944		1208											
30	Public services	34	395	68	69	99.3	90.7											
31	Rest world										3	174		90	132		21	
		44436	20949	14231	3077	3731.3	7442.7	35351	13974	66879	4114	30301	6921	25955	12694	1659	2197	5581

Key: U = Urban, R = Rural, R mdm/smlfmow = Rural medium and small farm owners

Table 1.3. Continued

Wants	Households		Firms	Government	Capital	Activities								Rest of world	Total
	18	19	20	21	22	23	24	25	26	27	28	29	30	31	
1 Food	6016	1557													44434
2 Non-food	2156	396													20947
3 Housing	731	199													14231
4 Health	379	84													3078
5 Education	186	25													3731
6 Social services	300	102													7442
Factors															
7 Urban wages						2730	442	128	7718	577	12266	4593	6897		35352
8 Rural wages						7093	297	29	1722	58	2466	923	1386		13974
9 Gross profits						23234	2144	513	10812	755	28444	4571			66898
Institutions															
10 U proprietors				15										11	4113
11 U high skilled				335										80	30300
12 U low skilled				35										18	6920
13 U selfempl / fw				162										68	25954
14 U inactive				1630										33	12694
15 R latifundists				25										4	1689
16 RuR mdm/sml owners				22										6	2195
17 R farm workers				38										15	5579
18 R nonfarm hshlds				70										26	9887
19 R inactive				307										6	2407
20 Firms				1284		-104	-342	3072	6647	-12	1177	113	13		16776
21 Government	274	148	3249	10565											32169
22 National capital	-155	-103	13528	7661										5229	28660
Activities															
23 Agriculture					2636	725	23	5909	15042	4	413	701	250	2322	42281
24 Mining					56	18	44	3	1826	36	174	5	6	1393	3686
25 Processed coffee								549				225	47	9194	10869
26 Industry					13250	4067	191	81	24165	454	9202	3664	1595	2657	103980
27 Electricity/gas/water					6	7	106	5	576	44	221	85	56		204
28 Modern services					12633	3573	726	576	18372	112	12214	233	668	2932	69797
29 Personal services					79	6	2	1	91	10	417	79	162	18	15291
30 Public services				9962		23	11	3	158	4	89	11	10		11123
31 Rest world	32			59		910	43		16851		2714	87	33		21150
	9919	2408	16777	32170	28660	42282	3687	10869	103980	2042	69797	15290	11123	24012	667811

3. Transforming the SAM into a Model

Analytically, input-output tables and SAM tables are treated in very similar ways. Particularly when analysing changing economic structures and performances, a main focus in this study, the SAM is an appropriate framework for conducting such an analysis in ways similar to the analysis of input-output tables. In input-output analysis, an endogenous vector of sectoral production, q, can be predicted from a matrix of input-output coefficients, L, and a vector of exogenous final demand, f, as in equation (1.1).

$$q = Lq + f = (I - L)^{-1} f \tag{1.1}$$

The SAM can be used similarly. In order to transform the social accounting matrix into a predictive model along the above lines, several steps must be performed.

First, the SAM accounts need to be subdivided into exogenous and endogenous components denoted by x and y, respectively, and regrouped accordingly, so that the exogenous accounts fall to the right and bottom of the endogenous accounts.

Following an established convention, which coincides with the focus of this chapter, the endogenous accounts specified as such are three; they are numbered as 21, 22 and 31. These belong to government, national capital and rest of the world. All three accounts can be seen to be relatively controllable, and as external to the otherwise endogenous market processes in the economy.

Consequently, the endogenous accounts will include the following four categories, falling together in 28 variables:

1. Wants, rows and columns 1 through 6;
2. Factor incomes, rows and columns 7 through 9;
3. Households and firms, rows and columns 10 through 20;
4. Production activities, rows and columns 23 through 30.

The shape of the SAM table is adjusted as follows. The outgoings of the exogenous accounts constitute a 28 x 3 submatrix to the right, which contains flows of sectoral export and investment demands and income transfers from the rest of the world and government. These are exogenous outgoings and can be summed into one exogenous vector, denoted by x. The endogenous accounts indicated above form a 28 x 28 submatrix within the regrouped SAM, containing all the flows from endogenous accounts to endogenous accounts. This is a submatrix of *y* by *y*. To the bottom of the exogenous and endogenous accounts is a residual submatrix of residual balances that contains the outgoings of the endogenous accounts into the exogenous accounts, that is imports, taxes and savings. These residual balances insure consistency in the use of the social accounting matrices as an invertable model. We need not go further in dealing with the residual balances, once the closure of the model in terms of the specified exogenous and endogenous variable is appropriately defined.

Second, the flows in the endogenous accounts need to be expressed as average propensities of their corresponding column totals. Thus each flow in the 28 x 28 matrix is divided by its respective column total to give the social accounting matrix of average propensities, which we shall denote throughout by *A*.

As a result of these manipulations, the SAM takes the form of table 1.4. Note that the *A* matrix appears in a partitioned form to facilitate a decomposition of the multipliers in the next section. The vector of row totals, *y*, represents the endogenous variables, whereas the vector *x* represents the exogenous variables.

Table 1.4. SAM in the Form of $A_y + x = y$

		Endogenous accounts *y*				Exog-enous account *x*	Totals
Receipt	*Expenditures*	*1.* *Wants*	*2.* *Factors*	*3.* *Institutions*	*4.* *Activities*	*Governm-ent capital, rest world*	*Totals*
Endogenous	1 *Wants*			A_{13}		X_1	Y_1
	2 *Factors*				A_{24}	X_2	Y_2
	3 *Institutions*		A_{32}	A_{33}		X_3	Y_3
	4 *Activities*	A_{41}			A_{44}	X_4	Y_4
Exogenous			*Residual Balances*				
Totals		Y_1	Y_2	Y_3	Y_4		

The vector of endogenous variables, *y*, can now be solved from equation (1.2).

$$y = Ay + x = (I - A)^{-1}x = M_a x \qquad (1.2)$$

where M_a is the aggregate multiplier matrix.

One possible use of eq. (1.2) is for predictive purposes for the short and medium terms with M_a and given values of x for 1970-1975, in constant 1970 prices, one can, in principle, solve to obtain predicted values of the 28 endogenous variables for 1970-1975. Using the SAM, we predict a 20% growth rate in total Gross Domestic Product (GDP) over 5 years, or about 3.7% per annum, compared to a realised growth of 4.9% per annum. We should note, of course, that macroeconomic forecasts for 1971-1975 have been particularly inaccurate for most countries. Predictions of the institutional incomes are underestimates as well. However, the predicted growth differences between the household groups provide important information that is otherwise not available. In particular, it is noted that the rural households have benefited relatively more than the urban households. The same reasons for the poor ability of the traditional input-output model to predict the value added also apply to the SAM; in particular, the use of constant coefficients in both the input-output model and the SAM reduces their ability to function as predictive tools. Of course, the use of the SAM as an analytical tool rests less in its predictive ability than in the study of the underlying economic structure through an analysis of its multipliers.

Table 1.5 displays the type of multipliers M_a which the inverted A matrix generates. We shall focus on a selection of these in this chapter. Specifically, these are the four submatrices of $M_{a,14}$, $M_{a,24}$, $M_{a,34}$ and $M_{a,44}$ corresponding, respectively, to the impacts of injections in activities (subindex 4) on wants (subindex 1), factors (subindex 2), institutions (subindex 3) and activities (subindex 4). We shall not deal with the other multipliers; some of these will be studied in later chapters.

Table 1.5. SAM Multipliers

	x_1	x_2	x_3	x_4
y_1	$M_{a,11}$	...	...	$M_{a,14}$
y_2		$M_{a,22}$	...	$M_{a,24}$
y_3	...	...	$M_{a,33}$	$M_{a,34}$
y_4	...	...	$M_{a,43}$	$M_{a,44}$

Table 1.6 gives the results for the relevant aggregate multipliers we are focussing on. Taking the first submatrix in table 1.5, rows 1 through 6, which shows the impact of injections in activities on wants, we note a high impact of injections in public services on food; surpassing that of injections in agriculture on food. In general, a higher impact of injections in services, as compared to other sectors, is generally established for the other wants categories as well.

In the second submatrix, rows 7 through 9, which relates to the impact of injections on the factor accounts, we find that labour income is highly affected by expansion in service activities. Other sectors with significant effects are mining and agriculture. Capital income is mostly affected by expansion in the agricultural, mining and service activities.

In the third submatrix, rows 10 through 20, injections in the services sectors are shown to have the highest income multipliers, followed by agriculture and mining. An injection of 1.0 mp has an income multiplier on the average of 2.21. The highest beneficiaries are the household groups belonging to urban high skill workers, and the rural nonfarm households, reflecting their greater income shares in the whole national income. The income multipliers will be discussed in further detail in the next section.

In the fourth submatrix, rows 23 through 30, the output multipliers are shown. Again, the services sectors show the highest output multiplier effects. The output multipliers reach an average of about 4.65, which is about 2.1 times the average of the income multipliers. This means that about half of the stipulated output is distributed as income to households and firms, and the other half leaks away in intermediate inputs, imports and domestic and foreign transfers. In a further analysis of the third and fourth matrices, it is instructive to decompose the multiplier results into separable effects, which will be attempted in the next two sections.

Table 1.6.   SAM Aggregate Multipliers Ma for Injections by Sector of Activity, Colombia, 1970

Sector, Institution	Agri-culture	Mining	Process-ed coffee	Ind-ustry	Electy, gas, water	Modern svcs	Person-al svcs	Public svcs
	23	24	25	26	27	28	29	30
1. Food	0.881	0.941	0.612	0.625	0.868	0.806	0.870	1.022
2. Non-food	0.407	0.440	0.446	0.296	0.417	0.385	0.414	0.484
3. Housing	0.268	0.302	0.302	0.200	0.289	0.263	0.281	0.327
4. Health	0.059	0.065	0.041	0.043	0.061	0.056	0.060	0.071
5. Education	0.071	0.080	0.050	0.053	0.076	0.070	0.074	0.086
6. Social services	0.144	0.161	0.101	0.106	0.151	0.139	0.148	0.170
7. Urb labour earnings	0.498	0.623	0.363	0.468	0.753	0.620	0.757	1.137
8. Rur labour earnings	0.347	0.278	0.226	0.191	0.217	0.211	0.254	0.338
9. Gross profits	1.533	1.708	1.075	1.050	1.419	1.403	1.341	1.163
10. Urb proprietors	0.081	0.093	0.057	0.061	0.087	0.081	0.093	0.092
11. Urb high skill worker	0.568	0.658	0.403	0.437	0.635	0.581	0.617	0.716
12. Urb low skill worker	0.097	0.121	0.071	0.091	0.146	0.120	0.147	0.221
13. Urb self-employed,fm	0.507	0.583	0.359	0.381	0.547	0.508	0.529	0.585
14. Urb inactive	0.213	0.246	0.151	0.162	0.234	0.216	0.227	0.259
15. Rur latifundists	0.039	0.039	0.0267	0.0251	0.0325	0.0320	0.0324	0.0321
16. Rur mdm/sml owner	0.052	0.048	0.035	0.032	0.039	0.038	0.041	0.046
17. Rur farm workers	0.137	0.110	0.089	0.075	0.086	0.093	0.101	0.134
18. Rur nonfarm hshlds	0.235	0.219	0.158	0.142	0.176	0.173	0.186	0.208
19. Rural inactive	0.050	0.046	0.033	0.030	0.037	0.036	0.039	0.045
20. Firms	0.355	0.395	0.249	0.243	0.329	0.325	0.310	0.269
Total income multiplier	6.542	7.156	4.848	4.711	6.600	6.156	6.521	7.405
23. Agriculture	1.574	0.600	0.971	0.588	0.583	0.534	0.638	0.682
24. Mining	0.035	1.045	0.025	0.049	0.056	0.036	0.039	0.042
25. Processed coffee	0.022	0.024	1.069	0.016	0.022	0.021	0.038	0.031
26. Industry	1.609	1.702	1.127	2.435	1.795	1.581	1.806	1.930
27.Electricity, gas, water	0.034	0.067	0.024	0.033	1.058	0.036	0.041	0.045
28. Modern Services	0.933	1.148	0.709	0.905	0.971	2.024	0.918	1.074
29. Personal services	0.290	0.321	0.204	0.215	0.306	0.284	1.302	0.361
30. Public services	0.019	0.024	0.014	0.016	0.022	0.019	0.020	1.023
Total output multiplier	4.516	4.931	4.143	4.257	4.813	4.535	4.802	5.188

Key: Urb=urban, Rur=rural, mdm/sml=medium/small, fm=family workers, hshlds=households

4. Decomposition of SAM Multipliers: $M_{a,34}$

Recalling equation (1.2) the aggregate multiplier matrix M_a can be decomposed into three multiplier matrices M_1, M_2 and M_3, as in equation (1.3).

$$y = A_y + x = (I - A)^{-1} x = M_a x = M_3 M_2 M_1 x \qquad (1.3)$$

In terms of the SAM, M_1, which is known as the transfer multiplier, captures effects resulting from direct transfers within the endogenous account, that is between production activities. The open-loop effects, M_2, capture the interactions among the endogenous accounts, that is from production to factors, institutions and wants. The closed-loop effects, M_3, ensure that the circular flow of income is completed among endogenous accounts, that is from production activities to factors to institutions to wants and then back to activities in the form of consumption demand, and so forth.[1] Because the multiplier matrix M_a and its partition into M_1, M_2 and M_3 is extensive, we limit the presentation to the aggregate and decomposed impacts of exogenous injections in sectoral activities on institutions and activities. This section addresses the impact on the institutions, $M_{a,34}$, and the next section considers the impact on the activities, $M_{a,44}$.

We can now study the third submatrix of multipliers in table 1.6 in more detail. This is the impact of sectoral injections on household incomes, $M_{a,34}$. It is worth using decomposition analysis in tracing how the results are obtained in the third submatrix. The decomposition of $M_{a,34}$ into its transfer, open and closed multiplier effects requires analyses of the three submatrices, as in equation (1.4).

$$M_{a,34} = (M_{3,33})(M_{2,34})(M_{1,44}) \qquad (1.4)$$
overall = (closed)(open)(transfer)

Tables 1.7, 1.8 and 1.9 show the $M_{1,44}$, $M_{2,34}$ and $M_{3,33}$ submatrices, respectively. Table 1.7 captures the transfer effect within the input-output accounts. The first column of table 1.7 shows that an initial injection in agriculture of 1.0 results in an addition to agriculture of 4.1%, mining 0.4%, industry 15.6%, electricity, water and gas 0.2%, modern services 14.1%,

---

[1] The formal derivation of the decomposed multiplier is described in, among others, Pyatt and Roe (1977), Bulmer-Thomas (1982), Pleskovic and Treviño (1985), Cohen and Jellema (1987). See also appendix to this chapter.

personal services 0.1% and government services 0.12%. The original injection of 1.0 leads to a total increase of 1.3459. These transfer effects will be traced through the rest of the system, $M_{2,34}$ and $M_{3,33}$, to illustrate how the system works.

Table 1.8, which presents $M_{2,34}$, captures the open-loop effects, the highest of which are those for rural households in the agriculture column. This pattern of a high concentration of rural factor income in agriculture is due to the dominating link between rural factors and rural households. In a similar way, the mining sector benefits the urban employers and capitalists, whereas the government sector benefits the other urban households.

The closed-loop multipliers as captured in $M_{3,33}$, table 1.9, are associated with the consumption patterns of the households. The increases in income resulting from open-loop effects are used mainly to purchase consumer goods, which increases output, and, in turn increases factor income that is paid out as institutional income.

Table 1.7. Transfer Effects in Sectoral Accounts, $M_{1,44}$

	Agri-culture	Mining	Proc-essed coffee	Industry	Electri-city, gas water	Modern services	Personal services	Public services
	23	24	25	26	27	28	29	30
23. Agricul-ture	1.041	0.028	0.600	0.207	0.052	0.042	0.108	0.060
24. Mining	0.003	0.016	0.003	0.026	0.025	0.007	0.007	0.005
25. Processed coffee	0.000	0.000	1.053	0.000	0.000	0.000	0.016	0.005
26. Industry	0.156	0.130	0.113	1.391	0.334	0.228	0.350	0.224
27. Electricity, gas, water	0.002	0.032	0.002	0.010	1.025	0.006	0.008	0.007
28. Modern services	0.141	0.275	0.154	0.326	0.151	1.268	0.108	0.129
29. Personal services	0.001	0.003	0.001	0.003	0.006	0.008	1.006	0.016
30. Public services	0.001	0.004	0.001	0.003	0.003	0.000	0.002	1.002
Total	1.346	1.486	1.923	1.966	1.596	1.560	1.604	1.447

Table 1.8. Open-loop Effects from Sectors to Institutions, M$_{2,34}$

	Agri-culture	Mining	Proc-essed coffee	Industry	Electri-city, gas water	Modern services	Pers-onal services	Public services
	23	24	25	26	27	28	29	30
10.Urb prprtrs	0.0247	0.0282	0.0024	0.0071	0.0260	0.0233	0.0239	0.0244
11.Urb high skill	0.1608	0.1896	0.0162	0.0537	0.1980	0.1672	0.1870	0.2326
12.Urb low skill	0.0125	0.0233	0.0023	0.0144	0.0549	0.0341	0.0583	0.1204
13.Urb slfmpl fw	0.1519	0.1743	0.0147	0.0451	0.1652	0.1463	0.1524	0.1632
14.Urb inactive	0.0617	0.0719	0.0061	0.0196	0.0722	0.0621	0.0675	0.0794
15.Rur latifundi	0.0155	0.0130	0.0009	0.0024	0.0075	0.0084	0.0073	0.0043
16.Rur mdm/sml	0.0224	0.0153	0.0009	0.0029	0.0078	0.0089	0.0095	0.0108
17.Rur farm wrk	0.0663	0.0318	0.0010	0.0066	0.0112	0.0140	0.0239	0.0493
18.Rur non farm	0.1012	0.0690	0.0041	0.0132	0.0350	0.0401	0.0429	0.0489
19.Rur inactive	0.0220	0.0145	0.0008	0.0029	0.0071	0.0082	0.0092	0.0113
20.Firms	0.1273	0.1347	0.0109	0.0241	0.0857	0.0944	0.0692	0.0000
Total	0.7663	0.7656	0.0603	0.1919	0.6706	0.6070	0.6565	0.7456

Table 1.9. Closed-loop effects between Institutions, M$_{3,33}$

	Urban					Rural				
	Propri etor	high skill	Low skill	Self empl/ fm	In active	Lati-fundi	m/s fm owner	Farm wrkrs	Non-farm	In-active
	10	11	12	13	14	15	16	17	18	19
10.Uprp	1.065	0.065	0.071	0.067	0.063	0.05	0.064	0.073	0.069	0.069
11.Uhsw	0.465	1.469	0.509	0.479	0.454	0.359	0.458	0.522	0.495	0.490
12.Ulsw	0.099	0.098	1.106	0.100	0.095	0.075	0.095	0.107	0.102	0.100
13.Usfw	0.405	0.409	0.445	1.418	0.397	0.313	0.4	0.457	0.433	0.429
14.Uinact	0.172	0.174	0.1891	0.178	1.169	0.133	0.167	0.194	0.184	0.182
15.Rlat	0.026	0.027	0.030	0.028	0.026	1.021	0.027	0.031	0.029	0.029
16.Rmsf	0.033	0.034	0.037	0.015	0.033	0.026	1.034	0.039	0.037	0.037
17.Rfwr	0.079	0.082	0.091	0.084	0.079	0.064	0.082	1.097	0.091	0.091
18.Rnfh	0.149	0.153	0.169	0.157	0.149	0.119	0.157	0.178	1.168	0.167
19.Rinact	0.032	0.033	0.036	0.033	0.032	0.025	0.033	0.038	0.036	1.036
20.Firms	0.255	0.26	0.284	0.266	0.253	0.200	0.256	0.295	0.279	0.277
Total	2.780	2.803	2.967	2.845	2.749	2.386	2.774	3.029	2.922	2.906

Reading the rows of table 1.9 and excluding the initial injections and a few exceptions, we see that the closed-loop multipliers are fairly constant. This can be interpreted as the result of similar expenditure and savings patterns over households. The closed-loop multipliers are generally much higher than either the transfer or open-loop multipliers, which reflects the fact that consumption is larger than other categories of final demand. An open-loop effect of 1.0 into any household creates between 2.3856 and 3.0293 of total institutional income. The national impact for transfer effects ranged between 1.3459 and 1.9658, whereas that for open-loop effects varied between 0.0603 and 0.7663 in tables 1.7 and 1.8, respectively. Being higher than the other multipliers, and given their low variance, the closed-loop multipliers tend to dampen the effects of the transfer and open-loop multipliers.

Table 1.10 summarises these interactions in a compact form. Columns 1 and 2 give the combined effects of the incomes of rural low wage households and all others of the transfer and open-loop multipliers following the exogenous initial injection in agriculture of one million pesos. Columns 3 and 4 complement the picture by introducing closed-loop effects. Column 5 gives the overall effects, which, when summed, result in the overall multiplier for rural low wage households, as was found in table 1.6, $M_{a,34}$ (17, 23), that is 0.137 units. Similarly, the overall multipliers can be obtained for other household groups and firms, resulting in a total overall multiplier effect of 2.335 units.

These results suggest that the marginal share of benefits to rural low wage households from agricultural expansion amounts to about 5.8%. Because the income share of rural workers in 1970 amounted to 3.5% we can expect an injection in agriculture to enhance the relative position of rural workers in the income distribution. The results also suggest that the significant gains obtained in the factor account by one group (in the open-loop effects) are reduced by losses through consumption to other groups (in the closed-loop effects). For Colombia, therefore, the effect of an injection in agriculture has a progressive effect on income distribution. The mining multiplier points in the same direction but less significantly. The energy multiplier distributes relatively more to urban than to rural households. The government sector multiplier appears to benefit household groups in various degrees at the expense of firms.

Table 1.10. Effects of an Injection of plus one million pesos in the Agricultural Sector on the Household Income of Rural Farm Workers and All Others, Colombia

	Open-loop effects of agriculture	Sum of open-loop effects of all sectors	Closed-loop effects of rural low wage worker	Closed-loop effects of all others	Sum of closed-loop effects	Simulated (%)	Actual 1970 (%)
	(1)	(2)	(3)	(4)	(5)	(6)	(7)
Rural farm workers	0.066	0.072	1.097	0.076	0.137	5.8	3.5
All others	0.700	0.765	1.792	2.704	2.198	94.1	96.5
Total	0.766	0.837	2.889	2.780	2.335	100.0	100.0

Note: transfer effect of the impulse on agriculture, 1.042, is multiplied by open-loop effects to give column 1 for agriculture, and for all sectors in column 2.

We may now extend the example of agriculture to other sectors using a more abridged presentation. Table 1.11 gives adapted overall and open-loop multipliers of initial injections in agriculture, mining, energy and government services. These four sectors happen to have the highest multiplier effects. The table also gives adapted closed-loop multipliers for the urban self-employed and the rural farm workers, which are the largest population groups in rural and urban locations, respectively. To assess the marginal effect of the adapted multipliers on income distribution, column 1 of table 1.11 gives the actual income shares in 1970, while column 2 gives the actual household shares in all households, and column 3 gives the actual income per household relative to an average of all households of 1.0. These columns indicate that lower rewards for urban high skill workers, proprietors, self-employed, inactive and rural latifundists (in decreasing order) and/or higher rewards for urban low skill workers and the rural population, represent a movement towards more equality at the individual household level.

The overall multiplier of an injection in agriculture promotes a redistribution of income from urban to rural population groups; the multiplier of mining points in the same direction, but less significantly. The multiplier of energy distributes relatively more to urban than to rural households. The multiplier of the government sector appears to benefit household groups in various degrees at the expense of firms.

The adapted multipliers can be partially decomposed in terms of adapted open-loop and closed-loop multipliers. The relative redistributionary effects of the open-loop multipliers as represented by the adapted $M_{2,34}$ appear to be very significant. Agricultural benefits are shown to be shared among rural and urban populations in proportions of 0.53 and 0.30, while the actual income shares are distributed in the proportions of 0.69 to urban and 0.15 to rural. $M_{2,34}$ shows that injections in mining also promote equality, while those in energy and government increase inequality. These significant redistributionary effects, whether they are positive or negative, are muffled by the closed-loop effects, $M_{3,33}$, which barely deviate from the actual income distribution. Table 1.11 shows that the multiplier effect for the two largest urban and rural population groups is divided among all urban and all rural according to the actual shares of 0.69 and 0.15. Approximately the same results are obtained from whichever group one starts with. The gains obtained on the factor account by one group are lost via consumption to other groups.

We may recall the discussion on the vanishing income redistribution effects, cf. Taylor and Lysy (1979). In the present context vanishing effects are the result of the interaction between three factors.

1. relatively weak transfer effects of agriculture, which is the potential sector for a sustained positive redistributionary effect;
2. sector-factor links producing multipliers, which are not very significant; and
3. very significant leakage from poorer to richer household groups - and otherwise - via their expenditure patterns.

In general, agricultural multipliers show more progressive redistributionary effects than industrial multipliers. It is also shown that the aggregate multipliers of injectors in an activity on all activities is higher for agriculture than for industry, so that, as far as these two sectors are concerned, progressive redistribution and higher growth can go hand in hand. The results direct attention to the presence of degrees of freedom in the selection of balanced socio-economic development policies, in spite of the existence of countervailing mechanisms, which cause parts of the redistribution and growth potentials to vanish.

Table 1.11. Percentage Distribution of Household Incomes in 1970 and of Multiplier Benefits according to the SAM

Household	Situation 1970			Adapted $M_{a,34}$			
	Income shares	House-hold shares	Relative income per household	21 Agri-culture	22 Mining	25 Energy	28. Govern-ment services
10.Urban proprietors	3.60	1.40	2.57	3.5	7	3.7	3.5
11.Urban high skill wrkr	26.36	19.02	1.39	24.3	25.7	27.0	27.5
12.Urban low skill wrkr	5.86	8.82	0.66	4.1	4.7	6.2	8.5
13.Urban selfempl & fw	22.67	20.12	1.13	21.7	22.8	23.3	22.4
14.Urban inactive	11.04	10.16	1.09	9.1	9.6	10.0	9.9
15.Rural latifundists	1.37	1.32	1.04	1.7	1.6	1.4	1.2
16.Rural mdm/sml ownr	1.63	2.98	0.55	2.2	1.9	1.7	1.8
17.Rural farm workers	3.48	12.59	0.28	5.9	4.3	3.7	5.1
18.Rural nonfarm	7.32	18.82	0.39	10.1	8.6	7.5	8.0
19.Rural inactive	1.79	4.77	0.38	2.2	1.8	1.6	1.7
20.Firms	14.87			15.2	15.4	14.0	10.3

Household	Adapted $M_{2,34}$				Adapted $M_{3,33}^{-1}$	
	21. Agriculture	22. Mining	25. Energy	28. Govern-ment services	13. Rural workers	16 Urban self-employed
10.Urban proprietors	3.2	3.7	3.9	3.3	3.6	3.6
11.Urban high skill wrkr	21.0	24.8	29.5	31.2	26.0	25.7
12.Urban low skill wrkr	1.6	3.0	8.2	16.2	5.4	5.3
13.Urban selfempl & fw	19.8	22.8	24.6	21.9	22.7	22.5
14.Urban inactive	8.1	9.4	10.8	10.7	9.6	9.6
15.Rural latifundists	2.0	1.7	1.1	0.6	1.5	1.5
16.Rural mdm/sml ownr	2.9	2.0	1.2	1.5	1.9	1.9
17.Rural farm workers	8.7	4.2	1.7	6.6	4.6	4.8
18.Rural nonfarm	13.2	9.0	5.2	6.6	8.5	8.8
19.Rural inactive	2.9	1.9	1.1	1.5	1.8	1.9
20.Firms	16.6	17.6	12.8	0.0	14.4	14.5

Note: Col.1=$Y/\Sigma Y$ where Y is income; Col.2=$P/\Sigma P$ where P is number of households
Col. 3 = col. 1/col. 2; Col. 4 to 13 are adapted from tables 1.4, 1.6 and 1.7.

5. Decomposition of SAM Multipliers: *Ma,44* and the Difference between SAM and Leontief Multipliers

Finally, we can now elaborate on the fourth submatrix of table 1.6, giving the aggregate multipliers of injections in activities on activities, Ma,44. These aggregate multipliers can also be decomposed into their transfer, open-loop and closed-loop effects, as in equation (1.5).

$$M_{a,44} = \left(M_{3,44}\right)\left(M_{2,44}\right)\left(M_{1,44}\right)$$ (1.5)

overall = (closed)(open)(transfer)

Because $M_{a,44}$ does not have an impact on accounts other than its own account 4. The open-loop effects are not applicable here and $M_{2,44}$ is an identity matrix. As a result, an analysis of the differences between the aggregate multiplier and that part which forms the transfer effects is sufficient to appreciate the nature of the remaining part, which forms the closed-loop effects.

The aggregate multipliers or $M_{a,44}$ can now be compared with the previously discussed transfer effects of activities on activities, $M_{1,44}$, found in table 1.7. The latter represents the Leontief open-model inverse. As expected, first, the SAM inverse contains more linkages than the Leontief open-model inverse, with the result that $M_{a,44}$ is substantially higher than $M_{1,44}$. Second, because of the heterogeneity of the linkages the structural pattern of $M_{a,44}$ is also different from $M_{1,44}$

The first point can be illustrated from table 1.12, which gives the frequency distribution of the size of the aggregate multipliers and the transfer effects, or the SAM-inverse and the Leontief inverse, respectively. The percentage of elements with negligible sizes, which form the great majority in the Leontief-inverse, is significantly reduced in the SAM-inverse reflecting the incorporation of many more indirect effects and additional interdependencies in a social accounting framework. Summing up elements < 0.2 gives a percentage of 86 in Leontief and only 50 in SAM.

The second point can be illustrated from table 1.13. Sectors are ranked according to the Leontief total column multipliers in the order of: industry 1.97, mining 1.49, service 1.45 and agriculture 1.35. Their contribution to production activity and their ranking are significantly different in the SAM total column multipliers: services 5.19, mining 4.94, agriculture 4.52 and industry 4.26. Policy making regarding allocations to activity with the object of achieving highest growth would have made wrong decisions in a structural analysis based on the Leontief framework as compared to a SAM framework.

Table 1.12. Size Distributions of the Off-diagonal Elements of the SAM-inverse and the Leontief-inverse in percentages; i.e. Aggregate Multipliers and Transfer Effects, respectively

Element size	< 0.050	0.051- 0.100	0.101 - 0.150	0.151 - 0.200	0.201 - 0.250	0.251 - 0.500	0.501 - 1.000	> 1.000
SAM aggregate multiplier	46.4	3.6	0.0	0.0	3.6	8.9	21.4	16.1
Leontief transfer effects	66.0	3.6	10.7	5.4	5.4	7.1	1.8	0.0

Source: Tables 1.7 and 1.8.

Table 1.13. Own Multipliers and Total Column Multipliers in the SAM-inverse and the Leontlef-inverses; i.e. Aggregate Multipliers and Transfer Effects, respectively

	Agriculture		*Mining*		*Industry*		*Services*	
Element size	1. own	2. total	1. own	2. total	1. own	2. total	1. own	2.total
SAM aggregate multiplier	1.57	4.52	1.05	4.94	2.44	4.26	1.02	5.19
Leontief transfer effects	1.04	1.35	1.02	1.49	1.39	1.97	1.00	1.45

Source: Tables 1.7 and 1.8.

The results should not be interpreted to mean that, if Colombia, for instance, had in the past expanded relatively more in agriculture, mining or services than in industry, it would have necessarily achieved a higher overall growth. For one thing, the exogenous expansion potential both domestically and in the rest of the world - denoted by x – was, and is, probably lower for the non-industrial sectors than for industry. Besides, neither the SAM nor the input-output model consider limits on the supply side, which are likely to be more demarcated for agriculture than for industry in most developing countries.

As is well known, labour use and capital use per unit of additional production can be multiplied by the contribution to production activities to give the employment and investment effects. It is obvious that, given the above, the impact of alternative allocations to activities on the marginal use of labour and capital would be less meaningful when they are derived from the partial framework of Leontief's transfer effects, than when they are derived from a more general framework incorporating SAM's aggregate effects.

6. Concluding Remarks

The use of the SAM as a framework for the analysis of economic development problems relating to economic growth, income distribution, sectoral strategies and transfer designs gas been demonstrated to be fruitful.

Even though the economic analysis gas been limited to one year only, the obtained results indicate durability that will be supported by cross-country and inter-temporal applications in later chapters.

There are limitations of the SAM multiplier approach as followed here. These will be discussed in later chapters, and their effects evaluated. For the moment it is sufficient to mention that these limitations relate to the assumption of excess capacity, linear relationships, aggregation errors, and closure rules.

Of special relevance for the validity of the results is the assumption of excess capacity. The SAM is a fixed price multiplier model, and hence supplied amounts are supposed to adjust to demanded amounts if the full potential of the multiplier effect is to be realised. If there is restricted capacity the result is immediate or repressed inflation. This may require a revision downward in the real sizes of multipliers. Applied to a developing country, the degrees of excess capacities in the economy will differ from one sector to another and by country. The full potential of the SAM multiplier effects are likely to more realised in countries with significant investments in increasing their overall production capacities.

The other limitations can be resolved by redesigning the SAM classifications, specifications and structures, as will be done in later chapters.

Chapter 2

Social Accounting and Development Performance: Growth and Distribution in Colombia, Korea, Pakistan and Surinam

1. Introduction

The role of the social accounting matrix, SAM, is sometimes seen as that of a helpful tool in the setting-up and estimation of corresponding models. An overview of modelling and social accounting matrices in Thorbecke (1984) concludes that the advantage of forcing a model into a social accounting framework is that one can discover inconsistencies of which the authors were not even aware. The discipline of building an explicit SAM ensures that the initial values of the variables in the system are internally consistent. There is another important role that a SAM can play, however. By appropriate manipulations, the table can be rearranged so as to give sets of exogenous variables and a coefficient matrix that can be subjected to a useful multiplier analysis, which gives insight into the working of the economic system.

The early empirical literature on the SAM has dealt in particular with the construction of social accounting data systems in the context of developing countries. For a few of these, counterpart computable general equilibrium models were also developed.[1] In contrast, published multiplier analysis of social accounting matrices, which is the focus of this chapter has been limited to a smaller number of developing countries.[2]

The purpose of this chapter is to examine the use of the SAM as a solid framework for conducting international comparisons of the structures of the socio-economic systems of different countries. In particular, an analysis of

---

[1] For an inventory of available SAMs in the mid-eighties, see Pyatt and Round (1985). This chapter supplements the list with four more SAMs.

[2] As of the 1980s, see the works by Pyatt and Roe (1977) for Sri Lanka, Hayden and Round (1980) for Botswana, Defourny and Thorbecke (1984) for Korea, and Cohen (1989) for the four countries studied in this chapter.

multipliers across countries should show meaningful, significant and stable results. The chapter is divided as follows: Section 2 deals with the construction and content of social accounting matrices for four countries, namely Colombia for 1970, Pakistan for 1979, (the Republic of) Korea for 1975 and Surinam for 1979. These were constructed by the author in collaboration with several associates. Section 3 presents the case for considering the SAM as a more complete analytical framework than such partial models as the input-output model; the section further states the steps for deriving the multipliers of the SAM. Section 4 discusses the decomposition of SAM multipliers into transfer, open loop and closed-loop effects, and examines the decomposed results for the relationship between economic growth and income distribution. Section 5 continues the decomposition analysis, focuses on the transfer effects, and examines comparative transfer effects in the broader and in the narrower analytical frameworks of social accounting and input-output, respectively. Section 6 ends with concluding remarks on the comparative analysis of the structural properties of the SAMs of the four countries.

2. Social Accounting Matrices of Colombia, Pakistan, Korea and Surinam

For obvious reasons, greater analytical insight is gained if basically comparable social accounting matrices are constructed for the individual countries to be compared. Table 1.3 in chapter 1, which gives the SAM for Colombia, was meant initially to serve as a benchmark example for the construction of the SAMs for the other three countries in the comparative analysis: Korea, Pakistan and Surinam. Although the Colombia SAM has been closely followed in the applications to Korea, Pakistan, and Surinam, certain modifications in the classifications for the latter countries were unavoidable. The results of the differentiated classification for the four countries are presented below in table 2.1 in a manner which nevertheless maximises the similarities between the four SAMs.

The first set of accounts in table 2.1 is the wants account. It is not obligatory to include this account in the SAM. However, by incorporating the wants account, the present SAMs increase the focus on a whole range of goods and services classified according to basic needs. Here they include food, housing, health, education and other goods and services. It is informative to know, for instance, how much expenditure on food products is taken up by specific household groups and how this expenditure is matched by agriculture and the non-agricultural sectors.

Table 2.1. Endogenous Account Classifications in the SAMs of Colombia, Korea, Pakistan and Surinam

(Common selections for the uniform comparative analysis are shaded)

Columbia	Korea	Pakistan	Surinam	Common
Wants	**Wants**	**Wants**	**Wants**	**Wants**
1 Food	1 Food	1 Food & drink	1 Food	Not applied
2 Non-food	2 Others	2 Clthng/ Footwr	2 Housing	
3 Housing	3 Housing	3 Personal effects	3 Clothing	
4 Health	4 Health	4 Rent	4 Education	
5 Education	5 Education	5 Fuel/lighting	5 Health	
6 Other services		6 Health	6 Others	
		7 Education		
		8 Others		
Factors	**Factors**	**Factors**	**Factors**	**Factors**
7 Urban lbr erng	6 Labour earngs	Not specified	7 Labour income	Not applied
8 Rural lbr erng	7 Capital earngs		8 Capital income	
9 Gross profits			9 Trad income	
Institutions	**Institutions**	**Institutions**	**Institutions**	**Institutions**
10 Urban proprietors	8 Urban high skill	9 Urban	10 Urban workers	1 Urban high skill
11 Urban high skill	9 Urban low skill	10 Urban	11 Urb slfmplyd/ fw	2 Urban low skill
12 Urban low skill	10 Urban slfmpl/fw	11 Urban manual	12 Rural land owners	3 Urban slfmpl/fw
13 Urb slfmpl/fw	11 Rural lrg hldng	12 Urb slfmpl/fw	13 Rural landless	4 Rural lg holdng
14 Urban inactive	12 Rural mdm hlh	13 Rural large	14 Rrl sfmplyd/ fw	5 Rural mdm hldg
15 Rural latifunds	13 Rural sml Inds	14 Rural mdm	15 Firms	6 Rural sml/ landls
16 Rural mdm/sml fr	14 Firms	15 Rural		7 Other househlds
17 Rural farm worker		16 Rural nfrm		8 Firms
18 Rural nnfrm hshl		17 Firms		
19 Rural inactive				
20 Firms				
Activities	**Activities**	**Activities**	**Activities**	**Activities**
21 Agriculture	15 Agriculture	18 Wheat & rice	16 Modrn agricult	9 Agriculture
22 Mining	16 Mining	19 Other agrclyr	17 Trad agriculture	10 Mining
23 Process coffee	17 Modern industry	20 Mining/qryng	18 Mining	11 Industry
24 Industry	18 Traditional industry	21 Large-scale mf	19 Industry	12 Services
25 Electricty, gas, water	19 Modern services	22 small-scale mf	20 Modern services	
26 Modern services	20 Traditional services	23 Construction	21 Trad services	
27 Personal services		24 Housing		
28 Public services		25 Water, Elec		
		26 Whls rtl trd		
		27 Transport, cm		
		28 Banking, insurance		
		29 Public services		

This interest in itemising the achieved consumption stems from the policy questions addressed by basic-need approaches and corresponding modelling systems. The second set of accounts is the factor accounts, which is subdivided into several types of labour and capital. This was feasible given the available data for Colombia, Korea and Surinam, but not for Pakistan. Household surveys and other income data in Pakistan do not allow an explicit specification of the factor accounts, so that institutional income had to be mapped directly to the activity accounts. This, by itself, is not a handicap.

In order to conduct the multiplier analysis, a factor account with the same subdivisions as the institution account is attached to the SAM. Activity receipts by institution are allocated to its corresponding factor as ingoings, and reallocated again from the factor concerned to the corresponding institution as outgoings.

The third set of accounts is that of the institutions, subdivided into current accounts of household groups, firms and government; and a national capital account. Household groups receive a mixture of labour and capital income. Firms and government receive capital income. Additional sources of income to households are transfers from government and transfers from the rest of the world. The outgoings of the different institutions can directly be read from their respective columns. The focus of attention of the disaggregations in the applications reported here lies with the household account. The disaggregation of households emphasises dualities in the location of population (rural, urban), mode of earning (modern employment, self-employment, inactive) and occupational characteristics of worker (within modern employment a distinction is made between employers, non-manual workers and manual workers). As a result, the general rule was to distinguish rural groups from urban groups, as is shown in table 2.1. In the national capital account, savings of all institutions are entered in the row, and disposal of these savings in investment is entered in the column.

The fourth set of accounts relates to the activities, which represent the well known input-output structure. The definition of sectors differed substantially by country, even though commonly used broad categories can be easily identified. Finally, the rest of the world account, RW, is always present in all SAMs. The row for RW registers imports as if they are all complementary, while the column of RW registers exports and net capital flow. The SAM of Pakistan differs in that the available input-output table for the country registered all imports as competitive. As a result of the absence of leakage through imports in the application, the impact multipliers are bound to be over estimated by comparison to other countries.

With regard to details of estimation and statistical sources, in all four SAMs the official national accounts statistics were used as the building blocks of these statistical applications. This is necessary because national accounts statistics form the reference framework for national policy-making. Besides, extended modelling in a later phase will have to work with time-series based on national accounts statistics. The above use of national accounts statistics implied rescaling statistics from other data sources to fit into these aggregates. Other data sources concerned are those of the input-output table, and the labour force survey combined with the household income and expenditure survey.

The data of the available input-output table had to be adjusted by applying the RAS-method to obtain a definite and consistent table for the selected year of the SAM.

The data of the household income and expenditure survey, which gives average values per type of earner, and the labour force survey, which gives the numbers of corresponding earners, were combined and used to fill the inner structure of the cross-accounts of households and factors and households and wants. This was done after rescaling to fit the national accounts aggregates. In filling the incomings in the household account, it was necessary to keep the receipts of households from other households at zero, and to assume that household receipts from the rest of the world are distributed among household types in proportion to each household group income. These assumptions reflect the general lack of data on income transfers between household groups.

As for the outgoings, the household income and expenditure survey, together with the labour force survey, provided the required data to fill consumption expenditure and direct taxes on household groups, after rescaling to fit the national accounts aggregates.

The difference between income and expenditure for each household group constitutes the entry in the capital account. Furthermore, groups with negative residuals, i.e. dissavings, were assumed to incur no outgoings to the rest of the world. Outgoings were proportionately distributed among households with positive residuals, or savings, on the basis of their income.

Finally, the submatrix that converts private consumption categories belonging to the wants account into final demand categories belonging to the activities account has been made consistent. This was done by applying the RAS-method to a converter matrix obtained from various sources and the already found column and row totals of private consumption and final demand categories.

3. The Social Accounting Matrix as a Model of Analysis

For a long time, much of the national planning of production and investment has been conducted within the narrow framework of the Leontief input-output model, thus dealing primarily with intersectoral delivery. This was done to the exclusion of other significant mechanisms in the economy such as those of factor remuneration, income transfers and expenditures by participating actors and their recycling back to sectoral activity. The SAM opens the way for inclusion of these channels in the circular flow. Needless to say, other things remaining the same, economic policy based on intersectoral accounts is inferior to that based on intersectoral, income, transfer and expenditure accounts.

The other argument in favour of working with the SAM is obvious. It is increasingly the case that policy-makers, economists and the larger public, in developing and developed countries alike, require the appraisal not only of the production objective, but also of other development objectives pertaining to income policy and the allotment of basic provisions and obligations among population groups.

Compared to the input-output model as depicted by Leontief, the social accounting model is a broadening of focus in development policy and thinking. In spite of compelling arguments in favour of the SAM, the use of SAMs for economic analysis is sporadic. It could be a matter of time before it catches up. Arguments that can be raised against the SAM include the static nature of the economic analysis obtainable from assuming constant coefficients, and the sometimes arbitrary classifications, unreliabilities and obsolescence imposed by the timing and the kind of data that go into the construction of SAMs. However, all these limitations also apply to the input-output model. Constant coefficients may be more objectionable in a SAM, but they can be minimised by appropriate classifications.

In the context of a comparative analysis of the structural properties of different socio-economic systems, the focus of this chapter, the SAM will prove to be an appropriate framework for comparison in ways similar to the comparative structural analysis in input-output tables, as first introduced by Chenery and Watanabe (1958). In the context of comparative cross-country analyses, the constancy of the coefficients can be an advantage. Impact multipliers based on constant coefficients obtainable from inverted social accounting tables can have the advantage of being more country-neutral in cross-country comparisons, in contrast to flexible models that involve non-uniformities in their treatment of individual case studies.

The algebraic derivations of multipliers can now be discussed. In the input-output model, an endogenous vector of sectoral production, q, can be predicted from an inverted matrix of input-output coefficients, L, and a vector of exogenous final demand, f, as in equation (2.1).

$$q = Lq + f = (I - L)^{-1} f \qquad (2.1)$$

SAMs can be used similarly. Several steps are required to transform the SAM into a predictive model along the lines of the input-output model. First, the accounts of the SAM need to be subdivided into endogenous and exogenous categories, and regrouped so that the exogenous accounts fall to the right and at the bottom of the endogenous accounts.

Following the procedure of the previous chapter, the endogenous accounts, denoted by y, would include the categories of wants, factor earnings, households and firms incomes, and production activities. These endogenous accounts form a matrix of rows y by columns y. Each flow in this matrix is divided by its respective column total to give the social accounting matrix of average propensities, denoted by A.

Accounts to be held exogenous are those of government, capital and rest of the world; all three can be postulated to be external to and constraining the otherwise endogenous market processes which characterise the remainder of the economy. The outgoings of the exogenous accounts constitute a submatrix to the right, containing flows of sectoral export and investment demand and income transfers from the rest of the world and government, which can be summed into one exogenous vector, denoted by x.

To the bottom of the exogenous and endogenous accounts is a submatrix that contains the residual outgoings of the endogenous accounts into the exogenous accounts, i.e. imports, taxes and savings. These residual balances assure a consistent closure of the SAM model.

As a result of the above manipulations, the SAM takes the form of table 2.2 (we have also encountered this table in the previous chapter). The vector of row totals, y, represents the endogenous variables, while the vector x represents the exogenous variables.

The vector of endogenous variables y can now be solved from equation (2.2).

$$y = Ay + x = (I - A)^{-1} x = M_a x \qquad (2.2)$$

where M_a is the aggregate multiplier matrix, which can be subjected to a standard reduced form analysis as is commonly done with input-output tables.

Table 2.2. SAM in the Form of $Ay + x = y$

	Endogenous Accounts y				Exogenous account	Totals
	1. Wants	2. Factors	3. Institutions	4. Activities	Government capital & rest of world	
Endogenous						
1. Wants			A_{13}		X_1	Y_1
2. Factors				A_{24}	X_2	Y_2
3. Institutions		A_{32}	A_{33}		X_3	Y_3
4. Activities	A_{41}			A_{44}	X_4	Y_4
Exogenous	*R e s i d u a l B a l a n c e s*					
Totals	Y_1	Y_2	Y_3	Y_4		

Because the multiplier matrices can be extensive (for Colombia they count 28 x 28), it is instructive to limit the presentation here to the impact of exogenously specified injections (changes) into sectoral activities on the variables of the wants, factors, institutions and activities accounts, and in particular the latter two.

Table 2.3 accordingly gives the relevant aggregate multipliers within M_a. Specifically, they fall into four compartments: $M_{a,14}$, $M_{a,24}$, $M_{a,34}$ and $M_{a,44}$ corresponding, respectively, to the impacts on wants (subindex 1, table 2.2), factors (subindex 2), institutions (subindex 3) and activities (subindex 4) as a result of injections into activities (subindex 4). The first, second and third compartments will be dealt with in this section, and the fourth compartment in the next.

In general, it can be seen that the magnitude of the multipliers is smallest for Surinam, followed by Korea and Colombia. The case of Pakistan, which shows the highest multipliers, is not strictly comparable because the SAM of Pakistan does not consider leakage through imports explicitly. However, the general validity and the general comparability of the relative distribution of the impact multipliers for Pakistan need not be disturbed by this difference in registration.

In the first compartment, which gives the impact of allocations to activities on the wants account, it is striking to note the relatively high impact of services on food (table 2.3, row 1). In Colombia, Korea and Surinam this impact surpasses that of agriculture on food. Pakistan, with a higher share of non-marketed and non-processed food, shows the opposite. The dominating impact of services, as compared with other sectors, is generally established for other wants categories as well. In terms of impact, the consumption of food is followed by that of other goods, housing, education and health, reflecting their decreasing shares in consumption expenditure. The main exceptions are in the relative positions of education and health, which are reversed in the cases of Pakistan (known for its very low expenditure on education) and Surinam (possibly as a result of its particularly high provisions for health).

In the second compartment, which relates to the impact of allocations on the factor accounts, it is found that, on a row-by-row basis, labour income is highly affected by expansion in service activities. Other sectors with significant effects are mining and agriculture. Capital income is mostly affected by expansion in agricultural activity, followed by mining and services. In column terms, the results show the multiplier ratio of labour income to capital income in Colombia to be highest in government services and lowest in electricity and agriculture, which are capital-intensive and land-extensive, respectively. Korea gives different results. The multiplier ratio of labour income to capital income is highest in mining and lowest in agriculture. In both countries, industry takes an intermediate position with the multiplier ratio of labour income to capital income varying between 0.6 for Colombia and 0.5 for Korea. The classification and computation of the factor accounts for Surinam is not strictly comparable with the other countries, while for Pakistan, as was stated earlier, the factor and institutions accounts are collapsed together.

In the third component, which gives the impact of injections to activities on the incomes of household groups, the following general results are found; these results will be further decomposed in section 5. The average size of the income multipliers is in descending order: Pakistan 2.85, Colombia 2.21, Korea 1.69, and Surinam 1.28. The services sector achieves the highest values. Income multipliers among the urban households are highest for the urban high skill workers, followed by the urban selfemployed. These results hold for Colombia, Pakistan and Surinam. In Korea, these two household groups exchange positions depending on which sector is injected. Generally speaking, in all four countries traditional services are relatively more beneficial to the selfemployed. Income multipliers among the rural households show diversified results for the four countries, reflecting the different rural structures in these countries. For instance, in Colombia the highest income multipliers go to the household groups of farm workers and non-farm workers, being the largest two groups population-wise.

Table 2.3. SAM Aggregate Multipliers by Activity for Four Countries

Country and item	21	22	23	24	25	26	27	28
COLOMBIA								
1 Food	0.8808	0.9411	0.6124	0.6252	0.8688	0.8059	0.8700	1.0221
2 Non-food	0.4077	0.4460	0.2852	0.2962	0.4173	0.3855	0.4141	0.4846
3 Housing	0.2696	0.3022	0.1893	0.2004	0.2869	0.2639	0.2816	0.3275
4 Health	0.0597	0.0650	0.0417	0.0432	0.0608	0.0561	0.0605	0.0712
5 Education	0.0712	0.0802	0.0502	0.0531	0.0760	0.0700	0.0746	0.0865
6 Other social services	0.1437	0.1608	0.1011	0.1061	0.1510	0.1396	0.1482	0.1701
7 Urban labour earnings	0.4983	0.6250	0.3634	0.4678	0.7529	0.6200	0.7571	1.1372
8 Rural labour earnings	0.3474	0.2783	0.2262	0.1908	0.2177	0.2109	0.2549	0.3384
9 Gross profits	1.5329	1.7075	1.0747	1.0505	1.4194	1.4032	1.3411	1.1634
10 Urban proprietors	0.0814	0.0934	0.0576	0.0608	0.0868	0.0810	0.0839	0.0917
11 Urban high skill wrkr	0.5680	0.6583	0.4035	0.4366	0.6352	0.5814	0.6173	0.7157
12 Urban low skill wrkr	0.0968	0.1211	0.0706	0.0909	0.1452	0.1204	0.1470	0.2209
13 Urban selfempl &fw	0.5075	0.5833	0.3595	0.3810	0.5466	0.5077	0.5285	0.5849
14 Urban inactive	0.2129	0.2459	0.1510	0.1621	0.2344	0.2159	0.2274	0.2588
15 Rural latifundists	0.0390	0.0397	0.0267	0.0251	0.0325	0.0320	0.0324	0.0321
16 Rural mdm/smlfrmwnr	0.0520	0.0485	0.0350	0.0316	0.0392	0.0383	0.0413	0.0459
17 Rural farm wrkr	0.1374	0.1101	0.0895	0.0755	0.0861	0.0834	0.1008	0.1338
18 Rural nonfarm hshlds	0.2350	0.2191	0.1580	0.1425	0.1768	0.1731	0.1864	0.2077
19 Rural inactive	0.5040	0.0463	0.0338	0.0303	0.0373	0.0364	0.0397	0.0451
20 Firms	0.3551	0.3955	0.2490	0.2433	0.3288	0.3251	0.3107	0.2695
21 Agriculture	1.5737	0.6004	0.9710	0.5876	0.5835	0.5337	0.6379	0.6819
22 Mining	0.0348	1.0495	0.0248	0.0483	0.0560	0.0366	0.0384	0.0417
23 Processed coffee	0.0224	0.0241	1.0688	0.0160	0.0224	0.0208	0.0379	0.0308
24 Industry	1.6098	1.7025	1.1272	2.4351	1.7949	1.5808	1.8056	1.9301
25 Electricity, gas, water	0.0336	0.0669	0.0243	0.0332	1.0581	0.0363	0.0410	0.0449
26 Modern services	0.9332	1.1483	0.7095	0.9055	0.9709	2.0243	0.9183	1.0742
27 Personal services	0.2901	0.3213	0.2038	0.2143	0.3056	0.2842	1.3023	0.3611
28 Public services	0.0195	0.0240	0.0140	0.0163	0.0219	0.0195	0.0204	1.2350
Total income multiplier (a)	0.3355	2.5612	1.6342	1.6797	2.35	2.2047	2.3255	2.6061
Total output multiplier (b)	4.5171	4.937	4.1434	4.3578	4.8133	4.5383	4.8027	5.1882

(a) Average all sectors=2.21. (b)Average all sectors=4.65

Table 2.3. (continued)

Country and item	15	16	17	18	19	20
KOREA						
1 Food	0.701	0.837	0.441	0.474	0.689	0.754
2 Others	0.380	0.445	0.237	0.254	0.367	0.407
3 Housing	0.113	0.143	0.073	0.079	0.117	0.123
4 Health	0.076	0.096	0.049	0.053	0.079	0.083
5 Education	0.084	0.099	0.053	0.056	0.082	0.099
6 Labour earnings	0.409	0.870	0.358	0.409	0.663	0.499
7 Capital earnings	1.477	1.217	0.789	0.809	1.078	1.502
8 Urban high skill worker	0.303	0.552	0.243	0.273	0.429	0.360
9 Urban low skill worker	0.175	0.329	0.142	0.160	0.254	0.207
10 Urban selfemployed/fw	0.440	0.382	0.239	0.248	0.335	0.450
11 Rural large holdings	0.306	0.269	0.168	0.174	0.235	0.316
12 Rural medium holdings	0.186	0.163	0.101	0.105	0.142	0.190
13 Rural small/ landless	0.106	0.093	0.058	0.060	0.081	0.109
14 Firms	0.380	0.313	0.202	0.209	0.277	0.386
15 Agriculture	1.534	0.598	0.365	0.383	0.491	0.511
16 Mining	0.021	1.026	0.031	0.030	0.029	0.020
17 Modern industry	0.991	1.057	1.885	0.910	1.081	0.886
18 Traditional industry	0.215	0.253	0.216	1.202	0.259	0.212
19 Modern services	0.487	0.674	0.400	0.414	1.514	0.637
20 Traditional services	0.239	0.368	0.271	0.277	0.341	1.316
Total income multiplier(a)	1.896	2.101	1.153	1.229	1.753	2.018
Total output multipliers(b)	3.487	3.976	3.168	3.216	3.715	3.582

(a) Average all sectors=1.692. (b) Average all sectors = 3.524

Table 2.3. (continued)

Country and item	18	19	20	21	22	23	24	25	26	27	28	29
PAKISTAN												
1 Food and drinks	1.47	1.46	1.08	0.93	1.29	1.23	0.79	1.09	1.42	1.06	1.19	1.22
2 Clothing, footwear	0.28	0.28	0.21	0.18	0.25	0.24	0.15	0.21	0.27	0.20	0.23	0.23
3 Personal effects	0.07	0.07	0.06	0.05	0.07	0.06	0.04	0.06	0.07	0.05	0.06	0.06
4 Rent	0.14	0.13	0.10	0.09	0.13	0.12	0.08	0.11	0.15	0.11	0.12	0.13
5 Fuel and lighting	0.14	0.13	0.10	0.09	0.12	0.11	0.07	0.10	0.13	0.10	0.11	0.11
6 Health	0.06	0.06	0.04	0.04	0.05	0.05	0.03	0.04	0.06	0.04	0.05	0.05
7 Education	0.03	0.03	0.03	0.02	0.03	0.03	0.02	0.03	0.03	0.03	0.03	0.03
8 Others	0.82	0.81	0.63	0.53	0.73	0.71	0.45	0.63	0.83	0.61	0.69	0.71
9 Urban employers	0.06	0.06	0.05	0.05	0.07	0.07	0.05	0.08	0.07	0.05	0.14	0.12
10 Urb non manual wrkr	0.17	0.17	0.15	0.12	0.16	0.15	0.11	0.28	0.23	0.15	0.23	0.27
11 Urban manual wrkr	0.19	0.18	0.15	0.17	0.21	0.22	0.13	0.19	0.17	0.23	0.16	0.21
12 Urban selfempl/fw	0.56	0.55	0.46	0.41	0.54	0.53	0.33	0.33	0.85	0.44	0.38	0.49
13 Rural large hldng	0.39	0.38	0.37	0.28	0.37	0.38	0.23	0.36	0.42	0.32	0.41	0.36
14 Rural medium hldng	0.44	0.44	0.37	0.29	0.39	0.38	0.24	0.35	0.42	0.34	0.40	0.37
15 Rural sml/lndlss wrkr	1.25	1.25	0.80	0.68	0.99	0.90	0.60	0.78	0.86	0.76	0.88	0.84
16 Rural nonfarm wrkr	0.16	0.16	0.08	0.08	0.12	0.11	0.07	0.08	0.11	0.09	0.09	0.10
17 Firms	0.23	0.22	0.16	0.16	0.22	0.19	0.43	0.15	0.19	0.22	0.17	0.22
18 Wheat and rice	1.41	0.40	0.27	0.25	0.66	0.39	0.21	0.27	0.36	0.27	0.30	0.31
19 Other agriculture	1.41	2.43	0.89	0.91	1.23	1.12	0.66	0.87	0.13	0.98	0.97	1.03
20 Mining, quarrying	0.12	0.13	1.10	0.14	0.13	0.20	0.08	0.13	0.12	0.13	0.11	0.12
21 Large scale mfctrng	1.78	1.68	1.41	2.34	1.75	1.85	1.08	1.30	1.61	1.88	1.51	1.63
22 Small scale mfctrng	0.69	0.69	0.52	0.44	1.80	0.84	0.40	0.52	0.68	0.50	0.57	0.58
23 Construction	0.01	0.01	0.01	0.01	0.01	1.01	0.11	0.01	0.02	0.01	0.02	0.01
24 Housing	0.14	0.14	0.11	0.09	0.13	0.12	1.08	0.11	0.15	0.11	0.12	0.13
25 Water, electy, gas	0.10	0.90	0.07	0.09	0.11	0.09	0.05	1.10	0.08	0.08	0.15	0.09
26 Whlsale, retail trade	0.67	0.67	0.57	0.45	0.61	0.50	0.28	0.36	1.45	0.43	0.40	0.42
27 Transport, cmnctn	0.68	0.60	0.48	0.43	0.65	0.54	0.32	0.43	0.57	1.44	0.55	0.57
28 Banking, insurance	0.11	0.11	0.10	0.09	0.11	0.12	0.07	0.08	0.11	0.09	1.12	0.11
29 Public services	0.39	0.39	0.31	0.25	0.35	0.34	0.21	0.30	0.39	0.30	0.33	1.37
Ttl income multiplier (a)	3.45	3.41	2.59	2.24	3.07	2.93	2.19	2.6	3.32	2.6	2.86	2.98
Ttl output multiplier (b)	4.57	5.19	3.58	4.19	5.52	5.41	3.6	4.21	5.06	4.84	4.77	4.91

Note: Factors account not shown since it corresponds to the institutions account in the application to Pakistan. (a) Average all sectors=2.853. (b) Average all sectors = 4.653.

Table 2.3. (continued)

Country and item	15	16	17	18	19	20
SURINAM						
1 Food	0.250	0.513	0.189	0.204	0.292	0.594
2 Housing	0.090	0.164	0.068	0.074	0.106	0.190
3 Clothing	0.071	0.132	0.054	0.058	0.083	0.153
4 Education	0.028	0.056	0.022	0.024	0.034	0.065
5 Health	0.065	0.130	0.049	0.053	0.076	0.151
6 Others	0.195	0.356	0.148	0.159	0.228	0.412
7 Labour income	0.511	0.420	0.436	0.495	0.701	0.486
8 Capital income	0.599	0.305	0.361	0.316	0.516	0.437
9 Traditional income	0.068	0.905	0.044	0.057	0.067	1.050
10 Urban workers	0.480	0.737	0.364	0.383	0.562	0.388
11 Urban selfemployed / fw	0.029	0.391	0.019	0.025	0.029	0.434
12 Rural landowners	0.039	0.513	0.025	0.032	0.038	0.596
13 Rural workers	0.318	0.231	0.248	0.265	0.386	0.262
14 Firms	0.210	0.109	0.129	0.112	0.181	0.142
15 Modern agrculture	1.066	0.115	0.037	0.178	0.049	0.097
16 Traditional agriculture	0.044	1.146	0.023	0.038	0.035	0.071
17 Mining	0.081	0.001	1.229	0.001	0.002	0.001
18 Industry	0.240	0.404	0.185	1.217	0.229	0.444
19 Modern services	0.465	0.734	0.373	0.378	1.513	0.850
20 Traditional services	0.047	0.171	0.035	0.039	0.054	1.231
Total income multiplier (a)	1.076	1.981	0.785	0.817	1.196	1.822
Total output multiplier (b)	0.877	2.456	1.845	1.673	1.833	2.597

(a) Average all sectors=1.2795. (b) Average all sctors=1.8802

In Korea, the income multipliers are highest for the larger farmers and lowest for landless workers. In Pakistan, the opposite is found, reflecting the magnitude of population shares of the various household groups. In Surinam, where plantation agriculture is very common, income multipliers for farm workers are higher than for the household group of self-employed and family helpers.

The exception is that injections in traditional services bring higher income multipliers to the self-employed and family helpers: a phenomenon also noted in the urban context.

The fourth compartment gives the impact of injections in sectoral activities on the sectoral activities themselves, after proceeding through and covering the whole circular flow. Here too, the ranking of the four countries is the same, with Pakistan and Colombia both having on average the highest multiplier at 4.65, followed by Korea at 3.52 and Surinam at 1.88. In all cases, the services sectors score the highest multipliers. Results of the fourth component will be decomposed and analysed further in section 6.

It is instructive to calculate a ratio obtainable by dividing the averages of the output multipliers by the income multipliers for each of the four countries, and then compare them. This will give an indication of the comparative size of circular flow of sectoral output required to create a unit of household income. The results show that Colombia and Korea, which are the most developed of the four countries, require more output per unit of income. The ratios are 2.10 and 2.08 for Colombia and Korea. The value for Pakistan is 1.63 and for Surinam 1.47. In spite of this disadvantage, both Korea and Colombia are able to generate bigger values of household incomes for their populations than Pakistan or Surinam. This is possible in view of the much greater circular flow of economic activities (greater volume of sectoral output) which characterises Korea and Colombia, as compared to Pakistan or Surinam.

4. Decomposition Analysis of SAM Multipliers

As was previously stated, the aggregate multiplier matrix can be decomposed into three multiplier matrices M_1, M_2 and M_3, as in equation (2.3) below. M_1, which is known as the transfer multiplier, captures effects resulting from direct transfers within endogenous accounts (for example, between production activities). The open loop effects, M_2, capture the interactions among and between the endogenous accounts (from production activities to factors, institutions and wants). The closed-loop effects, M_3, ensure that the circular flow of income is completed among endogenous accounts (from production activities to factors to institutions to wants and then back to activities in the form of consumption demand).

$$y = Ay + x = (I - A)^{-1} x = M_a x = M_3 M_2 M_1 x \tag{2.3}$$

The formal derivation of the decomposed multipliers proceeds by separating matrix $\tilde{A}$ from A, provided that $\tilde{A}$ is of the same size as A and that $\left(I - \tilde{A}\right)^{-1}$ exists. A pictorial presentation is found in the appendix to the chapter.

$$y = Ay + x$$
$$= \left(A - \tilde{A}\right)y + \tilde{A}y + x$$
$$= \left(I - \tilde{A}\right)^{-1}\left(A - \tilde{A}\right)y + \left(I - \tilde{A}\right)^{-1}x$$
$$= A^* y + \left(I - \tilde{A}\right)^{-1}x \tag{2.4}$$

Here, $\left(I - \tilde{A}\right)^{-1}$ refers to the transfer multiplier, M_1. Derivation of M_2 and M_3 proceeds further as in equations (2.5) to (2.7).

Both sides of equation (2.4) can be multiplied by A^*, substituting for A^*y from equation (2.4) and rearranging terms to give:

$$y = A^{*2} y + \left(I + A^*\right)\left(I + \tilde{A}\right)^{-1}x \tag{2.5}$$

The same manipulation can be repeated with A^{*2} up to A^{*k}, so that in general:

$$y = A^{*k} y + \left(I + A^* + A^{*2} + \ldots + A^{*(k-1)}\right)\left(I - \tilde{A}\right)^{-1}x \tag{2.6}$$

For any positive value for k it is true then that:

$$y = \left(I - A^{*k}\right)^{-1}\left(I + A^* + A^{*2} + \ldots + A^{*(k-1)}\right)\left(I - \tilde{A}\right)^{-1}x \tag{2.7}$$

Here then, $\left(I - A^{*k}\right)^{-1}$ is identified with M_3.. $\left(I + A^* + A^{*2} + \ldots + A^{*(k-1)}\right)$ is identified with M_2 and, as was just mentioned, $\left(I - \tilde{A}\right)^{-1}$ refers to M_1. The multipliers can also be rearranged in an additive form. The multiplicative decomposition can be rearranged, as done by Stone (1978), into four additive components, namely, the initial injection I and the net contributions of the transfer effect T, open loop effect 0 and closed-loop effect C, as follows:

$$M_a = I + \left(M_1 - I\right) + \left(M_2 - I\right)M_1 + \left(M_3 - I\right)M_2 M_1 = I + T + 0 + C$$

It is recalled that the general multiplier matrix M_a is decomposable into the three partial multiplier matrices of $M_3\, M_2\, M_1$ as in eq. (2.8).

$$M_a = M_3\, M_2\, M_1 \qquad\qquad (2.8)$$

This equation can correspondingly be rewritten for the specific multiplier matrices of $M_{a,34}$ and $M_{a,44}$, decomposable into their own partial multiplier matrices. In this section, attention will be directed to the decomposition of the third compartment in table 2.3, that is $M_{a,34}$, leaving the analysis of the fourth compartment in table 2.3, that is $M_{a,44}$, to the next section. A decomposition of $M_{a,34}$ into its transfer, open and closed multiplier effects requires an analysis of the three submatrices shown in eq. (2.9).

$$M_{a,34} = \left(M_{3,33}\right)\left(M_{2,34}\right)\left(M_{1,44}\right) \qquad\qquad (2.9)$$
overall = (closed)(open)(transfer).

Table 2.4 gives $M_{1,44}$, and table 2.5 gives $M_{2,34}$ and $M_{3,33}$, for the four studied countries.

Table 2.4 contains $M_{1,44}$, which capture the well known transfer effects within the input-output accounts. This will be referred to again later, but for the moment it should be noted that transfer effects are particularly important in industry, and that because of fewer linkages the multipliers for agriculture and the other sectors are lower.

In the case of Colombia, the first column of table 2.4 shows an initial injection into agriculture of 1.0 to result in an addition to agriculture of 1.0414, mining 0.0036, industry 0.1560, modern services 0.1411 etc. The original injection of 1.0 leads to a total increase of 1.3459. These transfer effects will be traced through the rest of the system, including $M_{2,34}$ and $M_{3,33}$ in order to illustrate the working of the system.

Table 2.5 contains also $M_{2,34}$, which capture open loop effects. Because of the high diversity of income sources in Colombia, and in particular, the significant presence of non-rural beneficiaries from agricultural expansion, the original injection of 1.0 into agriculture leads to a 0.22 increase in rural earnings as compared with a 0.55 increase in non-rural earnings.

Table 2.5 also presents closed-loop multipliers, as indicated in $M_{3,33}$. These multipliers are greatly influenced by the consumption patterns of the households. The increases in income resulting from open loop effects are used mainly to purchase consumer goods, which increase output, and, in turn, increase factor income that is paid out as institutional income, which is again spent mainly on consumption, and so on.

Table 2.4. Transfer Effects by Type of Activity in Four Countries

COLOMBIA	21	22	23	24	25	26	27	28
21.Agriculture	1.0414	0.0275	0.6002	0.2071	0.0524	0.0417	0.1077	0.0600
22.Mining	0.0036	1.0156	0.0030	0.0258	0.0245	0.0074	0.0070	0.0050
23.Proc coffee	0.0000	0.0001	1.0532	0.0001	0.0001	0.0001	0.0156	0.0047
24.Industry	0.1560	0.1299	0.1133	1.3908	0.3336	0.2279	0.3495	0.2241
25.Electricity,gas	0.0016	0.0316	0.0018	0.0098	1.0249	0.0057	0.0083	0.0071
26.Modern srvcs	0.1411	0.2754	0.1543	0.3262	0.1512	1.2676	0.1078	0.1293
27.Personal srvcs	0.0012	0.0025	0.0012	0.0033	0.0062	0.0079	1.0062	0.0157
28.Public srvcs	0.0010	0.0036	0.0010	0.0027	0.0028	0.0020	0.0015	1.0015

KOREA	15	16	17	18	19	20
15.Agriculture	1.115	0.039	0.070	0.066	0.031	0.007
16.Mining	0.004	1.007	0.020	0.019	0.013	0.003
17.Modern indstr	0.162	0.178	1.422	0.411	0.357	0.092
18.Trad industry	0.039	0.043	0.105	1.082	0.085	0.022
19.Modern srvcs	0.043	0.130	0.120	0.112	1.175	0.159
20.Trad srvcs	0.023	0.048	0.103	0.096	0.078	1.030

PAKISTAN	18	19	20	21	22	23	24	25	26	27	28	29
18.Wheat, rice	1.04	0.03	s	0.02	0.34	0.08	0.01	s	0.00	0.01	s	s
19.Other agricul	0.25	1.28	0.03	0.17	0.22	0.15	0.04	0.01	s	0.14	0.03	0.06
20.Mining	0.01	0.01	1.01	0.06	0.03	0.10	0.02	0.04	s	0.04	0.01	0.01
21.Large scale m	0.16	0.07	0.20	1.30	0.32	0.48	0.20	0.08	0.01	0.71	0.18	0.27
22.Small scale m	0.00	0.00	0.00	s	1.19	0.26	0.03	0.00	0.00	s	s	0.00
23.Construction	0.00	0.00	0.00	0.00	0.00	1.00	0.10	0.00	0.00	0.00	s	0.00
24.Housing	0.00	0.00	0.00	0.00	0.00	0.00	1.00	0.00	0.00	0.00	s	0.00
25.Water, elect	0.02	0.01	0.01	0.04	0.03	0.02	0.01	1.04	s	0.02	0.08	0.02
26.Wholesale	0.21	0.21	0.23	0.16	0.21	0.12	0.03	0.02	1.00	0.09	0.02	0.04
27.Transport	0.12	0.05	0.06	0.07	0.15	0.06	0.02	0.01	0.02	1.04	0.08	0.10
28.Banking ins	0.01	0.01	0.02	0.02	0.02	0.03	0.01	s	0.01	0.01	1.03	0.02
29.Public servic	s	s	0.01	s	s	0.01	s	s	s	0.01	0.01	1.04

SURINAM	15	16	17	18	19	220
15.Modern agric	1.027	0.037	0.007	0.146	0.003	0.007
16.Traditional ag	0.014	1.085	0.001	0.914	0.000	0.001
17.Mining	0.000	0.000	1.229	0.000	0.001	0.000
18.Industry	0.066	0.062	0.053	1.075	0.025	0.048
19.Modern srvcs	0.097	0.010	0.095	0.078	1.083	0.046
20.Trad srvcs	0.001	0.080	0.000	0.001	0.000	1.126

s = small, varying between .001 and .005

Table 2.5. Open-Loop and Closed-Loop Effects in Four Countries

Country and Institutions	Index (a)	Open loop effects		Closed loop effects					
		Agr (b)	Ind (c)	Urban groups			Rural groups		
				1	2	3	4	5	6
COLOMBIA									
1.Urb high skill	11	0.161	0.054	1.469	0.509	0.479	0.359	0.495	0.552
2.Urb low skill	12	0.013	0.014	0.098	1.106	0.100	0.075	0.102	0.107
3.Urb self-empl.	13	0.152	0.045	0.409	0.445	1.418	0.313	0.433	0.457
4.Rur large hld	15	0.016	0.002	0.027	0.030	0.028	1.021	0.029	0.031
5.Rur med hld	16	0.101	0.013	0.153	0.169	0.157	0.119	1.168	0.178
6.Rur smll/lndls	17	0.066	0.007	0.082	0.091	0.084	0.064	0.091	1.097
7.Other hshlds	e	0.130	0.033	0.305	0.333	0.313	0.234	0.325	0.313
8.Firms	20	0.127	0.024	0.260	0.284	0.266	0.200	0.279	0.295
Total		0.766	0.192	2.803	2.967	2.845	2.385	2.922	3.030
KOREA									
1.Urb high skill	8	0.081	0.048	1.293	0.310	0.297	0.231	0.254	0.274
2.Urb low skill	9	0.044	0.028	0.170	1.180	0.173	0.134	0.148	0.159
3.Urb self-empl.	10	0.190	0.040	0.314	0.341	1.321	0.249	0.278	0.304
4.Rur large hld	11	0.133	0.028	0.220	0.239	0.255	1.175	0.195	0.213
5.Rur med hld	12	0.080	0.017	0.133	0.144	0.136	0.105	1.118	0.129
6.Rur smll/lndls	13	0.046	0.010	0.076	0.082	0.078	0.060	0.067	1.074
7.Other hshlds	..	..	..	..	..	..	..	..	..
8.Firms	14	0.167	0.033	0.267	0.290	0.273	0.211	0.237	0.259
Total		0.741	0.204	2.473	2.586	2.503	2.165	2.297	2.412
PAKISTAN									
1.Urb high skill	10	0.000	0.004	1.143	0.145	0.143	0.147	0.154	0.162
2.Urb low skill	11	0.006	0.041	0.166	1.169	0.165	0.168	0.179	0.188
3.Urb self-empl.	12	0.025	0.049	0.417	0.425	1.415	0.410	0.455	0.479
4.Rur large hld	13	0.036	0.035	0.293	0.299	0.292	1.292	0.319	0.336
5.Rur med hld	14	0.070	0.030	0.311	0.318	0.310	0.306	1.340	0.358
6.Rur smll/lndls	15	0.300	0.047	0.786	0.805	0.782	0.765	0.865	1.913
7.Other hshlds	f	0.043	0.010	0.155	0.159	0.154	0.152	0.169	0.176
8.Firms	17	0.025	0.026	0.193	0.196	0.193	0.181	0.198	0.209
Total		0.505	0.242	3.464	3.516	3.454	3.421	3.679	3.821
SURINAM									
1.Urb high skill	10 g	..	..	..	..	..	..	..	..
2.Urb low skill	10 g	0.265	0.171	..	1.296	0.396	..	0.369	0.325
3.Urb self-empl.	11	0.000	0.000	..	0.045	1.061	..	0.060	0.049
4.Rur large hld	12 g	..	..	..	..	..	..	..	..
5.Rur med hld	12 g	0.000	0.000	..	0.059	0.080	..	1.079	0.064
6.Rur smll/lndls	13	0.171	0.121	..	0.203	0.272	..	0.254	1.224
7.Other hshlds	..	..	..	..	..	..	..	..	..
8.Firms	14	0.141	0.038	..	0.094	0.126	..	0.118	0.104
Total		0.577	0.330	..	1.697	1.935	..	1.880	1.766

a = For country index of household groups see table 2.3; b = Agriculture refers to sector in row 21 for Colombia, 15 for the Republic of Korea and 27 and 28 for Pakistan, as indicated in table 2.3; c = Industry refers to sector in row 24 for Colombia, 30 for Pakistan, 17 for the Republic of Korea and 18 for Surinam, as indicated in table 2.3; d = No separate column for firms is included since the closed-loop effects of firms amount to zero; e = Country groups 10, 14, 18 and 19; f = Country groups 19 and 25; g = Not separately calculated.

If this part of the table is read on a row-by-row basis, excluding the initial injections and the few exceptions, it appears that the closed-loop multipliers are fairly constant. This can be interpreted as the result of similar household expenditure and savings patterns. The closed-loop multipliers are generally much higher than either the transfer or open loop multipliers, which reflects the fact that consumption is larger than other categories of final demand or factor shares. For Colombia, an income receipt of 1.0 in any household group creates between 2.3856 and 3.0293 of total institutional income through the closed-loop effects. These can be compared with the impact for transfer effects by an activity, which ranged between 1.3459 and 1.9658 in table 2.4, and with that for open loop effects, which varied between 0.0603 and 0.7663 in table 2.5. Being higher than the other multipliers and given their low variance, the closed-loop multipliers tend to dampen the effects of the transfer and open loop multipliers.

Table 2.6 illustrates the combined working of the three decomposed effects. We trace the impact of an exogenous injection of one additional unit in the sector of agriculture on the incomes of household groups. We trace the impact via the transfer multipliers which affect sectoral activities, $M_{a,44}$. For instance, in Colombia the multiplier value for $M_{a,44}$ of an injection in agriculture on agriculture is 1.041, in row 1, column 2, and on industry 0.156, in row 1, column 3. These transfer effects are then combined with open-loop effects to give income increases per household group as in columns 2 and 3. The summing of these effects over all sectors gives column 4.

One may now proceed to track the closed-loop effects resulting from the combined transfer and open loop effects as obtained in column 4. To focus the analysis, we shall trace these effects for one household group only, namely that of the rural farm workers, this being usually the largest and poorest. Column 5 gives the applicable closed-loop effects for rural farm workers, already shown in row 6 in table 2.5. The multiplication of columns 4 by 5 results in column 6, which gives the aggregate effects. When these aggregate effects are summed, the overall multiplier for rural farm workers of 0.124 is obtained. The difference between this figure and the value of 0.137 in table 2.3 is the result of neglecting the impact of activities and institutions other than those specified in table 2.6. Similarly, overall multipliers can be obtained for other household groups and firms.

These results suggest that the marginal share of benefits to rural workers from agricultural expansion amount to about 5.8%. Since the income share of rural workers in 1970 amounted to 3.5%, it can be expected that an injection into agriculture will have the effect of enhancing the relative position of rural workers in the distribution of income.

The multipliers in the preceding tables are deceptive, in the sense that they do not allow an assessment of the benefit per household among the different household groups. In principle, dividing the multipliers by the number of households in each household group may give more insight. However, because of the underlying magnitudes of the database, it happens that the higher-in-rank average household always benefits more in absolute terms than the average household next in rank. Hence the need to consider relative effects. This is done in table 2.7, which adapts the multiplier effects of the preceding tables to give their relative distribution among the various institutional destinations.

Table 2.7 gives the percentage distribution of the multiplier benefit. The table is selective since it gives such results for initial injections into agriculture and industry only, and pursues the open and closed-loop multipliers for six population groups, which are generally comparable among the four countries studied. To assess the marginal effect of the multipliers on income distribution, column 2 of table 2.7 gives the actual income shares in the SAM. In general, higher multiplier shares than actual shares for the urban self-employed (group 3) and rural small owners and/or landless workers (group 6) would promote equality, and lower multiplier shares than actual shares for these two groups would decrease equality.

In the case of Colombia the aggregate multipliers of injections into both agriculture and industry promote a redistribution of income from urban to rural population groups. Other aggregate multipliers not included in the table are those of mining, which point in the same direction, but less significantly. The multipliers of energy distribute relatively more to urban than to rural households, while multipliers of the government sector appear to benefit household groups in various degrees at the cost of firms.

The relative redistributionary effects of the open loop multipliers appear to be very significant. Agricultural benefits are shown to be shared among the specified urban and rural populations in proportions of 0.43 and 0.24, while the actual income shares are distributed in the proportions of 0.55 and 0.12 to specified urban and rural populations, respectively. Not shown in the table are injections into mining, which promote equality and those into energy and government, which decrease equality.

These significant redistributionary effects, whether they are positive or negative, are neutralised to a great extent by the closed-loop effects. Table 2.7 shows that, for Colombia, the closed-loop effects are distributed among the urban and rural population groups in proportions which correspond closely to their actual shares. The gains obtained via the transfer and factor effects by a group are partly lost to other groups through consumption leakages.

Table 2.6. **Effects of an Exogenous Injection** *(+ 1.0)* **into Agricultural Activity on the Income of Rural Small / Landless Farm Workers**

Country and institutions	*1* Index	Transfer effects (TE) and open-loop effects				
		2 Agriculture	*3* Industry	*4* Sum of activities	*5* Closed-loop effects	*6* Aggregate effects
COLOMBIA		*TE* = 1.041	*TE* = 0.156			0.1241
1.Urb high skill	11	0.1674	0.0084	0.1994	0.0815	0.0163
2.Urb low skill	12	0.0130	0.0022	0.0200	0.0908	0.0018
3.Urb self-empl.	13	0.1528	0.0070	0.1858	0.0839	0.0156
4.Rur large hld	15	0.0161	0.0004	0.0177	0.0810	0.0011
5.Rur med hld	16	0.1054	0.0021	0.1132	0.0909	0.0103
6.Rur smll/lndls	17	0.0690	0.0010	0.0720	1.0966	0.0790
7.Other hshlds	..	..	..	..	..	..
8.Firms	20	0.1326	0.0038	0.1497	0.0000	0.000
KOREA		*TE* = 1.120	*TE* = 0.160			0.1058
1.Urb high skill	8	0.0900	0.0110	0.1010	0.0760	0.0077
2.Urb low skill	9	0.0450	0.0060	0.0510	0.0820	0.0042
3.Urb self-empl.	10	0.2130	0.0060	0.2090	0.0780	0.0163
4.Rur large hld	11	0.1460	0.0050	0.1510	0.0600	0.0091
5.Rur med hld	12	0.0900	0.0030	0.0930	0.0670	0.0062
6.Rur smll/lndls	13	0.0560	0.0020	0.0580	1.0740	0.0623
7.Other hshlds	..	..	..	..	..	..
8.Firms	14	0.1790	0.0050	0.1840	0.0000	0.0000
PAKISTAN		*TE* = 1.043	*TE* = 0.161			0.7530
1.Urb high skill	10	..	0.0010	0.0010	0.7860	0.0008
2.Urb low skill	11	0.0060	0.0070	0.0130	0.8050	0.0105
3.Urb self-empl.	12	0.0260	0.0080	0.0340	0.7820	0.0266
4.Rur large hld	13	0.0380	0.0060	0.0440	0.7650	0.3370
5.Rur med hld	14	0.0730	0.0050	0.0780	0.8650	0.0675
6.Rur smll/lndls	15	0.3130	0.0080	0.3210	1.9130	0.6141
7.Other hshlds	..	..	..	..	..	..
8.Firms	17	0.0260	0.0020	0.0280	0.0000	0.0000
SURINAM		*TE* = 1.027	*TE* = 0.066			0.2826
1.Urb high skill		..	..	..	..	..
2.Urb low skill	10	0.2720	0.0110	0.2830	0.2030	0.0574
3.Urb self-empl.	11	0.0000	0.0000	0.0000	0.2720	0.0000
4.Rur large hld	..	..	..	..	..	..
5.Rur med hld	12	0.0000	0.0000	0.0000	0.2540	0.0000
6.Rur smll/lndls	13	0.1760	0.0880	0.1840	1.2240	0.2252
7.Other hshlds	..	..	..	..	..	..
8.Firms	14	0.1450	0.0030	0.1480	0.0000	0.0000

Column 1: see tables 2.3 and 2.5. Column 2: (*TE* from table 2.4) x (column 2, table2.5).
Column 3: (*TE* from table 2.4) x (column 3, table 2.5). Column 4: column 2 + column 3 and
other activities. Column 5: row 6 from table 2.5. Column 6: (column 4) x (column 2.5).

Table 2.7. Percentage distributions obtained from SAMs

Country & institutions columns	Country index (1)	Actual income (2)	Aggregate multipliers (3) Agri	Ind	Open-loop effects (4) Agri	Ind	Closed-loop effects Urban groups 1	2	3	Rural groups 4	5	6
COLUMBIA												
1 Urb high skill	11	26.4	24.3	26	21	28.1	26	25.9	26	25.9	25.8	27.2
2 Urb low skill	12	5.9	4.1	5.4	1.7	7.3	5.4	5.4	5.4	5.4	5.3	5.3
3 Urb selfempl	13	22.7	21.7	22.7	19.8	23.4	22.7	22.6	22.7	22.6	22.5	22.5
4 Rur large hld	15	1.4	1.7	1.5	2.1	1	1.5	1.5	1.5	1.5	1.5	1.5
5 Rur med hld	16	7.3	10.1	8.5	13.2	6.8	8.5	8.6	8.5	8.6	8.7	8.8
6 Rur sml/lndl	17	3.5	5.9	4.5	8.6	3.6	4.5	4.6	4.6	4.6	4.7	4.7
7 Oher hshlds	..	17.9	17	16.9	17	17.2	16.9	16.9	17	17	16.9	15.4
8 Firms	20	14.9	15.2	14.5	16.6	12.5	14.4	14.4	14.4	14.4	14.5	14.5
KOREA												
1 Urb high skill	8	23	16.2	20.9	10.9	23.5	19.9	19.5	19.8	19.8	19.6	19.4
2 Urb low skill	9	13.6	9.4	12.2	5.9	13.7	11.5	11.3	11.5	11.5	11.4	11.3
3 Urb selfempl	10	20	22.9	20.9	25.6	19.6	21.3	21.5	21.4	21.4	21.4	21.5
4 Rur large hld	11	14	16.2	14.8	17.9	13.8	14.9	15.1	15	15	15	15.1
5 Rur med hld	12	8.5	9.9	8.7	10.8	8.3	9	9.1	9	9	9.1	9.1
6 Rur sml/lndl	13	4.8	5.7	5.2	6.2	4.9	5.2	5.2	5.2	5.2	5.2	5.2
7 Oher hshlds	..	..	..	..	..	..	..	..	..	..	..	..
8 Firms	14	16.1	19.8	17.4	22.5	16.2	18.1	18.3	18.2	18.1	18.3	18.3
PAKISTAN												
1 Urb high skill	10	6.9	4.9	5.4	0	1.7	5.8	5.8	5.8	6.1	5.7	5.7
2 Urb low skill	11	7.2	5.5	7.5	1.2	16.9	6.7	6.7	6.7	6.9	6.7	6.7
3 Urb selfempl	12	17.7	16.2	18.4	5	20.5	16.9	16.9	16.9	16.9	17	17
4 Rur large hld	13	12	11.2	12.5	7.1	14.5	11.9	11.9	11.9	12.1	11.9	11.9
5 Rur med hld	14	12.9	12.9	12.8	13.9	12.4	12.6	12.6	12.6	12.6	12.7	12.7
6 Rur sml/lndl	15	30.4	35.7	30	58.4	19.4	31.9	32	31.9	31.6	32.3	32.4
7 Oher hshlds	..	7.2	6.9	6.1	8.5	4.1	6.3	6.3	6.3	6.3	6.3	6.2
8 Firms	17	6.1	6.7	7.3	5	10.7	7.8	7.8	7.9	7.5	7.4	7.4
SURINAM												
1 Urb high skill	..	..	..	..	..	..	..	..	..	..	..	..
2 Urb low skill	10	46	44.6	46.9	45.9	51.8	..	42.5	42.5	..	41.9	42.4
3 Urb selfempl	11	3.3	2.7	3.1	0	0	..	6.5	6.5	..	6.8	6.4
4 Rur large hld	..	..	..	..	..	..	..	..	..	..	..	..
5 Rur med hld	12	4.4	3.6	3.9	0	0	..	8.5	8.6	..	9	8.4
6 Rur sml/lndl	13	32.2	29.6	32.4	29.6	36.7	..	29.1	29.1	..	28.9	29.2
7 Oher hshlds	..	..	..	..	..	..	..	..	..	..	..	..
8 Firms	14	14.1	19.5	13.7	24.4	11.5	..	13.5	13.5	..	13.4	13.6

Column 1: see tables 2.3 and 2.5. Column 2: calculated from the SAM. Column 3: calculated from the aggregate multiplier of table 2.4. Column 4: calculated from the open loop effect of table 2.5. Column 5: calculated from the closed-loop effect of table 2.5 after deducting the initial injection of one unit from the diagonals and totals.

The above results for Colombia can be briefly compared with those for Korea, Pakistan, and Surinam. The three economies of Colombia, Korea, and Pakistan appear to have in common a progressive redistributionary effect from richer towards poorer household groups following injections into agriculture or industry, although these effects are more significant in Korea and Pakistan than in Colombia. This is partly because of open loop effects, which are more discriminatory in Korea and Pakistan than in Colombia. It is also the result of closed-loop effects, which tend to shift resources from richer to poorer groups and firms. This reflects that consumption patterns among poorer household groups are more divergent and self-constrained in Korea and Pakistan than in Colombia. In general, firms in Korea and Pakistan are able to capture relatively more of the aggregate benefit than in Colombia.

In Surinam, the aggregate multipliers of modern agriculture favour firms and disfavour households, mainly because of open loop effects associated with the plantation-like nature of modern agriculture. Aggregate multipliers of industry, which correspond closely to open loop effects, provide an increase in the actual income shares. In Surinam, the closed-loop effects show a pattern favouring the self-employed in cities and the owner class in districts, but disfavouring wage earners in cities and landless workers in districts. These closed-loop effects are not sufficient to change the impact of the open loop effects, so that the final outcome generally favours firms at the cost of households.

Finally, some summarised figures are tabulated in table 2.8 for the two largest and poorest household groups in urban and rural areas, namely the urban selfemployed and family workers, and the rural small/landless workers. Table 2.8 shows the actual share of the income of these groups in the total national income, and the simulated share of the redistributionary impact for these household groups in the total income multiplier. The results are shown for injections into agriculture and industry.

The picture indicates the presence of a slightly progressive mechanism in Colombia, somewhat more progressive mechanisms in Pakistan, and even more in Korea. The contrary result, i.e. the absence of a progressive redistributionary mechanism, is found for Surinam.

In general, agricultural multipliers show more progressive redistributionary effects than industrial multipliers (except in Surinam, where agriculture is understood to refer to modern plantations). Moreover, the aggregate multipliers of injections into a particular activity for all activities is higher for agriculture than for industry (see table 2.3), so that, as far as these two sectors are concerned, progressive redistribution and higher growth can go hand-in-hand.

Table 2.8. Income Share of the Two Poorest Groups (Percentages)

	Actual share	Simulated share for injections in	
		Agriculture	*Industry*
COLOMBIA	26.2	27.6	27.2
KOREA	24.8	28.6	26.1
PAKISTAN	48.1	51.9	48.4
SURINAM	35.5	32.3	35.5

Source: Adapted from table 2.7.

The results direct attention to the presence of degrees of freedom in the selection of balanced socio-economic development policies, despite the existence of countervailing mechanisms that cause part of the redistribution and growth potential to vanish.

5. Decomposition Analysis of SAM Multipliers: Transfer Effects

With reference to table 2.3, the $M_{a,44}$ component gives the aggregate multipliers of injections into a particular activity on the activities account. As in the previous section, these aggregate multipliers can be decomposed into their transfer, open loop and closed-loop effects. Open loop effects, being expressions of cross effects between accounts, are not applicable in the present case. Therefore, an analysis of the differences between the aggregate multiplier and that part of it which forms the transfer effects is sufficient to appreciate the nature of the remaining part, which forms the closed-loop effects.

The aggregate multipliers of $M_{a,44}$ in table 2.3 can now be confronted with the previously discussed transfer effects of activities on activities, $M_{1,44}$, found in table 2.4. The latter represents the simpler inverse of Leontief.

As expected, first, the SAM contains more linkages than the Leontief, with the result that $M_{a,44}$ is substantially higher than $M_{1,44}$. Second, as a result of the heterogeneity of the linkages, the structural pattern of $M_{a,44}$ is also different from $M_{1,44}$.

The first point may be illustrated from table 2.9, which gives the frequency distribution of the size of the aggregate multipliers and the transfer effects, or the SAM-inverse and the Leontief-inverse, respectively. The percentage of elements of negligible size, which form the great majority in the Leontief-inverse in the four countries, is significantly reduced in the SAM-inverse, reflecting the incorporation of many more indirect effects and additional interdependencies in a social accounting framework. Summing up elements of less than 0.2 gives a result of 86% in the Leontief-inverse and only 50% in the SAM-inverse for Colombia. The reductions are from 100% to 70% for Surinam, from 93% to 17% for Korea, and from 90% to 42% for Pakistan. The additional interdependencies brought in by the SAM are, relatively speaking, the most extensive in the case of Korea.

Table 2.9. Size Distributions of the Off-Diagonal Elements of the SAM-Inverse and the Leontief-Inverse, Four Countries
(in percentages)

Element size	< 0.050	0.051- 0.100	0.101 – 0.150	0.151 – 0.200	0.201 – 0.250	0.251 – 0.500	0.501 – 1.000	> 1.000
COLOMBIA								
SAM multiplier	46.4	3.6	0.0	0.0	3.6	8.9	21.4	16.1
Leontief multiplier	66.0	3.6	10.7	5.4	5.4	7.1	1.8	0.0
KOREA								
SAM multiplier	16.7	0.0	0.0	0.0	10.0	43.3	23.3	6.7
Leontief multiplier	46.1	20.0	16.7	10.0	0.0	6.7	0.0	0.0
PAKISTAN								
SAM multiplier	8.3	11.4	21.2	0.8	2.3	22.7	21.2	12.1
Leontief multiplier	71.2	9.8	3.8	5.3	4.5	4.5	0.8	0.0
SURINAM								
SAM multiplier	46.7	10.0	3.3	10.0	6.7	16.7	6.7	0.0
Leontief multiplier	73.3	23.3	3.3	0.0	0.0	0.0	0.0	0.0

Source: Tables 2.3 and 2.4.

The second point can be illustrated from table 2.10. For Colombia, sectors are ranked according to the Leontief total column multipliers in the order of industry (1.97), mining (1.49), services (1.45) and agriculture (1.35). Their contributions to production activity and their ranking are significantly different in the SAM total column multipliers: services (5.19), mining (4.94), agriculture (4.52) and industry (4.26). A structural analysis based on the Leontief framework instead of the SAM framework would have led to the wrong decisions being taken on the allocations required to achieve the highest growth rates. Similar contrasts occur in the other countries. For instance, the attractive position occupied by industry, in a structural analysis based on the Leontief framework, as the foremost contributor to production activity, is taken over by the activities of service, mining and agriculture. These individually contribute more than industry in a SAM framework; this is true for Korea, Pakistan, and Surinam (in Surinam, mining precedes industry).

Table 2.10. Own Multipliers and Total Column Multipliers in the SAM-Inverse and the Leontief-Inverse, Four Countries

Element size	*Agriculture*		*Mining*		*Industry*		*Services*	
	1. own	2. total	1. own	2. total	1. own	2. total	1. own	2. total
COLOMBIA								
SAM multiplier	1.57	4.52	1.05	4.94	2.44	4.26	1.02	5.19
Leontief multiplier	1.04	1.35	1.02	1.49	1.39	1.97	1.00	1.45
KOREA								
SAM multiplier	1.58	3.50	1.03	3.98	1.89	3.17	1.61	3.82
Leontief multiplier	1.12	1.38	1.01	1.45	1.42	1.84	1.18	1.74
PAKISTAN								
SAM multiplier	1.41	7.51	1.10	5.82	2.34	5.49	1.37	6.37
Leontief multiplier	1.04	1.83	1.01	1.57	1.30	1.85	1.04	1.56
SURINAM								
SAM multiplier	1.07	1.86	1.23	1.88	1.22	1.85	1.51	1.88
Leontief multiplier	1.03	1.21	1.23	1.39	1.08	1.31	1.08	1.11

Source: Tables 2.3 and 2.4.

Note: Sectors are defined for each country as indicated in table 2.3.

The results should not be taken to mean that if Korea, for instance, had in the past expanded more in agriculture, mining or services than in industry it would have necessarily achieved a higher overall growth. For one thing, the exogenous expansion potential both domestically and in the rest of the world - denoted by x - was, and will probably remain, lower for the non-industrial sectors than for the industrial sector. In addition, neither SAM nor the input-output matrix takes into account limits on the supply side, which are likely to be more demarcated for the non-industrial sectors than for industry in most developing countries.

As is well known, labour use and capital use per unit of additional production can be multiplied by the contribution to production activities to give the employment and investment effects. It follows that the impact of alternative allocations to activities on the marginal use of labour and capital would be less meaningful when they are derived from the partial framework of Leontief's transfer effects, than when they are derived from a more general framework that incorporates the aggregate effects of SAM.

6. Concluding Remarks

This chapter reported primarily on the results of a multiplier analysis that has been applied to social accounting matrices of Colombia, Korea, Pakistan, and Surinam. The construction of these four matrices forms a major addition to the SAMs for other countries already available. Although the construction of each matrix in this paper is briefly introduced, more details on the estimation of the four SAMs are to be published elsewhere.

In addition to its use for calibrating economy-wide models, the SAM forms an appropriate framework for a comparative analysis of the structural properties of different socio-economic systems. The multipliers obtained are found to be significant, stable and meaningful. A few selected results on the aggregate multipliers and their decomposition into transfer, open loop and closed-loop effects are presented here for purposes of illustration.

The results indicate the absence of progressive redistributive mechanisms in Surinam. On the other hand, they show the presence of slightly progressive mechanisms in Colombia, somewhat more progressive mechanisms in Pakistan, and the most progressive in Korea. These results are partly due to open loop effects that link particular sectoral activities to particular factor incomes and particular household groups in both Pakistan and Korea, as compared with relatively weaker correspondence between activities, factors and households in Colombia. The results are also due to closed-loop effects that tend to shift relatively fewer resources from poorer to richer groups than the other way round. This reflects more self-oriented consumption patterns among poorer household groups in Pakistan and Korea, by comparison to more similar consumption patterns among both rich and poor household groups in Colombia.

In all four case studies, agricultural multipliers show more progressive redistributionary effects than industrial multipliers. The growth effect is also shown to be higher for agriculture than for industry, so that for these two sectors progressive redistribution and higher growth are not in conflict with each other. Other results point to the presence of degrees of freedom in selecting balanced socio-economic development policies, despite the existence of countervailing processes that cause part of the redistribution and growth potentials to vanish.

Furthermore, the SAM multipliers obtained in all four case studies differ appreciably from those derived from that part of the SAM-inverse that corresponds to the Leontief-inverse. This leads to the conclusion that when a development problem, such as the macro-analysis and broader planning of capital use, labour use and growth strategies, involves significant linkage effects on income and expenditure, it can be expected that results derived from the input-output model will be inferior to those derived from the social accounting framework. Although obvious, it should be emphasised that this conclusion does not deny the recognised usefulness of the input-output model in analytical and planning contexts other than those described in this chapter.

For an effective analysis of development mechanisms and problems in different socio-economic settings, it is desirable to construct and make available SAMs for many more countries and for more years. Difficulties relating to standardisation and comparability will take some time to solve, although the multiplier analysis presented here may help to provide clues as to which SAM classifications, entries and analytical designs are more meaningful in a comparative analysis of socio-economic systems and their implications for global policy-making.

Chapter 3

Cross-Country Analysis of SAMs for Ten Developing Countries

1. Introduction

This chapter extends the cross-country comparative analysis of social accounting matrices of the previous chapter to more dimensions and more countries. The chapter aims to highlight common results encountered in simulating the effects of injections in sectoral activities on the output of the sectoral activities themselves, and on the incomes of different household groups. This will enable the relationship between economic growth and income distribution in the countries studied to be traceable. The comparative analysis also aims at studying the effect of transfers to specific household groups on economic growth and income distribution among the household groups.

In the cross-country comparative analysis of social accounting statistics, greater analytical insight is gained if the compared social accounting matrices (SAMs) for the individual countries are classified and tabulated according to one common standard. This is not always feasible but can be broadly approximated. In the previous chapters, the SAMs for four countries, Colombia, Korea, Pakistan and Suriname, constructed by the same investigators, have been reviewed. This chapter also considers SAMs for six other countries: Egypt, Kenya, India, Indonesia, Iran, and Sri Lanka.[1] The SAMs of these countries are very diversified in content. However, appropriate aggregation and modifications can result in bringing the various SAMs to a common base. In the process, we necessarily exclude some valuable information on some countries, but enhance drawing more general conclusions on the relationships between growth and distribution.

The focus of attention in the applications reported here obviously lies with the specific disaggregation of the household and activity accounts.

---

[1] For the sources of the ten SAMs analysed in this chapter, see references in the appendix.

The disaggregation of households emphasises dualities in the location of population in urban and rural areas, and the differentiation within urban and rural groups by level of income earned. This differentiation is done by distinguishing urban households into three groups: employers, employees and self-employed; and breaking down rural households into three groups: large landowners, medium landowners and small/landless households. For a couple of countries a seventh residual group was incorporated so as to accommodate classifications which did not fit the standardised six categories. The SAMs of Egypt and India form exceptions to the above as they follow personal income distributions in distinguishing between household groups with different income levels.

The classification of activities had to be limited to four large groups of sectors: agriculture, mining, industry and services. Distinguishing more sectors would reduce the uniformity and comparability of the ten SAMs reported here.

In this chapter, we use general notations for the households and activities. Households are denoted by index h and activities by index s, while for the SAM aggregate multiplier we use M_a. The effect of an injection in sector s' on output of other sectors is $M_{a,ss'}$ which is what has thus far been referred to as output multipliers from sectoral injections. The effect of the injection in sector s' on (income of) household h is expressed by $M_{a,hs'}$, which has thus far been referred to as income multipliers from sectoral injections. Similarly, if the injection is in the form of an income transfer to household h' this will have both output effects on the sectors and income effects on the household groups. These are expressed as $M_{a,sh'}$ and $M_{a,hh'}$, respectively, or in words, output and income multipliers from household transfers.

2. Aggregate Multipliers

Table 3.1. gives the level of the output and income multipliers for injections in sectoral activities. India and Pakistan are shown to have the highest average output multipliers, 5.9 and 8.8 respectively, which is partly due to a treatment of imports in their SAMs that does not fully consider leakage due to imports. (Note that the size of the multiplier for Pakistan reported here is slightly different than in the previous section, this being due to aggregation errors.) At the other extreme, Suriname and Egypt show the lowest output multipliers, 1.9 and 2.5 respectively, reflecting low degrees of interdependence. The other countries fall in a middle range:

Colombia, Korea, Iran, Indonesia, Sri Lanka and Kenya, scoring 4.6, 3.6, 3.6, 3.4, 3.1 and 2.9 respectively.

In general, output multipliers are highest for impulses in the agricultural sector, followed by the services sector, which is second in 7 out of the 10 countries. Industry ranks between third and fourth. Mining does not show a common ranking among the ten countries.

Table 3.1. Income Multiplier $M_{a,hs}$, and Output Multipliers $M_{a,ss}$, from an Additional Unit of Sectoral Demand

		Agriculture	*Mining*	*Industry*	*Services*	*Average*
COLOMBIA 1970	income	2.146	2.512	1.651	2.230	2.135
	output	4.447	4.952	4.287	4.678	4.591
SURINAM 1979	income	1.153	0.777	0.816	1.220	0.992
	output	1.967	1.871	1.849	1.911	1.900
EGYPT 1976	income	1.570	0.854	0.893	1.473	1.073
	output	2.897	1.721	2.537	2.997	2.538
KENYA 1976	income	1.867	1.127	0.910	1.501	1.351
	output	2.872	3.099	2.541	2.934	2.861
INDIA 1968/69	income	4.427	3.384	3.328	3.599	3.684
	output	6.910	5.185	5.977	5.711	5.946
INDONESIA 1975	income	2.567	na	1.395	2.395	2.119
	output	4.176	na	2.414	3.579	3.390
IRAN 1970	income	2.584	1.470	1.752	2.085	1.973
	output	4.358	3.025	3.576	3.595	3.639
S. KOREA 1973	income	1.883	2.080	1.144	1.809	1.729
	output	3.514	3.994	3.198	3.766	3.618
PAKISTAN 1978/9	income	4.430	4.116	3.534	4.033	4.028
	output	9.457	8.911	8.227	8.483	8.770
SRI LANKA 1970	income	2.289	na	1.714	2.163	2.055
	output	3.334	na	2.929	3.007	3.090

na: not available

The five Asian countries of Iran, Pakistan, India, Sri Lanka and Indonesia show a particularly homogeneous pattern of sectoral ranking regarding their output multipliers.

Turning to income multipliers, it is observed from table 3.1 that for all countries together, the size of the income multipliers are about half the output multipliers, 0.53 on average. The difference is due partly to intermediate deliveries, and partly to government income and imports from the rest of the world. For individual countries it is noted that Egypt, Pakistan, Colombia, Kenya and Korea extract a lower income proportion from output, around 0.45, while Sri Lanka, Indonesia and India extract a higher proportion, around 0.64. In the latter countries it takes less of an output effort to produce a unit of household income.

3. Growth and Distributionary Bias of Sectoral Injections

Besides studying the level of a multiplier and the decomposable mechanisms which determine the level of the multipliers, it is interesting to study the structural distribution of the multiplier effects on the constituents of the specific account, since these have a significant impact on structure in the future. In order to do so, a Relative Distributive Measure of sector-sector effects, $RDM_{ss'}$, has been defined, cf. Cohen 1988).

$$RDM_{ss'} = \frac{\left(M_{a,ss'} - d_{ss'}\right)}{\left(\sum_s M_{a,ss'} - 1\right)} / \frac{Output_{s,0}}{\sum_s Output_{s,0}}$$

where s and s' denote receiving and injecting sectors, and $d_{ss'}$, (the Kronecker-symbol, equals 1 if $s=s'$ and 0 in other cases) is subtracted to obtain the share of s in the multiplier effects of s' on all sectors after deducting the initial injection. The result is divided by the actual output share of sector s in year 0, i.e. the year to which the SAM refers. For values of $RDM_{ss'} > 1$, < 1, and $= 1$, there are positive, negative and neutral redistributive effects. For instance, values of $RDM_{ss'} = 1$ mean that sectoral injections would exactly reproduce the sectoral distribution pattern of the base year.

Similarly, a relative distributive measure, $RDM_{hs'}$ for the multiplier effects of sectoral injections s' on the income of institutional group i, $M_{a,hs'}$ can be calculated.

$$RDM_{hs'} = \frac{M_{a,hs'}}{\sum_h M_{a,hs'}} / \frac{Income_{h,0}}{\sum_h Income_{h,0}}$$

Values of $RDM_{hs'} = 1$ mean that sectoral injections would reproduce exactly the share group i had in the base year in total income. A higher value would mean an increase in its income share; a negative value would mean a decrease.

We have calculated *RDM* for the ten countries in table 3.2 to give the relative distribution of the output multipliers over the sectors, and the relative distribution of the income multipliers on the household groups. A few comments will be made on the results obtained.

As regards the distributionary pattern of the output multipliers, in eight of the ten countries, agriculture gains from an injection in either agriculture or industry, scoring an *RDM* above unity. The results suggest that the value of *RDM* in favour of agriculture tends to diminish as a country develops. The growth bias changes in favour of mining, industry and services.

As regards the distributionary pattern of the income multipliers the results show that, for the ten countries, demand impulses in the agricultural sector bring about a more equal distribution of income.

Considering the countries individually, the results show demand injections in agriculture to be most progressive in Colombia, India, Iran, Korea and Pakistan and least progressive in Sri Lanka and Surinam.

These results are partly due to open-loop relationships that strongly link sectoral activities in agriculture to particular household groups, such as the rural poor in India, Iran, Korea and Pakistan. By contrast, there are relatively weaker correspondences between activities, factors, and households in the other countries. The results are also due to closed-loop effects that shift relatively fewer resources from poorer to richer groups than the other way around. This reflects more self-oriented consumption patterns among poorer household groups in India, Iran, Korea and Pakistan compared to the other countries, where rich and poor show more uniform consumption patterns.

It has been shown that the growth multiplier of agricultural injections is higher than that for industrial injections. It has also been shown that agricultural injections have more progressive redistribution effects than other sectoral injections. This means that, as far as agriculture is concerned, progressive redistribution and higher growth are not in conflict with each other. The results direct attention to the presence of degrees of freedom in selecting balanced socio-economic development policies, in spite of the existence of countervailing processes which cause parts of redistribution and growth potentials to vanish.

Table 3.2.   Distribution of Multiplier Effects of Sectoral Injections over Households and Sectors, as Compared with Original Distribution

	Actual distribution	Multiplier distribution			RDM		
		Average	Agricltr	Industry	Average	Agricltr	Industry
COLOMBIA							
Urban	62.09	62.89	59.64	63.74	1.10	0.96	1.03
Rural	37.90	37.11	40.36	36.25	0.98	1.06	0.96
Total	100.00	100.00	100.00	100.00			
Agriculture	20.52	19.15	21.62	20.34	0.93	1.05	0.99
Mining	1.42	1.15	0.93	1.45	0.81	0.65	1.02
Industry	40.92	44.30	43.66	44.12	1.08	1.07	1.08
Services	37.14	35.40	33.79	34.09	0.95	0.91	0.92
Total	100.00	100.00	100.00	100.00			
SURINAM							
Urban	57.47	57.63	56.61	57.83	1.00	0.99	1.01
Rural	42.53	42.38	43.39	42.18	1.00	1.02	0.99
Total	100.00	100.00	100.00	100.00			
Agriculture	7.48	13.81	14.03	25.57	1.85	1.88	3.42
Mining	29.23	6.46	0.07	0.06	0.22	0.00	0.00
Industry	18.08	25.00	27.38	25.47	1.38	1.51	1.41
Services	45.22	54.73	58.52	48.90	1.21	1.29	1.08
Total	100.00	100.00	100.00	100.00			
EGYPT							
Urban	66.39	56.39	25.77	63.59	0.85	0.39	0.96
Rural	33.61	43.61	74.24	36.40	1.30	2.21	1.08
Total	100.00	100.00	100.00	100.00			
Agriculture	21.43	27.17	35.03	30.19	1.27	1.63	1.41
Mining	5.39	9.32	5.07	4.50	1.73	0.94	0.83
Industry	39.24	36.20	37.41	38.14	0.92	0.95	0.97
Services	33.95	27.31	22.49	27.17	0.80	0.66	0.80
Total	100.00	100.00	100.00	100.00			
KENYA							
Urban	37.62	40.68	30.01	43.10	1.08	0.80	1.15
Rural	62.36	59.32	69.98	56.90	0.95	1.12	0.91
Total	100.00	100.00	100.00	100.00			
Agriculture	23.50	20.21	28.60	22.22	0.86	1.22	0.95
Mining	0.46	1.96	0.35	0.91	4.26	0.76	1.98
Industry	41.91	46.05	38.99	49.98	1.10	0.93	1.19
Services	34.13	31.78	32.07	26.89	0.93	0.94	0.79
Total	100.00	100.00	100.00	100.00			
INDIA							
Urban	60.40	56.40	45.58	57.38	0.93	0.75	0.95
Rural	39.60	43.60	54.42	42.62	1.10	1.37	1.08
Total	100.00	100.00	100.00	100.00			
Agriculture	37.02	43.58	48.68	40.52	1.18	1.31	1.09
Mining	2.20	2.11	1.79	2.70	0.96	0.81	1.23
Industry	35.84	27.35	25.07	30.22	0.76	0.70	0.84
Services	24.94	26.95	24.45	26.56	1.08	0.98	1.06
Total	100.00	100.00	100.00	100.00			

Table 3.2. (Continued)

	Actual distribution	Multiplier Distribution			RDM		
		Average	*Agriclt*	*Industry*	*Average*	*Agriclt*	*Industry*
INDONESIA							
Urban	34.46	28.96	23.17	33.76	0.84	0.67	0.98
Rural	65.53	71.04	76.83	66.25	1.08	1.17	1.01
Total	*100.00*	*100.00*	*100.00*	*100.00*			
Agriculture	36.14	66.58	73.07	56.05	1.84	2.02	1.55
Mining	NA	NA	NA	NA	NA	NA	NA
Industry	33.94	17.01	12.53	27.66	0.50	0.37	0.81
Services	29.92	16.41	14.40	16.29	0.55	0.48	0.54
Total	*100.00*	*100.00*	*100.00*	*100.00*			
IRAN							
Urban	74.93	69.26	54.77	73.38	0.92	0.73	0.98
Rural	25.07	30.74	45.23	26.62	1.23	1.80	1.06
Total	*100.00*	*100.00*	*100.00*	*100.00*			
Agriculture	22.46	27.67	32.71	27.72	1.23	1.46	1.23
Mining	7.75	12.11	7.80	9.82	1.56	1.01	1.27
Industry	33.99	31.94	31.90	32.67	0.94	0.94	0.96
Services	35.79	28.28	27.59	29.79	0.79	0.77	0.83
Total	*100.00*	*100.00*	*100.00*	*100.00*			
KOREA							
Urban	67.41	66.80	61.06	66.76	0.99	0.91	0.99
Rural	32.58	33.20	38.94	33.26	1.02	1.20	1.02
Total	*100.00*	*100.00*	*100.00*	*100.00*			
Agriculture	14.25	19.50	23.17	16.70	1.37	1.63	1.17
Mining	1.02	1.01	0.84	1.42	0.99	0.82	1.39
Industry	47.65	46.58	45.14	51.17	0.98	0.95	1.07
Services	37.08	32.91	30.85	30.71	0.89	0.83	0.83
Total	*100.00*	*100.00*	*100.00*	*100.00*			
PAKISTAN							
Urban	33.88	31.34	28.49	32.37	0.93	0.84	0.96
Rural	66.11	68.66	71.51	67.63	1.04	1.08	1.02
Total	*100.00*	*100.00*	*100.00*	*100.00*			
Agriculture	25.24	25.38	27.19	25.76	1.01	1.08	1.02
Mining	0.95	2.45	2.27	2.86	2.58	2.39	3.01
Industry	43.73	43.17	41.27	43.61	0.99	0.94	1.00
Services	30.08	29.00	29.26	27.77	0.96	0.97	0.92
Total	*100.00*	*100.00*	*100.00*	*100.00*			
SRI LANKA							
Urban	28.08	26.63	21.64	27.77	0.95	0.77	0.99
Rural	71.93	73.37	78.37	72.23	1.02	1.09	1.00
Total	*100.00*	*100.00*	*100.00*	*100.00*			
Agriculture	32.64	37.31	43.11	32.60	1.14	1.32	1.00
Mining	NA	NA	NA	NA	NA	NA	NA
Industry	32.13	30.13	26.15	35.04	0.94	0.81	1.09
Services	35.23	32.55	30.74	32.36	0.92	0.87	0.92
Total	*100.00*	*100.00*	*100.00*	*100.00*			

Although agricultural growth appears to favour both growth and equality, the weight which is given to agriculture in the exogenous impulses during the course of development is usually much lower than for industry, mining or services. Since the latter sectors may be inequality-biased, there is a tendency for the actual situation regarding income distribution to become worse. This tendency is not characteristic of the multiplier system because the multiplier analysis has just shown that there are possibilities for combining potential growth with more equality. This tendency is the result of: (1) the exogenously determined limited opportunities for expanding agricultural demand (i.e. it is more difficult to find foreign markets for agricultural exports than for non-agricultural exports), and (2) more restrictive production constraints in the case of agriculture as compared to industry, mining or services.

4.   Growth and Distribution Bias of Household Transfers

Table 3.3 summarises additional main results regarding multiplier effects of institutional transfers to household groups. The impact of institutional transfers on output and income is denoted by $M_{a,sh'}$ and $M_{a,hh'}$, respectively.

In all cases, average output multipliers of institutional transfers $M_{a,sh'}$ are lower than output multipliers of sectoral injections $M_{a,ss'}$ but income effects from institutional transfers $M_{a,hh'}$ are higher than income effects from sectoral impulses $M_{a,hs'}$.

For most of the ten countries institutional transfers to the poorer household groups - mostly in rural areas - bring with them the highest output and income multipliers. Injections into richer households - mostly urban - have lower output and income multipliers. These results suggest that a redistribution of incomes from urban to rural household groups may increase growth and equality.

For the sake of comprehensiveness it can be mentioned that for the ten countries the same analysis of decomposition and *RDM* has been applied to institutional transfers as well. In correspondence with the formula of RDM for sectoral injections, two types of *RDM* for household transfers can be formulated, giving $RDM_{sh'}$ and $RDM_{hh'}$.

Table 3.3. Income Multiplier M$_{a,hh'}$ and Growth Multiplier M$_{a,sh'}$ of an Additional Unit of Institutional Transfers

	Urban			Rural			Others	Average
	poor	middle	rich	poor	middle	rich		
COLOMBIA								
$M_{a,hh'}$	2.795	2.913	2.756	2.965	2.863	2.341	2.728	2.766
$M_{a,sh'}$	4.117	4.417	4.014	4.809	4.356	3.108	3.958	4.083
SURINAM								
$M_{a,hh'}$	1.896		1.669	1.839		1.735		1.785
$M_{a,sh'}$	1.539		1.147	1.450		1.261		1.349
EGYPT								
$M_{a,hh'}$	2.124	2.083	1.759	1.901	1.692	1.651		1.870
$M_{a,sh'}$	2.593	2.464	1.662	2.108	1.582	1.482		1.982
KENYA								
$M_{a,hh'}$	2.353	2.224	1.743	2.339	2.360	2.299	2.071	2.198
$M_{a,sh'}$	2.463	2.088	1.309	2.507	2.310	2.400	2.088	2.195
INDIA								
$M_{a,hh'}$		4.932			3.752			4.342
$M_{a,sh'}$		6.288			4.433			5.361
INDONESIA								
$M_{a,hh'}$	3.011		2.761	3.440		3.104	3.142	3.092
$M_{a,sh'}$	3.146		2.727	3.916		3.366	3.413	3.314
IRAN								
$M_{a,hh'}$		2.414			2.916			2.665
$M_{a,sh'}$		2.568			3.459			3.014
KOREA								
$M_{a,hh'}$	2.475	2.557	2.445	2.387	2.773	2.143		2.380
$M_{a,sh'}$	3.206	3.388	3.146	3.041	2.798	2.515		3.016
PAKISTAN								
$M_{a,hh'}$	4.421	4.496	4.435	4.875	4.579	4.359	4.433	4.520
$M_{a,sh'}$	7.525	7.698	7.536	8.561	8.123	7.378	7.579	7.774
SRI LANKA								
$M_{a,hh'}$		2.323		2.378		2.689		2.530
$M_{a,sh'}$		1.962		2.330		2.305		2.265

$$RDM_{hh'} = \frac{\left(M_{a,hh'} - d_{hh'}\right)}{\sum_h Ma, hh' - 1} / \frac{Income_{h,0}}{\sum_h income_{h,0}}$$

$$RDM_{sh'} = \frac{M_{a,sh'}}{\sum_s M_{a,sh'}} / \frac{Output_{s,0}}{\sum_s Output_{s,0}}$$

The results, which will not be presented here, confirm the general tendency of obtaining a high *RDM* for the poorer household groups, especially the rural ones, which is an indication of the existence of progressive inclinations in the mechanisms of income distribution. The fact that the actual distribution of income in the ten countries is worse than what the income multipliers indicate must be the result of regressive patterns of the actual exogenous impulses.

5.   SAM versus Leontief Multipliers

It was shown in the previous chapters that the social accounting model is a more complete description of the circular flow than the conventional input-output model as first introduced by W. Leontief. In this section we elaborate on the differences between the two. Of interest here is an analysis of the aggregate multiplier effects of sectoral injections on sectoral output $M_{a,ss'}$.

Recalling the decomposition of SAM multipliers into transfer, open-loop and closed-loop effects, $M_{a,ss'}$ can also be subdivided into these three effects. The case is somewhat simpler here since open-loop effects are not applicable. As a result, the aggregate multiplier $M_{a,ss'}$ consists of a transfer component $M_{1,ss'}$, which is nothing other than the Leontief multipliers, and a closed-loop component $M_{3,ss'}$, which constitute the indirect effects that are carried throughout the circular flow as modelled by the SAM.

An analysis of the differences between the aggregate multiplier and that part forming the transfer effects is sufficient to appreciate the nature of the remaining part forming the closed-loop effects. In table 3.4 we compare the aggregate multipliers of $M_{a,ss'}$ with those of transfer effects of activities on activities, $M_{1,ss'}$, the latter representing the Leontief multipliers.

The attractive position that industry occupies in a structural analysis based on the Leontief-model as the foremost contributor to production activity from an additionally allocated unit is taken over by the activities of services, agriculture, and mining, which contribute individually more than manufacturing in a SAM framework. These results are consistent for the 10 countries, with the Leontief-model multipliers being about one-third of the SAM multipliers, depending on the country and the sector.

Table 3.4   Aggregate SAM Multipliers and the Leontief Multipliers: Ten Countries

		Agriculture	Mining	Manufacturing	Services
COLOMBIA	SAM	4.447	4.953	4.287	4.679
	Leontief	1.478	1.499	1.985	1.558
SURINAM	SAM	1.968	1.871	1.849	1.912
	Leontief	1.218	1.385	1.316	1.121
EGYPT	SAM	2.898	1.722	2.537	2.997
	Leontief	1.321	1.348	1.575	1.353
KENYA	SAM	2.871	3.099	2.540	2.934
	Leontief	1.160	2.118	1.755	1.615
INDIA	SAM	6.910	5.184	5.977	5.711
	Leontief	1.350	1.240	1.936	1.411
INDONESIA	SAM	4.176	nc	2.414	3.579
	Leontief	1.584	nc	1.345	1.240
IRAN	SAM	4.357	3.025	3.576	3.594
	Leontief	1.396	1.454	1.668	1.344
KOREA	SAM	3.515	3.995	3.198	3.767
	Leontief	1.388	1.451	1.847	1.619
PAKISTAN	SAM	9.463	8.924	8.110	8.610
	Leontief	1.865	1.888	2.187	1.671
SRI LANKA	SAM	3.335	NC	2.929	3.007
	Leontief	1.378	NC	1.524	1.193

nc = not computed

6. Conclusions

In addition to its use for purposes of calibrating economy-wide models, the SAM forms an appropriate framework for appraising policy issues relating to growth and distribution, and for a comparative analysis of the structural properties of different socioeconomic systems. In all ten case studies, agricultural multipliers show more progressive redistributive effects than manufacturing multipliers. We also showed that the growth effect is higher for agriculture than for industry, so that as far as these two sectors arc concerned progressive redistribution and higher growth are not in conflict with each other.

In general, the Asian countries we studied show more progressive mechanisms. These results are due partly to open-loop effects and partly to closed loop effects. The former link particular sectoral activities to particular factor incomes and particular household groups more strongly in the Asian context, as compared to relatively weaker correspondence between activities, factors, and households elsewhere. The latter tend to shift relatively more resources from richer to poorer groups than vice versa, reflecting more self-oriented consumption patterns among poorer household groups in the Asian context, as compared to more similar consumption patterns among rich and poor household groups elsewhere. Furthermore, the SAM multipliers obtained in all ten case studies differ appreciably in value and rank from those derived from that part of the SAM inverse that corresponds to the open-model Leontief inverse.

For an effective analysis of development mechanisms and structural problems in different socio-economic settings it is desirable to construct and make available social accounting matrices for many more countries and for more years. Difficulties relating to standardisation and comparability will take time to solve. However, the multiplier analysis as presented here may contribute to giving clues as to which SAM classifications, entries and analytical designs are more meaningful and operational in a comparative analysis of socio-economic systems with respect to issues of growth and equity.

Chapter 4

Inter-Temporal Analysis of Social Accounting

1. Introduction

In chapter 1 the social accounting matrix, SAM, was introduced and analysed for one country, Colombia, for one year, 1970. This chapter will extend the framework of analysis to the study of inter-temporal changes in the economic structure by contrasting the SAMs over time. For this purpose, two comparable SAMs for Colombia for 1970 and 1980 will be employed to extend the analysis.

The chapter is divided as follows. Section 2 reflects on the changing shares of various accounts in the SAM over the period of ten years. Section 3 applies a comparative inter-temporal multiplier analysis and demonstrates how a decomposition of multipliers adds insights to the understanding of mechanisms behind the shifting positions of activities and institutions in the economy. The analysis will highlight the transfer-, open- and closed-loop effects behind the changing patterns of growth and distribution over time. Section 4 applies another kind of decomposition of inter-temporal economic performance. This decomposition will attempt a separation between the endogenous and exogenous factors in accounting for changes in growth and distribution over the ten-year period.

2. The Changing Structure of the SAM: the Case of Colombia 1970-1980

Next to the SAM of Colombia for 1970, discussed in chapter 1, another SAM for the same country has been constructed for 1980. With a view to concentrating the analysis on the major accounts of activities and institutions, we opted for a somewhat simplified SAM for both years. Two main simplifications were introduced.

The first simplification is to leave out the explicit inclusion of the wants account. As a result, the expenditure of the institutions on the wants categories will now go directly to the activities. This implies some loss of information, which can influence the multiplier effects, however, this is outweighed by the advantage of gaining focus.

The second simplification is the reduction of the classification of institutions. The two SAMs now distinguish between seven household groups. Four groups reside in urban areas; these are proprietors of large estates and business (Uprp), urban high skill workers (Uhsw), urban low skill workers (Ulsw), and urban tiny establishments of self-employed and family workers (Usfw). Three groups reside in the rural areas; these are the large landowners or rural latifundists (Rltf), the medium and small farmowners (Rmsf), and the rural landless who are either farm or non-farm workers (Rfnw). The other institutions distinguished remain the same; these are the firms, government, and the aggregate national capital account for all institutions together.

As far as other accounts of the SAM are concerned, these remain the same. The factors account distinguishes three factors; these are urban labour earnings, wage labour earnings, and profits.

The activities account distinguishes eight sectors of production. The sectors are agriculture (Agrc); mining (Mnng); processed coffee (Pcff); industry (Inds); electricity, gas and water (Elgw); modern services (Mdsr); personal services (Prsr) and public services (Pbsr). Next to these is the rest of the world activity.

The two SAMs are in current prices. This is a handicap since the real changes do not necessarily correspond to the nominal changes. At the same time, it is generally admitted that it is not feasible to convert such a combined matrix of production values, earnings and expenditures into constant prices. There are not only unresolved methodological problems in implementing such conversions, but also a lack of appropriate data. Economists are inclined to mitigate the handicap by considering how the relative structural distribution of the entities changes over time rather than the growth rates of variables over time. They also look for the directions in magnitudes to which a comparative nominal analysis points rather than at the absolute magnitudes, thus allowing for discounts due to price changes. This is what will also be done in this chapter.

As this chapter is interested in structural changes in the endogenous and exogenous components of the SAM, the intervening price effects have to be singled out in some way. This is mainly achieved by looking at the so-called *A* matrix of the SAMs of 1970 and 1980. The SAM can be written in a model form $y = A y + x$ where x and y are the vectors of exogenous and endogenous variables, respectively; and where the A matrix expresses each transaction of the endogenous accounts as a proportion of the total transactions performed by the endogenous account holder, i.e. the column.

In keeping with the previous chapters, the variables of government, capital and rest of world are assigned as the exogenous variables, while the other variables are endogenous. As a result, the *A* matrix is a coefficient matrix for the endogenous variables. Although the inflationary effects of price movements are not eliminated in a comparison of the *A* matrices for 1970 and 1980, these two matrices present structural distributions among the endogenous variables, in relation to the residual balances represented by the exogenous variables, which are valid for the two years. This makes a comparison meaningful and helpful in some ways by showing how the economic structure has changed.

Tables 4.1.1 and 4.1.2 display *A* matrices of Colombia for 1970 and 1980, together with the residual balances relating to the exogenous variables. The following remarks can be made about the changing structures in the tables. As regards the factors account, the shares of urban labour earnings decreased along most sectors of economic activity, while the shares of rural labour earnings increased on the whole. The share of profits from the various activities shows little change over the ten years.

Comparing the two *A* matrices, we see that the distribution of labour factor payments among the urban household groups shifts from the high income groups of urban proprietors and high skill workers (Uprp and Uhsw) to the urban low skill workers and self-employed and family (Ulsw and Usfw). The distribution of labour factor payments among the rural household groups is fairly stable. In contrast, profits are redistributed to the advantage of urban proprietors and to the disadvantage of all other population groups.

The expenditure pattern of most households has also changed towards more saving and less consumption, the exception being urban high skill workers. Furthermore, the overall tendency is for households to spend smaller shares on products of agriculture, coffee and public services, and more on electricity, gas and water.

As for the activities account, a stable structure is observed with only a few modifications. This is partly due to the methods and data that go into the construction of the input-output transactions. Furthermore, drastic changes in the interindustry structure cannot be expected in a period of ten years.

Finally, a comment should be made about the changing share of the exogenously stipulated variables in the total economy. This share is obtained by dividing the sum total of the accounts of government, capital and rest of the world by the grand total of all accounts in the SAM. This share amounted to about 22% in 1970, and surged to about 30% in 1980, a relative increase of 36%. As a result, the endogenous part of the economy

Table 4.1.1. The A Matrix Expressed in Promiles, Colombia 1970

1970	Ulb	Rlb	Prft	Up	Uh	Uls	Usf	Rlt	Rm	Rfn	Flr	Ag	Mn	Pcf	Ind	Elg	Mds	Prs	Pbs
	Wants Factors			*Institutions*								*Activities*							
Wants																			
Factors																			
U lbr												65	120	12	74	283	176	300	620
R lbr												168	80	3	17	28	35	60	125
Profits												550	582	47	104	370	408	299	
Sbttl												783							
Institutions																			
U prp	45		48																
U hsw	426		292																
U lsw	228																		
U sfw	301		291																
R ltf		37	20																
R msf		524	89																
R fnw		440																	
Firms			232																
Sbttl	100																		
Activities																			
Agrcltr				93	121	158	132	116	185	216		17	6	544	145	2	6	46	22
Mnng				2	1	1	1	1	1	1			12		18	18	2		1
Coffee				5	7	10	8	7	11	13				51				15	4
Indstry				344	395	490	420	353	540	603		96	52	7	232	222	132	240	143
El,g,w				21	10	5	10	13	5	5			29		6	21	3	6	5
Md srv				222	203	164	192	107	98	88		85	197	53	177	55	175	15	60
Pr srv				173	148	150	145	99	127	117			1		1	5	6	5	15
Pb srv				9	8	8	8	5	7	6		1	3		2	2	1	1	1
Subttl				869	893	986	916	701	974	951		199	300	655	581	325	325	328	251
residue		-1	28	131	107	14	84	299	26	-49	18	-82	283	224	-6	56	13	4	
Total	1000	1000	1000	1000	1000	1000	1000	1000	1000	1000	1000	1000	1000	1000	1000	1000	1000	1000	1000

Key: W=wants, U=urban, R=rural, lbr=labour, prp=proprietor, hsw=high skill worker, lsw=low skill worker, sfw=self employed and family workers, ltf=latifunda, msf=medium and small farmers, fnw=farrm and nonfarm workers. Sbttl=subtotal Md srv=modern services, Pr srv=personal services, Pb srv=public services.

Table 4.1.2. The A Matrix Expressed in Promiles, Colombia 1980

1980	Wants Factors			Institutions								Activities							
	Ulb	Rlb	Prft	Up	Uh	Uls	Usf	Rlt	Rm	Rfn	Fir	Ag	Mn	Pcf	Ind	Elg	Mds	Prs	Pbs
Wants Factors																			
U lbr													74	70	55	207	151	226	594
R lbr												208	208	29	16	22	68	39	54
Profits												481	507	15	127	346	428	412	
Sbttl												689	610	101	204	621	618	692	763
Institutions																			
U prp	36		159																
U hsw	193		224																
U lsw	366		2																
U sfw	404		236																
R ltf		56	63																
R msf		504	65																
R fnw		440																	
Firms			240																
Sbttl	999	1000	989																
Activities																			
Agrcltr				92	50	102	101	93	134	240		11	2	411	117	1	3	33	21
Mnng				1	2	2	1	1	1	1		1	12		27	17	3		
Coffee				3	6	6	5	3	4	3				118				27	12
Indstry				261	534	525	439	272	379	245		135	50	7	213	267	133	206	114
El,g,w				13	14	11	15	13	18	13			18	1	9	31	5	7	13
Md srv				75	239	263	180	79	133	51			143	45	191	58	189	15	46
Pr srv				90	202	223	153	67	113	43				1	6	8		6	22
Pb srv				3	4	3	4	4	5	4		1		1	1	1			
Subttl				538	1051	1135	898	532	787	600		241	226	582	559	381	342	294	228
residue	1		11	462	-51	-135	102	468	213	400		70	164	317	237	-2	40	14	9
Total	1000	1000	1000	1000	1000	1000	1000	1000	1000	1000		1000	1000	1000	1000	1000	1000	1000	1000

Key: W=wants, U=urban, R=rural, lbr=labour, prp=proprietor, hsw=high skill worker, lsw=low skill worker, sfw=self employed and family workers, ltf=latifunda, msf=medium and small farmers, fnw=farrm and nonfarm workers. Sbttl=subtotal Md srv=modern services, Pr srv=personal services, Pb srv=public services.

is reduced in size that will also reduce the size of the SAM multipliers, as will be examined in the next section. The endogenous part, relative to the whole circular flow, falls from 78% to 70%, which is a relative reduction of 12%.

3. Changing Multipliers over Time

In this section we shall continue the line set out in the previous chapters in the analysis of multiplier effects. A comparison of the results of a multiplier analyses for two periods will reveal changes in the structures and mechanisms of the economic system which occurred between these two periods. The inversion of matrix A gives multipliers of injections in activities and households on all four SAM accounts, namely (1) wants, (2) factors, (3) institutions consisting mainly of household groups, and (4) activities. As indicated above, to increase focus we shall restrict the analysis in this chapter to the multipliers effects of injections in activities on the activities themselves, that is the multipliers of account 4 on 4, or $M_{a,44}$, and of injections in activities on the household groups, or $M_{a,34}$. In terms of table 1.4 in chapter 1, the focus will be on the sector output multipliers of $M_{a,44}$, and especially the household income multipliers of $M_{a,34}$. These two multiplier effects allow the analyst to study the growth pattern of the economy and its redistributionary patterns, respectively. This section is organised as follows. First, the $M_{a,44}$ and $M_{a,34}$ are displayed, the latter in more detail. Second, the $M_{a,34}$ multipliers are then decomposed in transfer, open- and closed-loop effects. Third, the working of these mechanisms and their outcome are demonstrated for two household groups: the household group of urban proprietors, which has profited much during the ten year period, and the household group of rural small and medium sized farmers, which benefited the least.

Table 4.2.   Total output multipliers by sectoral injection, M$_{a,44}$.
1970 and 1980

	Agrc	Mnng	Pcff	Inds	Elgw	Mdsr	Prsr	Pusr	Average
1970	4.52	4.94	4.14	4.26	4.81	4.54	4.80	5.19	4.65
1980	3.74	3.48	3.51	3.72	4.19	4.04	4.09	4.62	3.92

Results of $M_{a,44}$ for the two years are found in table 4.2. They show a reduction in the average value of output multipliers from 4.65 in 1970 to 3.92 in 1980, less 16%. This can partly be explained by the increase in the size of the exogenous part and the corresponding reduction of the endogenous part of the SAMs between 1970 and 1980, amounting to 12%. The relative fall in the multipliers is greater than that of the endogenous part by some 4 percentage points, which is an indication of a genuine weakening in the internal dynamics of the circular flow. The biggest reduction occurs in the mining sector, less 30%, and the lowest in the services sectors, less 11%.

Table 4.3. **Household income multipliers by sectoral injection, $M_{a,34}$, 1970 and 1980**

1970	Agrc	Mnng	Pcff	Inds	Elgw	Mdsr	Prsr	Pusr	average
Uprp	0.096	0.110	0.068	0.072	0.102	0.095	0.099	0.107	0.094
Uhsw	0.659	0.763	0.468	0.506	0.734	0.673	0.713	0.824	0.668
Ulsw	0.113	0.142	0.083	0.106	0.171	0.141	0.172	0.259	0.149
Ufsw	0.596	0.684	0.422	0.446	0.640	0.595	0.618	0.681	0.585
Rltf	0.043	0.044	0.029	0.028	0.036	0.035	0.036	0.035	0.036
Rmsf	0.318	0.298	0.214	0.193	0.240	0.235	0.253	0.281	0.254
Rfnw	0.153	0.122	0.099	0.084	0.096	0.093	0.112	0.149	0.113
Firms	0.355	0.395	0.249	0.243	0.329	0.325	0.310	0.269	0.309
Total	2.334	2.559	1.633	1.678	2.348	2.192	2.314	2.605	2.208

1980	Agrc	Mnng	Pcff	Inds	Elgw	Mdsr	Prsr	Pusr	average
Uprp	0.215	0.210	0.139	0.162	0.222	0.228	0.225	0.203	0.201
Uhsw	0.344	0.342	0.236	0.273	0.386	0.386	0.390	0.420	0.347
Ulsw	0.112	0.122	0.106	0.118	0.195	0.171	0.194	0.352	0.171
Usfw	0.423	0.426	0.306	0.351	0.512	0.499	0.515	0.634	0.458
Rltf	0.101	0.088	0.063	0.070	0.094	0.095	0.094	0.087	0.087
Rmsf	0.263	0.161	0.162	0.151	0.203	0.186	0.196	0.254	0.197
Rfnw	0.158	0.071	0.096	0.078	0.105	0.087	0.098	0.162	0.107
Firms	0.308	0.299	0.194	0.227	0.306	0.319	0.310	0.253	0.277
Total	1.923	1.719	1.303	1.431	2.023	1.973	2.022	2.366	1.845

Table 4.3 gives more details about the household income multipliers, $M_{a,34}$. Here too, as can be expected, the multipliers for 1980 are lower than those for 1970 by about 10% on average (2.366/2.605), for the same reasons given above. The reduction in income multipliers is less than that in output multipliers, implying an economic improvement in the form of a higher value added per unit of output.

The reduction in income multipliers is different depending on the sector injected and the household group considered. Reviewing the columns it is seen that because mining decreases the most, households which are more dependent on this sector suffer the most, while those dependent on the services sector are relatively better off. Reviewing the rows it is observed that two household groups, those of urban proprietors and rural latifundists, were able to increase their income multipliers along all sectors. For instance, the former increased their average income multiplier emanating from a unit injection in economic activity from 0.094 to 0.201. Irrespective of the sector in which the impulse is injected these two groups, which were the richest, secured an even higher income multiplier over the decade under consideration. In contrast, the other groups experienced a deterioration in their income multipliers.

4. Decomposed Multipliers

Until now the comparison has centred on the aggregate multipliers M_a. The decomposition of the aggregate multipliers into meaningful effects will be the focus of this section. M_a can be decomposed into three multiplier matrices M_1, M_2, M_3, as in eq. (1).

$$y = Ay + x = (I- A)^{-1}x = M_a x = M_3 M_2 M_1 x \tag{1}$$

In terms of the SAM, M_1, which is known as the transfer multiplier, captures intra effects resulting from transfers which happen between one variable and other variables belonging to the same endogenous account (*i.e.* effects of an impulse in one production activity on all production activities, or in other words, the Leontief multipliers). The open-loop effects M_2 capture the effects of one endogenous account on other endogenous accounts (*i.e.* from production to factor income to household income). The closed-loop effects M_3 ensure that an effect from a specific account is subjected to circular flows through all endogenous accounts (i.e. from household income to product consumption, to production activities, to factor income, to household income, and so on, again and again through all four types of endogenous accounts).

We shall treat below the decomposition of the impact of injections in activities on the output of all activities, $M_{a,44}$, and deal later with the decomposition of the impact of the same injections on incomes of households, $M_{a,44}$.

The decomposition of $M_{a,44}$ in the three effects is shown in eq. (2).

$$M_{a,44} = M_{3,44} * M_{2,44} * M_{1,44} \tag{2}$$
$$\text{aggregate} = \text{closed} * \text{open} * \text{transfer}$$

The aggregate multiplier thus falls into the transfer effects (which correspond with the Leontief multipliers), $M_{1,44}$ *and* the closed-loop effects, $M_{3,44}$.

For 1970, table 4.2 gave an average of aggregate multipliers $M_{a,44}$ at 4.65. Table 4.4 gives the average of transfer effects (Leontief multipliers) $M_{1,44}$ at 1.617. Note that the open-loop effects are not applicable in this decomposition since $M_{2,44}$, being an identity matrix, does not engage accounts other than the entities in its own account. As a result, the remainder is accounted for by the closed loop effect $M_{3,44}$. The closed loop effects stand for carrying the generated production increase through factor incomes, household incomes, product consumption, back to production activities in the form of final demand, and so on, again and again. The results are evidence of the fact that the SAM includes significantly more linkages than the Leontief multipliers, which are restricted to the input-output matrix.

Table 4.4. Transfer Multipliers $M_{1,44}$. 1970 and 1980

1970	Agrc	Mnng	Pcff	Inds	Elgw	Mdsr	Prsr	Pusr
Agrc	1.041	0.027	0.600	0.207	0.052	0.042	0.108	0.060
Mnng	0.004	1.016	0.003	0.026	0.024	0.007	0.007	0.005
Pcff	0.000	0.000	1.053	0.000	0.000	0.000	0.016	0.005
Inds	0.156	0.130	0.113	1.391	0.334	0.228	0.349	0.224
Elgw	0.002	0.032	0.002	0.010	1.025	0.006	0.008	0.007
Mdsr	0.141	0.275	0.154	0.326	0.151	1.268	0.108	0.129
Prsr	0.001	0.003	0.001	0.003	0.006	0.008	1.006	0.016
Pusr	0.001	0.004	0.001	0.003	0.003	0.002	0.002	1.001
Total	1.346	1.486	1.928	1.966	1.596	1.560	1.604	1.447

1980	Agrc	Mnng	Pcff	Inds	Elgw	Mdsr	Prsr	Pusr
Agrc	1.037	0.016	0.487	0.162	0.048	0.032	0.082	0.050
Mnng	0.007	1.016	0.005	0.039	0.030	0.011	0.009	0.006
Pcff	0.000	0.000	1.134	0.000	0.000	0.000	0.031	0.014
Inds	0.209	0.110	0.121	1.366	0.394	0.231	0.299	0.184
Elgw	0.003	0.021	0.003	0.015	1.037	0.008	0.010	0.015
Mdsr	0.171	0.208	0.149	0.348	0.178	1.794	0.102	0.109
Prsr	0.002	0.002	0.002	0.005	0.008	0.011	1.007	0.028
Pusr	0.001	0.001	0.001	0.002	0.001	0.002	0.001	1.001
Total	1.430	1.376	1.900	1.937	1.697	2.089	1.542	1.407

As was seen in table 4.2 for 1980, the results show a reduction in aggregate multipliers to an average value of 3.92. Table 4.4 shows practically no change in the average value of transfer effects, at 1.672. As the open-loop effects are not applicable, the closed-loop effects must have become weaker over time. While the techno-economic substructure of the economy, as represented by the transfer effects among production activities, was able to maintain its multiplier strength, it appears that the other chains in the circular flow, relating to income and expenditure, have lost influence during the decade.

We can now consider in eq. (3) the decomposition of the aggregate multiplier effect of sectoral injections on household incomes, $M_{a,34}$. Sectoral injections create transfer effects $M_{1,44}$ addressed just previously. These are carried through open-loop effects $M_{2,34}$, thereby creating household incomes, after which these household incomes are engaged in a circular flow through the whole system and back to incomes via the closed-loop effect of $M_{3,33}$.

$$M_{a,34} = M_{3,33} * M_{2,34} * M_{1,44} \qquad (3)$$

It was seen in table 4.3 that income multipliers $Ma,34$ have fallen from an average of 2.20 to 1.85. This is not due to a weakening of the transfer effects of economic activities, for we have just seen that the average strength of the transfer effects, $M_{1,44}$ remained the same over the decade. Although output might have been maintained, the income component of this output, i.e. the value added, which is distributed on households via the open-loop effects, has deteriorated over time.

Table 4.5.   Open-Loop Multipliers $M_{2,34}$, 1970 and 1980

1970	Agrc	Mnng	Pcff	Inds	Elgw	Mdsr	Prsr	Pusr
Uprp	0.029	0.033	0.003	0.008	0.031	0.028	0.028	0.028
Uhsw	0.188	0.221	0.019	0.062	0.228	0.194	0.215	0.264
Ulsw	0.015	0.027	0.003	0.017	0.064	0.040	0.068	0.141
Usfw	0.179	0.205	0.017	0.053	0.193	0.172	0.178	0.187
Rltf	0.017	0.014	0.001	0.003	0.008	0.009	0.008	0.005
Rmsf	0.137	0.094	0.006	0.018	0.048	0.055	0.058	0.065
Rfnw	0.074	0.035	0.001	0.007	0.013	0.016	0.027	0.055
Firms	0.127	0.135	0.011	0.024	0.086	0.094	0.069	0.000
Total	0.766	0.766	0.060	0.192	0.671	0.607	0.651	0.745

1980	Agrc	Mnng	Pcff	Inds	Elgw	Mdsr	Prsr	Pusr
Uprp	0.078	0.083	0.005	0.022	0.063	0.074	0.074	0.022
Uhsw	0.113	0.128	0.017	0.039	0.117	0.125	0.136	0.115
Ulsw	0.012	0.028	0.026	0.020	0.076	0.056	0.083	0.218
Usfw	0.125	0.149	0.032	0.052	0.165	0.162	0.188	0.240
Rltf	0.042	0.034	0.002	0.009	0.026	0.029	0.029	0.009
Rmsf	0.136	0.048	0.009	0.019	0.057	0.047	0.054	0.085
Rfnw	0.092	0.013	0.007	0.010	0.030	0.017	0.024	0.074
Firms	0.116	0.122	0.004	0.031	0.083	0.103	0.099	0.000
Total	0.713	0.605	0.101	0.203	0.617	0.613	0.687	0.763

The open-loop effects $M_{2,34}$ in table 4.5 show falling factor payments from output in agriculture, mining, and electricity, and slightly rising factor payments from output in the other sectors. It is in the open-loop effects that that the two household groups of urban proprietors and rural latifundists manage to extract higher incomes in all sectors, in contrast to urban high-skill workers who lose in all sectors. The other household groups show a mixed picture.

The next step is the closure of the model through the closed-loop effects. These are presented in table 4.6. They show the effect of a flow of income to households on all households $M_{3,33}$. Row-wise, the two richer groups of urban proprietors (Uprp) and rural latifundists (Rltf) have been able to retain greater parts of the closed-loop effects. An indication of the magnitude is found in the last column, which sums the closed-loop effects over all households. From this we can see that urban proprietors have been able to increase their multiplier units from 1.5 to 2.0; while rural latifundists achieved an increase from 1.2 to 1.4. This can be explained by a movement of all households towards an expenditure pattern, and in turn to production and remunerative structures corresponding with that expenditure pattern, which indirectly benefits these two groups most.

Table 4.6. Closed-Loop Multipliers $M_{3,34}$, 1970 and 1980

1970	Uprp	Uhsw	Ufsw	Ulsw	Rltf	Rsmf	Rwlw	Firms	Total
Uprp	1.075	0.076	0.083	0.0783	0.059	0.060	0.086	0.000	1.518
Uhsw	0.534	1.539	0.585	0.551	0.416	0.566	0.605	0.000	4.795
Ulsw	0.115	0.114	1.123	0.116	0.087	0.118	0.125	0.000	1.798
Usfw	0.470	0.476	0.517	1.486	0.367	0.501	0.536	0.000	4.352
Rltf	0.029	0.029	0.032	0.030	1.023	0.032	0.034	0.000	1.209
Rmsf	0.201	0.206	0.227	0.212	0.162	1.224	0.242	0.000	2.474
Rfnw	0.087	0.090	0.100	0.092	0.071	0.099	1.108	0.000	1.647
Firms	0.254	0.258	0.282	0.264	0.200	0.274	0.295	1.000	2.827

1980	Uprp	Uhsw	Ufsw	Ulsw	Rltf	Rsmf	Rwlw	Firms	Total
Uprp	1.104	0.203	0.222	0.174	0.102	0.152	0.117	0.000	2.071
Uhsw	0.174	1.343	0.374	0.293	0.171	0.255	0.193	0.000	2.804
Ulsw	0.075	0.154	1.166	0.129	0.077	0.110	0.077	0.000	1.788
Usfw	0.224	0.444	0.484	1.378	0.220	0.328	0.245	0.000	3.323
Rltf	0.045	0.086	0.095	0.075	1.004	0.066	0.052	0.000	1.423
Rmsf	0.099	0.183	0.203	0.161	0.098	1.145	0.122	0.000	2.011
Rfnw	0.052	0.093	0.104	0.084	0.052	0.077	1.068	0.000	1.530
Firms	0.145	0.283	0.310	0.243	0.143	0.213	0.165	1.000	2.499

Among the major losers are the groups of urban high skill workers (Uhsw) and rural small and medium farmers (Rmsf). Their summed closed-loop multiplier effects fall from 4.8 to 2.8, and from 2.5 to 2.0, respectively. These groups have expenditure patterns, and indirectly corresponding production and remunerative structures, which do not benefit them in the final analysis, but leaks to the previously identified favoured groups of urban proprietors and rural latifundists.

It is instructive to follow the consequences of a unit injection in a selected activity, say agriculture, and then trace the chain of the three multiplier effects for individual household groups in order to see how this has changed over time. We shall do this for a household group that improved its position appreciably, urban proprietors Uprp, and a group which experienced declines in its multiplier effects, rural medium and small farmowners Rmsf. Table 4.7 shows the results for these two groups.

To simplify matters we illustrate the transfer and open-loop effects through the three main sectors of agriculture, industry and modern services; these are shaded in tables 4.4 and 4.5. The relevant closed-loop effects are the shaded rows in table 4.6.

First, we consider the income outcome for the household group Rmsf from a unit injection in agriculture. Table 4.4 show agriculture to increase its own output by 1.041, or only 4% more, while the other sectors under consideration, industry and modern services, increase their outputs by 0.156 and 0.141. When these transfer effects are multiplied by the corresponding shaded open-loop effects for the three sectors in table 4.5, they result in income increases for the eight household groups as given in the columns for the three sectors in table 4.7. The fourth column in table 4.7 sums these combined transfer and open-loop effects which go to each household group. The relevant closed-loop effects of Rmsf across each household group are reproduced in the fifth column in table 4.7. When the fourth and fifth columns are multiplied by each other and summed, the aggregate multiplier in the sixth column is obtained, giving for Rmsf an ultimate drop from 0.317 in 1970 to 0.213 in 1980. Table 4.7 gives the results for Uprp in columns 7 and 8, showing their aggregate multiplier to increase from 0.096 in 1970 to 0.262 in 1980. These figures are less than those in table 4.3, which is due to the simplification of tracing the effects through three sectors instead of all eight sectors.

The combined transfer and open-loop effects do not change for Rmsf; they stay at 0.153 in both years. In multiplier terms, Rmsf maintains the same level of value added from economic activities. In contrast, Uprp is one of the very few household groups which increased these effects, from 0.036 to 0.098. This was possible for Uprp by employing more of their factors of production, obtaining a higher remuneration per factor, or a combination of both, which is the more likely case. It is in the closed-loop effects that the greatest shifts occur. Rmsf, together with most other groups, experienced a leakage of their expenditure to their disadvantage. These expenditures, extended by production and income mechanisms, are transformed to the advantage of Uprp. In column 5 it is noted, for instance, that Rmsf extracted from Uprp a portion of 0.201 in 1970; this portion fell to 0.099. In contrast, column 7 shows that Uprp extracted from Rmsf a portion of 0.08 in 1970, this portion increased to 0.152.

Table 4.7. The Multiplier Effects of a Unit Injection in Agriculture: Tracing the Three Multiplier Effects on Incomes of Household Groups Rmsf and Uprp

1970	tranfer effect * open-loop effects for any household group				Rmsf closed-loop effects	Rmsf aggregate multiplier	Uprp closed-loop effects	Uprp aggregate multiplier
	Agrc col.1	Inds col.2	Mdsr col.3	Sum col.4	col.5	col.6	col.7	col.8
Uprp	0.031	0.001	0.004	0.036	0.201	0.007	1.075	0.038
Uhsw	0.196	0.010	0.027	0.233	0.206	0.048	0.076	0.018
Ulsw	0.015	0.003	0.006	0.024	0.228	0.005	0.083	0.002
Usfw	0.187	0.008	0.024	0.219	0.212	0.046	0.078	0.017
Rltf	0.018	0.000	0.001	0.019	0.162	0.003	0.059	0.001
Rmsf	0.143	0.003	0.008	0.153	1.224	0.187	0.080	0.012
Rfnw	0.077	0.001	0.002	0.080	0.242	0.019	0.086	0.007
Firms	0.133	0.004	0.013	0.150	0.000	0.000	0.000	0
Total	0.798	0.030	0.086	0.914		0.317		0.096

1980	tranfer effect * open-loop effects for any household group				Rmsf closed-loop effects	Rmsf aggregate multiplier	Uprp closed-loop effects	Uprp aggregate multiplier
	Agrc col.1	Inds col.2	Mdsr col.3	Sum col.4	col.5	col.6	Col.7	Col.8
Uprp	0.081	0.005	0.013	0.098	0.099	0.010	1.104	0.108
Uhsw	0.118	0.008	0.021	0.147	0.183	0.027	0.203	0.03
Ulsw	0.012	0.004	0.010	0.026	0.203	0.005	0.222	0.006
Usfw	0.130	0.011	0.028	0.169	0.161	0.027	0.174	0.029
Rltf	0.044	0.002	0.005	0.051	0.098	0.005	0.102	0.005
Rmsf	0.141	0.004	0.008	0.153	1.145	0.175	0.152	0.023
Rfnw	0.095	0.002	0.003	0.100	0.122	0.012	0.117	0.012
Firms	0.120	0.006	0.018	0.144	0.000	0.000	0.000	0
Total	0.740	0.042	0.105	0.887		0.000		0.213

The multiplier results can be presented in another way which highlights the growth and redistributionary bias in the economy. This is done in table

4.8. The first and second columns give the actual proportional distribution of income and population over the household groups and firms, while the third column divided the first by the second column to indicate the relative richness of one group to another. For instance, in 1980 the urban proprietors are on average 6.8 times richer than the next group of urban high skilled workers (9.64/1.42). The remaining columns in the table give for each household group its proportional share in the generated aggregate multiplier, distinguished by sectoral injection. These shares can be called the SAM multiplier shares. We include an average column for these shares. A case of a household group where the average SAM multiplier share is higher than the actual share, as shown in the last column of the table, indicates that the circular flow in the economy favours this household group, and will ultimately enhance its future share to a level above its actual share. Household groups with a SAM multiplier share lower than their actual share will score values below unity in the last column; these are at a disadvantage as regards future growth and distribution. It is observed that in 1970 the rural household groups are favoured by the circular flow, they score above unity in the last column. In contrast, in 1970 the urban household groups are disfavoured, scoring below unity in the last column.

If one considers 1980, the picture tends to reverse. The urban proprietors, who are the wealthiest, are the household group which consistently shows a favourable bias. The circular flow is also biased in favour of urban high skilled workers. All other household groups are in a weakened position in 1980 by comparison to 1970. In general, it can be said that the rural bias of 1970 is transformed into an urban bias in 1980, but only partially so, since two other urban groups either maintain or experience a deterioration in their material role in the circular flow. Correspondingly, all rural household groups are losers, but small and medium farmers, wage earners and landless farmers lose much more than the latifundists.

The results also show that in 1970 all sectors had multipliers with progressive effects on income distribution, the exception being public services. In 1980, the mechanisms are significantly altered. Only processed coffee and public services are slightly progressive, while the other sectors are either regressive or cause no change in the income distribution. This means that the trade-off between policies for growth and equity must have increased in the ten years, which is a particularly difficult problem for policy makers. The possibilities of material progress for all population groups may be significantly limited.

Table 4.8. An Alternative Presentation of Shifts in Aggregate Multipliers, 1970 and 1980

1970	Actual income share	Population share	Relative richness	Agriculture	Manufacturing	Coffee	Ind	Elgw	Md sr	Pr sr	Pu sr	Average	Average/ actual
Uprp	0.043	0.02	2.53	0.041	0.043	0.042	0.043	0.044	0.044	0.043	0.041	0.042	0.992
Uhs	0.313	0.229	1.37	0.283	0.298	0.287	0.301	0.313	0.307	0.308	0.316	0.302	0.962
Uls	0.070	0.106	0.66	0.049	0.055	0.051	0.063	0.073	0.064	0.075	0.099	0.066	0.950
Usf	0.270	0.243	1.11	0.255	0.267	0.259	0.266	0.272	0.271	0.267	0.261	0.265	0.983
Rltf	0.016	0.015	1.03	0.018	0.017	0.018	0.016	0.015	0.016	0.015	0.014	0.016	1.050
Rmsf	0.101	0.247	0.41	0.136	0.116	0.131	0.115	0.102	0.107	0.109	0.108	0.116	1.145
Rfnw	0.039	0.143	0.28	0.065	0.048	0.061	0.050	0.041	0.042	0.048	0.057	0.052	1.312
Firm	0.149			0.152	0.154	0.152	0.145	0.140	0.148	0.134	0.103	0.141	0.948
Total	1.00	1.00		1.000	1.000	1.000	1.000	1.000	1.000	1.000	1.000		

1980	Actual income share	Population share	Relative richness	Agriculture	Manufacturing	Coffee	Ind	Elgw	Md sr	Pr sr	Pu sr	Average	Average/ actual
Uprp	0.108	0.011	9.64	0.112	0.122	0.107	0.113	0.110	0.116	0.111	0.086	0.110	1.015
Uhs	0.189	0.133	1.42	0.179	0.199	0.181	0.191	0.191	0.196	0.193	0.178	0.188	0.996
Uls	0.100	0.332	0.30	0.058	0.071	0.081	0.083	0.096	0.087	0.096	0.149	0.090	0.901
Usfw	0.252	0.188	1.34	0.220	0.248	0.235	0.246	0.253	0.253	0.255	0.268	0.247	0.981
Rltf	0.047	0.010	4.85	0.053	0.051	0.049	0.049	0.046	0.048	0.047	0.037	0.047	1.009
Rmsf	0.108	0.141	0.76	0.137	0.094	0.125	0.105	0.100	0.094	0.097	0.107	0.107	0.995
Rfnw	0.061	0.185	0.33	0.082	0.041	0.074	0.055	0.052	0.044	0.049	0.069	0.058	0.952
Firm	0.134			0.160	0.174	0.149	0.159	0.131	0.162	0.153	0.107	0.149	1.115
Total	1.00	1.00		1.000	1.000	1.000	1.000	1.000	1.000	1.000	1.000		

5. Decompositional Analysis of Inter-Temporal Change

An analysis of SAM output multipliers for Colombia for the period between 1970 and 1980 showed diminishing multiplier effects for all sectors (table 4.2 shows that these have fallen by 16% on average). The diminishing multiplier effects over time can be reasoned in terms of changes in external and internal mechanisms. First, there is an increased dependence on the exogenous variables in influencing the course of the economy, i.e. the external mechanisms. The exogenous variables, it is recalled, are those of the government, capital, and the rest of the world. The share of these in the total circular flow has gone up significantly between 1970 and 1980. Consequently, the share of the endogenous part of the circular flow has gone down by about 12%. Second, within the endogenous part there appears to be a weakening of the internal circular flow mechanisms. There is the double hypothesis of an increased dependence of the economy on external exogenous variables combined with a weakening of internal multiplier effects as the economy grows over time. This hypothesis will be studied further in chapter 8. This section will decompose inter-temporal performance in terms of SAM multipliers and exogenous changes, and give evidence supporting the above hypothesis.

The availability of SAMs for 1970 and 1980 allows a decomposition of economic performance of the economy over time into a part due to changes in SAM multipliers and the part due to changes in exogenous variables.

Keeping in mind that we have solved the vector of endogenous variables y from exogenous variables x and coefficient matrix A and x as in eq. (4):

$$y = Ay + x = (I - A)^{-1} x = M_a x \qquad (4)$$

where M_a is the aggregate multiplier matrix. Rewriting this equation for the two periods of 1970 and 1980 and subtracting gives the change in the endogenous variables, Δy, as in eq. (5).

$$\Delta y = y_{80} - y_{70} = M_{a,80} \, x_{80} \quad - M_{a,70} \, x_{70} \qquad (5)$$

Changes in the endogenous sector can be explained in terms of two effects: a change in the multiplier matrix $(M_{a,80} - M_{a,70})$ and a change in the exogenous vector $(x_{80} - x_{70})$. The assumption of a zero value for one effect enables measurement of the other effect. This is done by adding, subtracting, and simplifying terms to give eq. (6).

$$
\begin{aligned}
\Delta y &= y_{80} - y_{70} & = M_{a,80} \, x_{80} \quad - M_{a,70} \, x_{70} \\
&= M_{a,80} \, x_{80} - M_{a,80} \, x_{70} + M_{a,80} \, x_{70} - M_{a,70} \, x_{70} \\
&= M_{a,80} \, \Delta x \qquad\qquad + \Delta M_a \, x_{70} \qquad (6)
\end{aligned}
$$

As a result, the change in an endogenous variable is decomposed into a change in exogenous variables (at constant SAM multipliers) and a change in SAM multipliers (at constant exogenous variables).

The two expressions in eq. (6) are sufficient to explain the variations in the endogenous variables, if both SAMs used in the decomposition were available in constant prices. In order to give a treatment in real volumes, the price changes have to be excluded from the analysis, which means that the SAMs have to be deflated to a common basis.

As is generally known price deflation of such matrices poses enormous difficulties as regards the choice of neutral handling methods, as well as the lack of crucial data. In the circumstances, we opt for rough approximations in an attempt to eliminate major price effects.

For instance, it is kept in mind that eq. (6) can alternatively be reformulated to give a decomposition of performance starting from a different base year, say 1970, as in eq. (7):

$$\Delta y = \Delta M_a \, x_{80} + M_{a,70} \, \Delta x \tag{7}$$

The results obtained from application of eq. (6) can be compared with those obtainable from eq. (7); if the results are approximately the same, then it can be postulated that price changes must have been neutral and did not influence the changes in real volumes. Indeed, we have applied both equations, and the similarity in results obtained using eq. (6) and (7) can be interpreted as evidence that selection of a base year, 1970 or 1980, for decomposition of past performance does not significantly influence the obtained results. Consequently, one can speculate that the results in this section may not have been very different if the two SAMs were deflated to the same prices. (This would in any case not be feasible to perform).

In passing it is noted that a more general formula than either eqs. (6) or (7) is eq. (8). This equation was also calculated, but again, the results did not deviate significantly from eq. (6), the results of which will further be presented in table 4.9.

$$\Delta y = \Delta M_a \, x_{70} + M_{a,70} \, \Delta x + \Delta M_a \, \Delta x \tag{8}$$

Table 4.9 explains the changes over the ten years in output and their distribution over the sectors, and similarly the changes in income and their distribution across the different household groups and firms, in terms of the exogenous and endogenous components in eq. (6).

Results show that the increase in the total output of 154268 mp is accountable in terms of a bigger increase in the exogenous component of 406761 mp, and a significant reduction in the multiplier effects that is equivalent to −252503 mp. The results reflect the weakening in most sectors of the internal endogenous mechanisms referred to earlier. In the exogenous component capital investment played a dominant role, followed by trade and transfers with the rest of world, and government.

Table 4.9.   An Explanation of Changes in Factor Earnings, Household Income and Sectoral Output between 1970 and 1980

(Changes in mil. pesos.)

	Total	%	Due to exogenous change x	%	Of which is accountable by: Capital	Government	Rest world	Due to endogenous change M	%
Factors									
U lab	12932	36.6	79839	225.8	38961	20480	20378	-66907	-189.2
R lab	10591	75.8	13468	96.4	6916	1796	4757	-2877	-20.6
Profits	44649	66.8	105946	158.4	47211	8087	40648	-61296	-91.6
Income									
Uprp	15134	309.5	-2832	-579.3	-16412	-4383	-7529	43459	888.9
Uhsw	-817	-2.3	122455	340.0	57892	29406	35157	-123272	-342.3
Ulsw	10815	131.5	-1778	-21.6	-132	-1520	-126	12593	153.1
Usfw	7826	25.4	51315	166.3	29535	9997	11784	-43490	-141.0
Rltf	6822	359.2	-13890	-731.2	-7708	-2594	-3587	20712	1090.4
Rmsf	6514	48.0	26704	196.6	13105	4613	8986	-20190	-148.6
Rfnw	5250	83.7	6467	103.1	3024	1325	2118	-1217	-19.4
Firms	11441	68.2	21697	129.3	9318	3794	8585	-10256	-61.1
Subttl	62986		184645		88621	40637	55388	-121660	
Output									
Agrc	10620	25.1	102378	242.1	47129	19617	35633	-91758	-217.0
Mnng	4137	112.2	-654	-17.7	-976	-283	605	4791	130.0
Pcff	7292	67.1	3288	30.3	1060	74	2155	4003	36.8
Inds.	64135	61.7	180036	173.1	88530	35531	55976	-115902	-111.4
Elgw	2901	142.2	-1819	-89.2	-907	-765	-146	4720	231.4
Mosr	47346	67.8	89908	128.8	46934	15888	27086	-42561	-61.0
Prsr	10226	66.9	21881	143.1	10346	3927	7609	-11655	-76.2
Pusr	7600	68.3	11741	105.6	1918	8662	1160	-4141.3	-37.2
Subttl	154258		406761		194034	82651	130076	-252503	

There are three sectors showing the opposite tendency, these are mining, processed coffee and electricity, gas and water.

The dominance of positive exogenous effects over negative endogenous effects also occurs more regularly in accounting for the changes in income over the ten years. Most household groups are affected accordingly. The three exceptions are the groups urban proprietors (Uprp), urban low skill workers (Ulsw), and rural latifundists (Rltf).

In conclusion, it can be stated that the internal endogenous mechanisms in the economy worked in favour of these groups, while the exogenously held government, capital investment and the rest of the world worked to their disadvantage.

Chapter 5

Social Accounting and Circular Flow Planning Models: an Application to Pakistan

1. Introduction

There is an important role for the social accounting matrix, SAM, in setting up and estimating SAM-corresponding policy making models. This chapter and the following three chapters develop economic models primarily meant for policy making in the areas of economic growth and income distribution, primarily based on the SAM framework. While this chapter develops and applies such models to Pakistan, the next chapter applies other refinements to Indonesia. The other chapters apply further refinements to more developing countries.

To start with, most of the past models developed and applied for Pakistan served analytical purposes, were demonstrative in nature or were not updated. As a result, they are practically irrelevant for today's appraisal of future prospects. In the last two decades, a few models that have been updated regularly may turn out to be more useful in policy preparation. In particular, PIDE's econometric model is the most widely publicised, cf. Naqvi *et al.* (1983). In the category of activity models one simple but handy model is that by Cohen, Havinga and Saleem (1985). In the category of activity and factor planning models a regularly updated and used manpower planning model that elaborates on the labour force matrix of Pakistan, is in Cohen (1985). Finally, two research reports by the author, published by Pakistan Institute of Development Economics, in PIDE (1985) and PIDE (1986), apply various circular flow models based on the SAM.

The chapter will examine several extensions of policy making models that belong to the family of SAM-corresponding models. Section 2 deals with the simplest form, which is a SAM multiplier model which gives multiplier effects of injections in sectoral activities and transfers to household groups on growth and income. Section 3 treats a more flexible model, which is a SAM-consistent policy making model, SAM/POL.

SAM/POL incorporates changing coefficients of consumption, investment, deliveries, government, budget and payments deficit, and aims at checking plan targets.

Section 4 adapts the model to consider the effects of structural adjustment; this is modelled in SAM/ADJ. Section 5 extends the model further in the direction of introducing relationships regarding demand for and supply of labour and capital. Section 6 adds concluding remarks on other developments in economic modelling for Pakistan.

Relative prices are taken as given in the models treated in this chapter, meaning that the markets clear via quantity adjustments, and not price adjustments. In the next chapter the focus shifts to SAM-based computable general equilibrium models, which allow for both price and quantity adjustments.

2.   SAM Multiplier Models

2.1. The SAM of Pakistan

By way of introduction it may be restated that the SAM is nothing more or less than the transformation of the circular flow of goods and services among agents into a matrix of transactions between the various agents, as in table 5.1 for Pakistan. When appropriately manipulated, this table can give a model-representation of the economy that forms a useful framework for tracing the effects of structural adjustments in public expenditure, investment schedules, and trade and transfers with the rest of the world on sectoral growth and institutional incomes.

For the purpose of this chapter, table 5.1 represents an abridged SAM with emphasis on the agricultural sectors and the rural households groups. Agriculture is divided tentatively into two sectors: wheat and rice, and other agriculture. The remaining sectors are industry and services.

As the SAM in table 5.1. shows, wheat and rice had in 1979/80 a total production of 28.8 million rupees, out of which 8.1 is registered as a direct consumption of food, 0.1 as stock additions, 1.3 as net export, and 19.3 as intermediate deliveries for processing in the various sectors of the economy before being converted into final goods for domestic consumption or exports. The part for processing forms a high percentage of 67%.

Other agriculture shows a different pattern. Out of a total production of 88.6 mln. Rs. the direct food consumption is 40.1, stock additions is 0.6, net exports 5.4, and intermediate deliveries for further processing is the remaining sum of 42.5. The part for processing forms a lower percentage of 48%.

Although about one-quarter of the total agricultural production was accounted for by wheat and rice in contrast to three-quarters for other crops, table 5.1 shows wheat and rice to have in 1979/80 relatively stronger linkages in the input-output sense than other crops (intermediate deliveries of 67% as compared to 48%, respectively).

Furthermore, table 5.1 distinguishes between four rural household groups:

1. households with large landholdings, above 25.0 acres
2. households with medium landholdings, between 12.5 and 25.0 acres
3. households with small or no landholdings, below 12.5 acres
4. non-farm households.

These, in addition to two urban household groups of wage employment and self-employment.

It is noted, from the SAM, row 5, that the income receipts of the large landholdings group depend for only 4% (i.e. 1.1/27-4) on wheat and rice, and for 12% (i.e. 3.4/27.4) on other agriculture. It can be calculated further that their dependence on non-agricultural sectors, on government services, and on foreign remittances amounts to 62%, 15% and 7%, respectively. The medium landholdings group, row 6, is slightly more dependent on its income on wheat and rice whose share is 7%, and on other agriculture which forms 23%, but similarly, the lion's share of income for both the large and medium landholdings groups comes from non-agricultural activities and foreign remittances. The situation is very different for the small landholdings groups, row 7, whose income depends on wheat and rice for 13%, and on other agriculture for 40%. It is also striking to note the high dependence of non-farm households, row 8, on wheat and rice and on other agriculture, forming 14% and 44%, respectively. These facts show that the lot of richer households in rural areas is much less tied to what happens to agriculture than is generally assumed.

The dependence of poorer households in rural areas is about evenly divided between agricultural and non-agricultural incomes, a fact which could suggest that policy emphasis on rural industrialisation is just as important as that on crop cultivation.

Table 5.1.   **SAM Pakistan 1979/1980** (in billions of rupees)

	1.	2.	3.	4.	5.	6.	7.	8.	9.	10.
	Food , Drinks	Non-Food	Urban Wage Employment	Urban Self Employment	Rural Large Holdings	Rural Medium Holdings	Rural Small/No Hldgs	Rural Non-Farm	Firms	Government
Wants										
1 Food, drinks			15.5	16.1	8.7	13.9	36.7	4.9		
2 Non-food			18.0	19.4	14.9	13.1	.33.0	3.9		
Institutions										
3 Urb wage empl										0.2
4 Urb self empl										
5 Rur large hldng										
6 Rur mdm hldng										
7 Rur sml/no hld										
8 Rural non-farm										0.2
9 Firms										1.1
10 Government				0.9	0.9		0.1		3.6	
11 Aggr capital			4.0	4.1	3.8	1.6	0.4	0.2	10.3	5.1
Activities										
12 Wheat, rice	8.1									
13 Other agrcltr	40.1									
14 Non-agrcltr	47.5	78.3								
15 Public srvcs		24.6								22.1
16 Indirect taxs										
17 Rest World Errors, omissions	0.1		0.5							
Total	95.8	102.9	38.9	40.5	27.4	28.6	70.2	9.0	13.9	28.7

Table 5.1. (Continued)

	11.	12.	13.	14.	15.	16.	17.		
	Aggr Capital Account	Wheat and Rice	Other Agriculture	Non-Agriculture	Public Services	Indirect Taxes	Rest of World	Errors and Omissions	Total
Wants									
1 Food, drinks									95.8
2 Non-food								0.6	102.9
Institutions									
3 Urb wage empl		0.2	0.6	21.4	12.6		4.3	-0.5	38.9
4 Urb self empl		0.7	2.4	28.0	4.8		4.5		40.5
5 Rur large hldng		1.1	3.4	17.0	4.2		1.7		27.4
6 Rur mdm hldng		2.1	6.5	14.6	3.6		1.8	0.1	28.6
7 Rur sml/no hld		8.9	28.1	23.2	5.6		4.4		70.2
8 Rural non-farm		1.3	4.0	2.3	0.6		0.5		9.0
9 Firms		0.7	2.3	9.8	2.0		-3.0	0.1	13.9
10 Government			0.1	0.9	0.8	23.9	-2.4		28.7
11 Aggr capital					0.0	0.0	11.3	0.8	41.6
Activities									
12 Wheat, rice	0.1	1.0	2.2	16.1	0.9		1.3		28.8
13 Other agrcltr	0.6	5.1	18.8	17.6	13.1		5.4	0.1	88.6
14 Non-agrcltr	40.9	9.3	19.8	121.9	1.8		-32.7	-0.6	297.5
15 Public srvcs				0.7	0.1		0.8	0.2	50.2
16 Indirect taxs		-1.8	0.3	25.3					23.9
17 Rest World									
Errors, omissions	41.6	0.1	0.1	-1.1	0.1		2.0		1.7
Total		28.8	88.6	297.5	50.2	23.9		1.7	988.2

2.2. *The SAM multipliers*

An interesting feature is that the SAM is a square matrix. As such it represents a model of the economy. By appropriate manipulations of this square matrix, it is possible to derive SAM-multipliers. To transform the social accounting matrix into an economy-wide model along the above lines requires performing several steps. First, the accounts of the SAM need to be subdivided into endogenous and exogenous and regrouped accordingly so that the exogenous accounts would fall to the right and bottom of the endogenous accounts. The choice regarding subdivision into x exogenous and y endogenous variables can lead to lengthy discussions on alternative closure rules. We shall assume for a typical developing country, variables relating to expenditure and revenue of government, capital and rest of world as exogenous, the remaining variables are endogenous.

Each flow in the endogenous matrix is divided by its respective column total to give the matrix of average propensities, denoted by A. The vector of endogenous variables y can now be solved from equation (1):

$$y = Ay + x = (I - A)^{-1} x = M x \qquad (1)$$

where M is the SAM multiplier matrix.

There are two uses of equation 1. For years that are directly before and after the year of computation the SAM multipliers can be employed to tell us what are the effects of restructuring the sectoral demand - via restructuring of investment outlay, budget expenditure or foreign trade - on the two dimensions of growth of output and the generation and distribution of income by population groups. These two types of effects will be called the growth and the income effects, and we will mainly concentrate on them. In a similar way, one can assess the effects of transfers to specific household groups (by government or rest of world) on growth of output and on the generation and distribution of income.

For purposes of presentation, table 5.2 gives the impact multipliers of the SAM for 11 selected exogenous impulses. The impact of exogenous injections to sectoral activities on the functioning of the whole economy is found in columns 12 to 15. The impact of exogenous transfers to household groups are found in columns 3 to 9.

Let us first consider the growth and distributionary effects of exogenous injections in sectoral activities. Column 12 would imply that an additional million rupees(mr) of demand for wheat and rice by government and/or exports ultimately leads to an additional 1.6 mr production of wheat and rice, 1.8 other agriculture, 5.9 non-agriculture, and 0.5 services; giving a total of 9.7 mr.

Table 5.2. Aggregate multipliers, Pakistan 1979-1980

	Institutions							Activities			
	urban wage earners	urban self-employed	rural large holdings	rural medium holdings	rural small holdings	rural non-farming	firms	wheat and rice	other agricultural	non-agricultural	public services
Products											
Food & drinks	1.760	1.775	1.668	1.975	2.094	2085.000	0.000	1.869	1.786	1.483	1.631
Non-food	1.912	2.000	1.980	2.043	2.141	2.076	0.000	1.956	1.865	1.587	1.754
Total	3.672	3.719	3.647	4.018	4.236	4.161	0.000	3.825	3.650	3.070	3.385
Institutions											
Urban wage earners	1.492	0.499	0.495	0.534	0.562	0.550	0.000	0.570	0.535	0.544	0.751
Urban self-employed	0.563	1.571	0.563	0.615	0.648	0.635	0.000	0.688	0.646	0.649	0.669
Rural large holdings	0.396	0.401	1.394	4.320	0.455	0.447	0.000	0.504	0.477	0.444	0.484
Rural medium hld	0.416	0.422	0.413	1.456	0.481	0.473	0.000	0.569	0.543	0.457	0.490
Rural small/no hld	1.037	1.049	1.019	1.142	2.205	1.188	0.000	1.571	1.518	1.094	1.143
Rural non-farming	0.130	0.132	0.127	0.143	0.152	1.149	0.000	0.203	0.198	0.135	0.141
Firms	0.231	0.234	0.230	0.253	0.266	0.261	1.000	0.300	0.284	0.260	0.273
Total	4.265	4.307	4.241	4.575	4.769	4.703	1.000	4.406	4.200	3.583	3.950
Activities											
Wheat and rice	0.468	0.474	0.458	0.516	0.545	0.538	0.000	1.574	0.532	0.498	0.462
Other agriculture	1.423	1.438	1.372	1.583	1.675	1.660	0.000	1.800	2.757	1.356	1.386
Non-agriculture	4.953	5.019	4.945	5.405	5.693	5.585	0.000	5.858	5.449	5.952	5.065
Public services	0.487	0.495	0.504	0.521	0.546	0.529	0.000	0.501	0.477	0.409	1.485
Total	7.331	7.426	7.279	8.026	8.460	8.312	0.000	9.733	9.216	8.214	8.390

The contribution of an expansion in wheat and rice to the overall growth of output is highest, followed by other crops, industry and services. Note that the narrower input-output framework, lays emphasis on the intra-activities accounts, and gives higher values of multipliers for industry than for agriculture. This has had the effect of encouraging investment in industry at the cost of agriculture. We have here different results from the broader SAM framework as it considers the whole circular flow including the activities accounts. The SAM would recommend expansion of agriculture at the cost of industry. Of course, both the input-output and the SAM frameworks consider the demand side only. Realistic planning requires considering both demand and supply sides.

Secondly, we consider the income distributionary effect. Wheat and rice lead with an income impact multiplier of 4.4. The rural small/no holdings group gains, collecting 1.6 out of the 4.4, or 36%. This is a higher share than the actual share of the income of this group in 1979-80 that amounted to 31%. As a result, it can be concluded that additional demand for wheat and rice is progressive in its income redistribution effect. The same applies to other agriculture. These progressive effects are due to two causes. First, the persistence of a strong link between the agricultural factors of production and factor income for rural households at the lower end of the income scale. Second, the ability of these households to plough back their consumption expenditures and those of other households to their benefit. In several countries where such an analysis has been made it was found that the consumption pattern of poorer households is inefficient in the sense that it leads to an income leakage to richer households. In this respect, Pakistan is better off.

We may turn now to the growth and distributionary effects of exogenous transfers to household groups. The same mechanisms assure that an addition of one million rupees of transfers (through direct government subsidies, price policy or foreign remittances) to any household group results in a growth of output of between. 7.3 and 8.5, and a growth of income of between 4.2 and 4.8 million rupees (columns 13 to 18). Here too, the highest growth and income effects are in the case of transfers to the rural small/no holdings group: total output would grow by 8.5 million rupees while total income would increase by 4.8 million rupees. The rural small/no holdings group retains 46% (i.e. 2.2/4.8) of the income increase which is much higher than their actual income share (31% as quoted above), testifying to significant progressive redistribution effects due to the transfer.

The income increases calculated above are spent in favour of higher food consumption of about 2.1, higher non-food consumption of about another 2.1, and the rest goes into savings of about 0.6.

Discounting errors that may have gone in the calculation of a social accounting matrix of Pakistan, the SAM analysis suggests that there is evidence towards inclusion of Pakistan in a selected group of countries that manifest both positive growth and positive distributionary effects as far as agricultural injections are concerned.

To balance our exposition, we conclude this section by making several limitations of the SAM-multiplier approach explicit. (1) The evaluation of the multipliers of the SAM-model cannot be done in isolation from the closure rules applied. (2) In the multiplier model, supplied amounts are supposed to adjust to demanded amounts. They will, but if there is restricted capacity, the result is inflation. This may require a revision downwards in the real sizes of multipliers in situations with limited capacity. (3) The SAM-multiplier model is more comprehensive than the input-output multiplier model, but also many more linear relationships have to be assumed: constant shares of factor remunerations in total output, of household incomes in the various factor payments, of commodities in household expenditure, and of sectors in commodity production. (4) The poor data available on factor accounts stand in the way of linking household earnings to income by sectoral sources in more disaggregated and relevant ways.

3. SAM-Corresponding Policy Making Models (SAM/POL)

Policy making models can be made consistent with SAM. Resulting models, named SAM/POL, are flexible and can be made capable of forecasting future development and analysing alternative policy options. Such a flexible model has been implemented for Pakistan giving yearly solutions for the period from 1980 to 1993, which is the final year of the Seventh Plan. A full description and discussion of estimation of the model as well as the results of various simulations are found in a research report by the author, PIDE (1986).

The SAM/POL model consists of 30 types of equations resulting in a total of 201 equations comprising a disaggregation in 8 products, 12 sectors, and 10 household groups. It is a circular flow model with binding constraints on the supply side.

Meant as a planning model the revenue and expenditure of the government sector are fully modelled in relation to domestic institutions as well as foreign sources.

The estimates of the coefficients of the model are derived in one of four ways: (1) proportions directly derived from the SAM such as the input-output coefficients, (2) consumption propensities and intercepts estimated by regressions from cross-sections of the Household Income and Expenditure Survey, (3) averages of several years, and (4) being a simulative model a number of calibration parameters are incorporated especially in the consumption functions to permit a correspondence between the simulated results of the model in the period of 1978-81 to 1984-85 and the observed values for the same period.

The exogenous variables in the model include, besides population *POP*, those of exports *EXP*, imports *IMP*, factor income from rest of world to households *ROW*, firms OFR_f and government *OFRg*, and other budgetary variables such as government consumption CON_g, government investment INV_g, and indirect taxes less subsidies ITX_g, (direct taxes are the result of tax rates applied to tax-payer incomes). Table 5.3 sums up the trends of the exogenous variables.

Once tested and well-callibrated this model can be used effectively for planning purposes. A simple but meaningful evaluation of the ability of the model to reflect the actual course of the *ex post* period is by comparing model predictions with actual observations for 1979-80 to 1984-85. The relative differences between predicted and actual values for variables of consumption, investment and the GDP are not significant, they do not exceed 8% up and 2% down. Besides, the predicted changes in capital utilisation are within permissible limits. As a result, the model forms a reasonable basis for following up and analysing development in the rest of the decade.

Table 5.4 gives the performance of the economy in the periods of the Sixth Plan and the Seventh Plan. The annual growth rate of consumption increases from 5.1% in the Sixth Plan to 5.7% in the Seventh Plan. Contrariwise the growth of investment is reduced from 7.5% to 6.4% This is due to a generally very low rate of investment at the start of the Sixth Plan (1982-83) which was still associated with the depressed investment climate in the world at large in the wake of the past oil price increases. The annual growth rate of investment in the Seventh Plan (6.4%) is a respectable one and exceeds that of consumption (5.7%) by about 0.7%. The balance of the trade gap is assumed to show a significant improvement. While at the end of the Sixth Plan the trade gap as a proportion of the GDP will form 2.9% (i.e. 11.9/413.3), it is predicted to fall down at the end of the Seventh Plan to 1.3% (i.e. 7.1/557.2). As a result of these developments, GDP that may grow at an average of 5.7% in the Sixth Plan, is predicted to grow at a higher rate in the Seventh Plan, i.e. 6.2%.

Table 5.3 Trends of Exogenous Variables,
in billions of rupees of 1979-80; and population, POP, in millions

Exogenous variables	1985-86 Actual	1992-93 Projected	1985-86 – 1992-93 Annual percentage growth
1. POP	96.0	116.5	2.8
2. EXP	47.0	73.6	6.6
3. IMP	60.0	80.6	4.3
4. ROW	26.2	21.3	-3.0
5. OFR_f	-6.9	10.0	5.4
6. OFR_g	-5.5	-8.0	5.4
7. CON_g	35.7	59.3	7.5
8. INV_g	34.2	60.9	8.6

The second part of table 5.4 gives the breakdown of the value added by twelve sectors. All sectors show higher growth in the Seventh Plan period as compared to the Sixth Plan period except construction. The growth rates by sector vary within a very small range. As a result of the above trends the percentage distributions of the value added on the sectors do not undergo basic changes. This tendency for converging growth rates is typical of demand-oriented input-output models. Inclusion of supply constraints for agriculture would have probably resulted in a more realistic agricultural growth of about 4.7% as compared to the 5.7% generated by SAM/POL work to adapt the model accordingly is under progress. Even if agriculture would grow at the lower rate, the GDP growth would be lowered marginally, so that a rounded target of 6% annual growth in the GDP is well within reach for the Seventh Plan.

The third part of table 5.4 deals with the breakdown of the disposable income by twelve institutions: 10 household groups, firms and government. In the first place, total disposable income grows at about one-half percent less than the value added, i.e. at 5.2% and 5.8% annually during the Sixth and Seventh Plans, respectively.

The highest growth is among the group of urban employers, and firms, but each institution is getting more income. It is important to note that the shares for rural groups remain stable over the ten years of the Sixth and Seventh Plan periods. Among the urban groups there are important shifts. The employers move over the two periods from a share of 0.35% to 0.49%, manual workers move slightly from 7.0% to 7.1%. These gains are at the cost of, on the one hand, the urban professional jobs and urban non-manual jobs who together fall from 8.0% to 7.7%, and on the other hand the urban self-employed who fall from a share of 14.8% to 14.0%.

More meaningful trends from the welfare point of view are in the fourth part which shows the levels and growth rates for disposable income per capita. This is projected for rural landless in 1992-93 at 1.58 thousand rupees followed by rural non-farm 2.43 thousand rupees rural small 3.13 thousand rupees and rural medium 3.92 thousand rupees. Among the urban groups, there is hardly a difference between non-manual, manual and self employed, they all earned about 4.8 thousand rupees per capita, followed with a distance by the urban professionals at 7.5 thousand rupees and the urban employers at 17.6 thousand rupees.

Average annual growth of disposable income for the Sixth Plan is 1.8 percent. Groups which fell significantly below this rate are the urban self-employed who, due to population pressure, have gained hardly anything, plus 0.19%. However, the situation for the Seventh Plan shows a closing of ranks. Total disposable income per capita is forecasted to grow at 2.7% per annum, while that of the rural self-employed is closer at 1.8% per annum. Although the signs of dualities are very striking when one analyses absolute gaps between rural and urban incomes, a comparison between relative growth rates of disposable income per capita of the various household groups shows that the discrepancies will be somewhat less in the Seventh than in the Sixth Plan, with the one striking exception of the group of urban employers.

The fifth part of table 5.4 treats past and future performance regarding essential needs. The three poorest groups which form the bulk in rural areas are bundled together to give their food expenditure per capita.

Table 5.4 The Sixth and Seventh Plans of Pakistan

All values in billions of rupees and in prices of 1979-80; Populations in 1000s;Values per capita in 1000 rupees

I Expenditure	Value			% Distribution			% Annual Growth	
	1982-3	1987-8	1992-3	1982-3	1987-8	1992-3	6th Plan	7th Plan
Consumption	275.13	352.23	464.95				5.065	5.71
Investment	50.76	72.91	99.31				7.511	6.37
Export/imports	-13.44	-11.38	-7.06				-2.406	-0.85
GDP	312.46	413.25	557.19	100	100	100	5.751	6.15
II Sectoral Product								
Wheat	15.99	20.77	27.47	5.12	5.03	4.93	5.370	5.75
Other agriculture	55.69	72.08	95.54	17.82	17.44	17.15	5.295	5.79
Mining	3.60	5.08	7.58	1.15	1.23	1.36	7.130	3.33
Large manufacturing	35.04	113.45	154.60	27.22	27.45	27.75	5.934	5.38
Small manufacturing	13.34	17.24	22.69	4.27	4.17	4.07	5.263	5.64
Construction	12.08	17.27	23.49	3.87	4.18	4.22	7.410	6.34
Ownership/dwelling	8.91	11.13	14.49	2.85	2.69	2.60	4.550	5.41
Electricity	7.71	10.14	13.63	2.47	2.45	2.45	5.632	3.09
Trade	42.86	56.14	75.32	13.72	13.58	13.52	5.547	6.05
Transport	19.60	25.49	34.10	6.27	6.17	6.12	5.396	5.99
Banking	7.23	9.50	12.74	2.31	2.30	2.29	5.613	6.04
Government services	40.41	54.97	75.56	12.93	13.30	13.56	6.343	6.57
GDP	312.45	413.25	557.19	100.00	100.00	100.00	5.751	6.15
III Disposable income								
U professionals	7.42	9.07	11.49	2.26	2.14	2.05	4.098	4.84
U clerical	20.35	24.85	31.69	6.21	5.87	5.65	4.076	4.98
U manual	23.00	29.69	39.83	7.02	7.02	7.11	5.239	6.05
U employers	0.84	1.49	2.75	0.26	0.35	0.49	12.145	13.03
U self-employed	53.31	62.42	78.46	16.26	14.76	14.00	3.206	4.68
R large farm holdings	36.33	76.74	62.11	11.08	11.05	11.08	5.163	5.85
R medium farm hldgs	37.30	47.78	63.28	11.38	11.29	11.29	5.077	5.78
R small farm hldgs	88.09	111.97	147.38	26.87	26.47	26.30	4.914	5.64
R landless workers	0.98	1.22	1.59	0.30	0.29	0.28	4.478	5.44
R non-farm workers	11.52	14.84	19.82	3.51	3.51	3.54	5.195	5.95
Firms	2.48	12.09	27.69	0.76	2.86	4.94	37.276	18.02
Government	46.24	60.88	74.38	14.10	14.39	13.27	5.655	4.08
Total	327.86	423.04	560.47	100.00	100.00	100.00	5.230	5.78

Key: U = Urban, R = Rural

Table 5.4 (Continued)

IV Disposable income per capita	Value			% Distribution	% Annual Growth	
	1982-3	1987-8	1992-3		6th Plan	7th Plan
U professionals	6.16	6.71	7.54		1.705	2.36
U clerical	3.36	4.17	4.65		1.523	2.21
U manual	3.67	4.14	4.33		2.427	3.14
U employers	6.98	10.89	17.55		9.29	10.00
U self-employed	4.52	4.57	4.98		0.189	1.75
R large farm holdings	4.13	4.63	5.36		2.306	2.90
R medium farm hldgs	3.05	3.4	3.92		2.217	2.90
R small farm hldgs	2.46	2.73	3.13		2.059	2.77
R landless workers	1.28	1.39	1.53		1.634	2.56
R non-farm workers	1.36	2.09	2.43		2.332	3.07
Average disp/cap	3.16	3.45	3.93		1.753	2.65
GDP/capita	3.54	4.07	4.73		2.671	3.26
V Basic needs: consumption p.c (a)						
1 Food per household						
a. Rural	1.16	1.29	1.46		2.081	2.59
b. Urban	1.74	1.80	1.99		0.673	1.997
c. Nation	1.35	1.48	1.63		1.873	2.582
2. Rent, fuel						
a. Rural	0.25	0.28	0.31		2.079	2.587
b. Urban	0.58	0.60	0.66		0.673	1.997
c. Nation	0.35	0.38	0.43		1.805	2.567

(a) = Consumption in 1000 rs per capita, values in prices of 1979-80

In 1992-93 this is projected at 146000 rupees per capita. By comparison, the food consumption of the self-employed in urban areas, which form 70 percent of urban dwellers, is projected at 199 000 rupees per capita, the latter being well above the national average of 168 000 rupees per capita. In terms of other essential needs, such as rent, fuel, health and education, the expenditure per capita is .31, .66 and .43 for rural poor, urban self-employed and the national average, respectively. The position of rural poor regarding non-food items is only half of that of urban dwellers. These happen also to be the areas that policy-makers have emphasised for the Seventh Plan.

Table 5.4 (Continued)

VI Labour wage rate	Value						% Annual Growth	
	1982-3	1987-8	1992-3				6th Plan	7th Plan
U professionals	20.83	23.93	27.66				2.807	2.945
U clerical	12.74	14.50	16.66				2.627	2.807
U manual	12.15	14.48	17.38				3.568	3.72
U employers	25.15	43.02	71.78				11.333	10.78
U self-employed	14.91	15.83	17.81				1.202	2.388
R large farm holdings	14.51	16.79	19.76				2.957	3.312
R medium farm hldgs	12.86	14.81	17.38				2.869	3.247
R small farm hldgs	6.83	7.81	9.12				2.72	3.131
R landless workers	2.12	2.38	2.76				2.394	2.993
R non-farm workers	3.55	4.07	4.77				-2.80	3.203
VII Employment in 1000s								
U professionals	317.8	356.9	402.4	1.19	1.06	1.14	2.353	2.425
U clerical	1393.4	1577.7	1803.0	5.22	5.15	5.12	2.515	2.706
U manual	1659.8	1900.5	2184.5	6.22	6.2	6.21	2.746	2.824
U employers	29.4	33.5	38.3	0.11	0.11	0.11	2.613	2.738
U self-employed	3142.3	3644.8	4198.5	11.77	11.89	11.93	3.011	2.869
Rural	20161.0	23144.1	26570.0	75.5	75.49	75.49	2.798	2.799
Total	26703.6	30657.4	35196.6	100.0	100.0	100.0	2.080	2.080
VIII Utilisation								
Utilisation UTL	-83.37	-36.18	-70.91				-15.376	14.406
Budget deficit / GDP%	3.52	5.01	8.21				7.328	10.377

(b) = Wage rate in 1000 Rs. per capita. Values in prices of 1979-80

The sixth and seventh parts of table 5.4 deal with the labour market. Part VII of table 5.4 gives the employment trends. They do not vary between the two plan periods. Rural Employment would grow at the national average of the two plan periods. Rural Employment would grow at the national average of 2.8%, urban self-employed to grow at a higher rate of 3.0% and the other urban labour types at rates between 2.3% and 2.7%. In absolute terms, there is a striking increase in the remuneration gap between, on the one hand, the employers' income, and on the other hand, the professionals, non-manual and manual workers.

The income gap between wage and non-wage employment is less pronounced. Of course, the very low levels of remuneration in rural areas compared to urban areas are self-evident.

A final part of table 5.4 concerns the variable on the change in utilisation, UTI, which varies within an acceptable range, and the budget deficit share as a percentage of the GDP which is projected to increase significantly from 5.0% to 8.2% This increase seems high by present international standards and may require taking corrective measures to reduce it. It goes without saying that the growth and development prospects discussed in this paper may be affected by the type of corrective measures taken in reducing the budget deficit.

4. Simulating the Effects of Structural Adjustment (SAM/ADJ)

In the fifties and sixties development planning was seen as the vehicle of structural change. Development planning was supposed to bring about gradual but enforced change towards a developed economy through government actions. For several reasons, development plans have been giving way to short-term adjustment programmes aiming at balancing in a couple of years demand and supply of major commodities, the trade-balance, and the government budget, and, affecting cuts in subsidies and enhancing revenues. Adjustment programmes have been compared to crisis management; they are often characterised by abrupt effects, and they require that the country concerned has to adjust under unfavourable conditions.

The need for adjustment programmes arises because of an imbalance between domestic demand and supply, reflected in a growing external deficit, inflationary pressures and slowing growth. Although the imbalances might have been partly due to external factors such as worsening terms of trade and rise in foreign interest rates, domestic policies in some countries have expanded demand too rapidly with little emphasis on the growth of productive capacity.

It is relevant to distinguish between two aspects of adjustment programmes which we may call balancing and structural. The essence of a balancing adjustment programme is to ensure that the supply-demand imbalance is eliminated in an orderly way, before the economy becomes seriously distorted and external finance is exhausted. The programme, therefore, has to include a variety of monetary and fiscal policies at the domestic level that reduce demand with minimal adverse effects on growth prospects, supplemented by devaluations and financial capital inflow at the external level.

In contrast, the essence of a structural adjustment programme is the redirection of the economy towards a more efficient and socially acceptable allocation of resources that could compensate for adverse effects of balancing adjustments on growth and equity. The objectives here are to increase the supply of goods and its fairer distribution.

Otherwise said, the difference between stabilisation and structural adjustment policies is that stabilisation policies, in particular those practised by the International Monetary Fund (IMF) usually take the structure of the economy more or less for granted, while structural adjustment and particularly the more recent approaches of the World Bank focus on the problems of specific segments of the economy and design policies, compensatory measures and development projects to improve the efficiency and enhance the prospects of that particular segment.

There are sound theoretical arguments for treating both balancing and structural adjustment together but there are as yet no accepted theoretical frameworks for a simultaneous treatment, even though Robinson and Tyson (1984) come very close to devising such a framework. Besides, a simultaneous treatment may not be operational given the limited planning staff capabilities in the context of many countries of the third world. It is, therefore, desirable to decompose the policy problem in short-term balancing adjustment strategies which focus on monetary variables, and the more medium-term structural adjustment strategies which focus on real variables taking as given the already predetermined monetary balances. This paper does not deal with balancing strategies, it considers structural adjustment only.

In doing so, we propose to examine the initial conditions which prevail in the particular economy and to assess the effects of structural adjustment measures on growth and income distribution. This requires a disaggregated framework which incorporates the structure of production (by providing production accounts) and the resulting factorial and household income distributions (by household groups). The framework must also supply initial values for variables in other accounts, e.g. capital, trade and government) which are directly or indirectly influenced by the adjustment measures. The SAM provides the comprehensive and consistent disaggregated general equilibrium data system required to capture the initial conditions and the structure of the socio-economic system.

The remainder of this section examines the use of the SAM/ADJ model in simulating alternative policies of medium-run structural adjustments.

Simulations relating to four variables will be reported upon in table 4.5: *consumption, investment, exports* and *transfers* to household groups.

First, the following variants of *consumption* behaviour have been simulated:

(a) A shift to imitative consumption. For each want j = 1, ..., 8 and all household groups h = 1, ..., 10 propensities to consume of each household group were set equal to those for professionals.

(b) A shift to basic needs. The propensities to consume of low-income household groups have been changed so as to reflect a higher concentration on the basic necessities of food, rent, fuel, health and education, at the cost of lower consumption of clothing and others.

The results show that imitative consumption retards growth and is detrimental to the income levels of low income groups. In contrast, the basic needs simulation is found to promote growth and equality. Improvement in the satisfaction of basic needs remains marginal however.

Second, regarding *investment* behaviour two simulations were run:

(a) The behavioural coefficient of lagged investment has been multiplied by 10% representing a better climate for private investment.

(b) The exogenous values of public investment have been multiplied by 10% to represent a greater involvement of public investment.

Both simulations lead to better performances regarding growth and improvement of earning levels of low income groups. The addition to GDP as a result of the public investment stimulus is twice that of private investment stimulus, considering that the absolute level of the two stimuli is about the same.

Third, regarding *export* growth two variants were run:

(a) 10% higher exports in wheat and rice (sector 1) and other agriculture (sector 2), and

(b) 10% higher exports in large scale manufacturing (sector 4) and small scale manufacturing (sector 5).

The GDP results respond better to higher imports of manufacturing (GDP increases from 540 to 559 billion rupees) than to higher imports of agriculture (GDP rises here to 550 billion rupees). Although disposable incomes of the low income groups increase more under the manufacturing than the agricultural scenario, their relative position falls down relative to higher income groups. Some of these results are at variance with the SAM inversion model, the differences are due to the introduction in the SAM/ADJ model of varying proportions over time of consumption, investment and intermediate deliveries which favour manufacturing over agriculture in the longer run. The refinements make a SAM/ADJ planning model a more relevant policy-making instrument than a SAM inversion model.

Fourth, several variants of *transfers* among household groups were simulated, all of them assumed to happen by state intervention in such a way that the government budget is not affected. The burdens and benefits of the transfers are distributed in accordance with the disposable income ratios of the respective household groups as generated by the model in 1986/87. The four variants are described below (see also table 4.5). They represent:

(a) 10% transfer from income of urban rich to urban poor
(b) 10% transfer from income of urban rich to rural poor
(c) 10% transfer from income of rural rich to rural poor
(d) 10% transfer from income of rural rich to urban poor

Table 4.5 Incidence of the Four Variants

	Taxed rural groups					Taxed urban groups				
Receiving Groups	*11*	*12*	*13*	*14*	*15*	*21*	*22*	*23*	*24*	*25*
Rural										
11 large holdings										
12 medium holdings										
13 small holdings	*c*	*c*				*b*	*b*	*b*		
14 landless	*c*	*c*				*b*	*b*	*b*		
15 non farm	*c*	*c*				*b*	*b*	*b*		
Urban										
21 professionals										
22 clericals										
23 manual workers						*a*	*a*	*a*		
24 employers	*d*	*d*				*a*	*a*	*a*		
25 self-employed	*d*	*d*				*a*	*a*	*a*		

The results of the simulation in table 5.6 show that variants (*a*) and (*d*) do not have a significant impact, variant (*c*) which stands for transfers from rural rich to rural poor promotes output growth and income equality, variant (*b*) which stands for transfer from urban rich to rural poor diminishes growth and is regressive in its distributionary effects.

Table 5.6. Basic and Simulation Runs of SAM/ADJ model for Pakistan, 1992/93

All values in billions of rupees and in prices of 1979/80; population in 1000s except rural employment in millions; values per capita in 1000 rupees per capita

		Consumption pattern		Higher invest		Higher export		Transfers			
	Basic run	limit 1a	Basic 1b	Priv 2a	Gov. 2b	3a	3b	4a	4b	4c	4d
I. Expenditure											
Consumption	CON	465	454	454	465	467	460	464	457	448	472	458
Investment	INV	99	94	99	104	106	99	100	99	99	100	99
Exports-Imports	X-M	-7	-11	-11	-11	-11	-9	-5	-11	-11	-11	-11
Gross Dom. Prod.	GDP	557	537	542	558	562	550	559	545	536	561	546
II. Value Added											
Wheat and Rice	VAD1	28	26	27	28	28	28	28	27	27	28	27
Other Agriculture	VAD2	95	89	96	96	97	96	96	95	93	97	95
Mining	VAD3	8	6	6	7	7	6	7	6	6	7	6
Large scale manufacturing	VAD4	155	146	149	154	155	151	156	150	147	154	150
Small scale manufacturing	VAD5	23	21	22	23	-23	22	23	22	22	23	22
Construction	VAD6	23	24	23	25	25	23	23	23	23	24	23
Ownership	VAD7	14	27	15	14	15	14	14	14	14	15	14
Electricity	VAD8	14	12	13	14	14	13	14	13	13	14	13
Wholesale	VAD9	75	70	74	75	76	74	75	73	72	76	74
Transport	VAD10	34	31	32	34	34	34	34	33	33	34	33
Banking	VAD11	13	12	12	13	13	13	13	13	12	13	13
Services	VAD	76	74	74	76	75	75	76	75	74	76	75
Total GDP		557	538	543	559	549	549	559	544	536	561	545
III. Disposable Incomes											
All Households	DISh	447	445	449	458	461	452	457	447	437	465	448
Firms	DISf	26	26	25	28	28	26	28	26	27	24	26
Government	DISg	74	73	74	74	75	74	75	74	74	73	74
Total		547	544	548	560	564	552	560	547	538	562	548
IV. Disposable Income											
Rural large holding		5.36	5.15	5.23	5.30	5.39	5.20	5.33	5.23	5.14	4.97	4.84
Rural medium holding		3.92	3.77	3.85	3.90	3.95	3.80	3.91	3.83	3.77	3.65	3.55
Rural small holding		3.13	3.00	3.09	3.10	3.16	3.10	3.13	3.07	3.13	3.15	3.24
Rural landless		1.53	1.52	1.59	1.50	1.60	1.50	1.59	1.56	1.59	1.61	1.65
Rural non farming		2.43	2.34	2.39	2.40	2.45	2.40	2.43	2.38	2.43	2.43	2.51

Table 5.6 (Continued)

Urban professional	7.54	7.46	7.45	7.50	7.52	7.46	7.50	6.88	6.82	7.52	7.44
Urban clerical	4.65	4.60	4.59	4.63	4.64	4.60	4.63	4.24	4.20	4.64	4.59
Urban manual	4.33	4.73	4.77	4.82	4.84	4.78	4.82	4.42	4.37	4.83	4.76
Urban employers.	17.55	17.01	16.60	17.50	17.70	17.00	17.86	17.51	17.46	16.86	16.74
Urban self employed	4.98	4.85	4.81	4.96	5.00	4.85	4.94	5.18	4.45	5.93	4.81
Total DIS/ POP	3.93	4.67	4.71	4.81	4.84	4.74	4.81	4.70	4.62	4.83	4.70
GDP/ POP	4.73	4.65	4.70	4.79	4.83	4.72	4.79	4.68	4.60	4.81	4.69
V. Basic needs											
Food: Low	1.46	1.42	1.45	1.47	1.48	1.45	1.46	1.44	1.46	1.47	1.54
Food: All	1.63	1.63	1.65	1.68	1.69	1.66	1.68	1.65	1.61	1.71	1.65
Rent etc: Low	0.31	0.30	0.31	0.31	0.32	0.31	0.31	0.31	0.31	0.31	0.32
Rent etc: All	0.43	0.42	0.42	0.43	0.43	0.42	0.42	0.43	0.41	0.44	0.42
VI. Labour Market Wage											
Rural large	19.76	19.03	19.31	19.79	19.93	19.47	19.72	19.31	18.98	19.81	19.32
Rural medium	17.38	16.74	17.08	17.43	17.55	17.17	17.37	17.02	16.73	17.47	17.03
Rural small	9.12	8.77	9.04	9.17	9.23	9.06	9.14	8.96	8.80	9.21	8.97
Rural landless	2.76	2.65	2.80	2.30	2.82	2.78	2.78	2.73	2.69	2.82	2.74
Rural non farm	4.77	4.59	4.71	4.79	4.82	4.73	4.77	4.68	4.60	4.81	4.68
Urban professional	27.66	27.50	27.47	27.66	27.74	27.51	27.63	27.43	27.23	27.75	27.42
Urban clerical	16.66	16.56	16.52	16.67	16.71	16.57	16.65	16.51	16.37	16.72	16.51
Urban manual	17.38	17.27	17.20	17.44	17.51	17.26	17.42	17.19	17.00	17.47	17.19
Urban employers	71.78	69.31	67.63	71.58	72.63	69.27	73.03	68.21	71.39	63.77	68.46
Urban self employed	17.81	17.41	17.27	17.81	17.98	17.42	17.74	17.26	15.88	19.38	17.25
VII. Employment											
Rural total	26.6	26.6	26.6	26.6	26.6	26.6	26.6	26.6	26.6	26.6	26.6
Urban professional	402	401	400	403	405	401	403	400	397	404	400
Urban clerical	1803	1791	1786	1804	1809	1793	1803	1785	1771	1808	1786
Urban manual	2184	2172	2167	2195	2203	2173	2138	2166	2150	2191	2166
Urban employers	38	38	38	38	39	38	38	38	38	38	38
Urban self employed	4198	4225	4237	4186	4170	4224	4196	4240	4275	4185	4239
VIII. Other											
Change in capital utilisation	-70.9	-64.8	-57.6	-56.3	-57.2	-53.4	-61.7	-57.4	-57.3	-57.7	-57.4
Budget deficit in % of GDP	8.21	8.53	8.52	8.1	8.1	8.4	8.16	8.52	8.63	8.36	8.51

The model results suggest, therefore, that rural income transfer policies are the most effective. These results of the SAM planning model are fairly consistent with those of the SAM planning model.

5. Extensions to Workforce Development, SAM/EXT

This section reports on linking the SAM/ADJ model of the previous section with a manpower planning model which has been updated and used regularly in the past seven years to give rolling forecasts of manpower imbalances, cf, Cohen(1985). The manpower planning model was used in 1980-81 for elaborating implications of the Fifth Plan and formed later in 1982-83 one of the basis for the preparation of manpower policy in connection with the Sixth Plan. It was used again in 1985 as an aid in judging the magnitudes of educated unemployment.

Wage employment is forecasted by applying GDP growth and wage employment output elasticities to wage employment levels. Non-wage employment is obtained in several steps. First, tentative non-wage employment is obtained from applying GDP growth and non-wage employment output elasticities to non-wage employment levels. Definite non-wage employment is obtained by adjusting the tentative figures proportionately upwards or downwards so that the following holds:

total supply = open unemployment + wage employment + nonwage
                   employment

whereby total supply and open unemployment are given exogenously. The implicit adjustment factor is an indication of the increment in under-employment. A positive factor means an increase in underemployment.

Due to the low growth in production and the low absorption in productive employment, 1983-84 was a year in which the additions to underemployment amounted to about 1.05 million. They fell back to 0.64 in 1984-85 and are predicted to fall down further. There may even be a favourable decrease in underemployment of .04 million in 1987-88 and of .28 million in 1992-93, see table 5.7.

So there seems to be little ground for worrying about an increase in under-employment. More significant is the stalemate that is taking place between wage and non-wage employment. Wage employment which in 1982-83 amounted to 31.5% of total employment is predicted to fall down to 28.7% in 1987-88 and to stabilise at 28. 5% in 1992-93, meaning that non-wage employment will retain the major share of about 71.0%. This tendency towards relatively less wage employment and more non-wage employment in Pakistan is also typical of India, Bangladesh and Indonesia, all of them populous countries. These tendencies emphasise that the employment/development pattern in these countries will have to be necessarily different than what has historically taken place in western countries and many small countries of the third world.

The demand forecast by mode of employment and sector are extendable to give forecasts by 7 broad occupational groups and 3 educational levels, as in table 4.8. These are confronted with supply forecasts from the educational system, and their appropriate conversions into occupational groups. The supply forecasts are based on a prolongation of policies of the Sixth Plan and would be revised as soon as policy directions become known. Note that the balances are not corrected for the return of migrants.

Table 5.7. Employment Forecasts (in thousands)

Sector (code)	1982-83 (actual)			1987-88 (Predicted)			1992-93(Predicted)		
	Wage	Non-wage	Total	Wage	Non-wage	Total	Wage	Non-wage	Total
Agriculture (1, 2)	1795	11256	13051	1979	15030	17009	2200	17631	19831
Industry (3, 4, 5, 8)	1884	1945	3829	2225	2214	4439	2591	2201	4792
Construction (6)	935	276	1211	1213	308	1521	1516	298	1814
Services (7, 9-12)	3300	3733	7033	3356	4326	7682	3738	5021	8759
Total employment	7914	17210	25124	8773	21878	30651	10045	25151	35196
Un-employment			1018			625a			718a
Total supply			26145			31276			35914
Under-employment			x+1005			x-42			x-279
Addition to under-employ			1005 b			-42			-279

(a) Target 2 percent of total supply (b) 1983-84

Future imbalances direct attention to relative shortages for the more educated by 1992-93. These forecasts point to a direction, which is the opposite of that depicted in the preparation of the Fifth and Sixth Plans. There, higher education formed a relative surplus while the lower educational levels showed relative shortages.

The reversal is due to the more modern structure of the economy in 1992-93, a higher economic growth up to 1992-93 and the materialisation of previously taken policy measures to expand at the lower end of education and restrain at the upper end of education.

The occupational imbalances are more significant. They point to the necessity of reorienting the training of graduates from the more favoured higher and middle level occupations i.e. professional, administrative, clerical and related jobs to the less favoured lower level occupations such as farm and production workers. There appears a relative shortage for the latter workers. The general tendency of a shortage for agriculturally and industrially trained workers in Pakistan has been a feature of previous forecasts for the Fifth and Sixth Plans, as well.

The magnitudes of the occupational imbalances can imply tensions in the labour market in the form of an unnecessarily prolonged search for desirable jobs, and a voluntary surge in unemployment.

Table 5.8. Conditional Forecasts of Demand, Supply and Imbalances

Type of manpower in thousands	Demand D	Supply S	Imbalance (S-D)/S
By Occupation			
Professional	902	1158	.22
Administrative	255	532	.52
Clerical	1344	1692	.21
Sale & service workers	5209	9697	.46
Agriculture & production	27487	22835	-.20
Total	35197	35914	.02
By Education			
Below primary	23563	24800	.05
Primary	4194	3915	-.07
Middle secondary	2769	2884	.04
High secondary	2680	2653	-.01
Intermediate	1063	916	-.16
Degree	590	490	-.20
Post-degree	338	257	-.32
Total	35197	35974	.02

6. Concluding Remarks

Until the early-eighties, the factor and product markets were modelled in terms of constant or variable exogenous prices. This meant that the clearance of the market happened exclusively via quantities. The SAM proves to be a flexible model for simulating and appraising policy within market clearance via quantities. In contrast, the main feature of computable general equilibrium,CGE, models is the generation of endogenous prices within competitive factor and product markets. These models take also the SAM as the accounting framework for the bench year for which the equilibrium is calibrated, but they separate price and guantity variables and model their interdependence explicitly.

One such demonstrative application of A SAM/CGE model for Pakistan is by Dhanani (1987). In that application parameters of the production and consumption functions are derived from an updated SAM of table 5.1. This makes feasible a comparison of results between the SAM inversion, SAM/POL. It is appropriate here to end this chapter with some concluding remarks on these results, pending a full application of CGE models in the next chapter.

As reported earlier the SAM inversion model has an output multiplier effect for a unit of investment increase of about 8.0, but this is excessively high and is handicapped by a SAM which excludes import leakage. The SAM/POL model gives an output multiplier of 3.4 for a unit of investment increase. In the SAM/CGE real investment was allowed to increase by 20%, and the effect of this policy was a simulated increase in real GDP by 2.9%; implying that an additional 10.0 billion rupees of investment would lead to an increase in the GDP of 9.0 billion rupees, or of gross output of about 18.0 billion rupees. As an approximation, the output multipler in the SAM/CGE would roughly be around 1.8 for a unit of investment increase, (all calculations at average investment and output levels of 1980). These two contrasting results from the two models would suggest that market clearance via quantity adjustments is good for 1.8/3.4, or a share of 53%, leaving slightly less than the half for market clearance via adjustments in prices. The next chapter will elaborate more on this theme.

Chapter 6

Social Accounting and Computable General Equilibrium Models: an Application to Indonesia

1. Introduction

The empirical application of general equilibrium models can be traced back to 1960 when Johansen presented his multisectoral model for the Norwegian economy. Since the mid-seventies, the stream of Computable General Equilibrium (CGE) models has grown remarkably, which mainly can be attributed to the availability of faster and cheaper computers and to the renewed recognition of the importance of relative prices for the allocation of resources. CGE models proved to be very useful tools for the analysis of tax reforms, international trade, resource allocation and income distribution. The majority of CGE models are applied to developing countries, there are increasingly more applications to advanced countries as well.[1]

In principle, the application of a Computable General Equilibrium (CGE) model requires the construction of a Social Accounting Matrix that fits to it. A CGE model describes the whole circular flow of a market economy, while maintaining accounting consistency both at the macro level as on the level of individual actors. A Social Accounting Matrix (SAM) is a statistical representation of that circular flow, in which transactions between the actors distinguished in the system are consistently accounted for.

Another common feature between CGE models and the SAM is the emphasis on disaggregation. Total production in the SAM is disaggregated by several production accounts, while CGE models distinguish between several types of producers. In the same way, consumption in the SAM is disaggregated by several household accounts that can serve to define the different types of consumers in a CGE model. The different types of labour

---

[1] For a survey for developing countries see Decaluwe and Martens (1988).

and capital distinguished in the SAM factor accounts can be used to define the different types of labour and capital in a CGE model. It is also possible to include separate want accounts in the SAM if one wants to introduce goods and services by type of want in the CGE model.

A SAM can be transformed into an economy-wide model by separating the SAM into endogenous and exogenous accounts, y and x respectively, and expressing the transactions between the endogenous accounts in terms of their column totals to give a coefficient matrix A. The resulting model is the familiar multiplier equation $y = (I - A)^{-1} x$. The CGE approach offers another opportunity to transform a SAM into an economy-wide model without using any supplementary data.[2] Under certain assumptions (Cobb-Douglas production, utility and aggregation functions) the SAM provides all data necessary to construct a simple CGE model. The objective of this chapter is to demonstrate the basic links between the primary form of CGE models and the SAM and to show how under a few assumptions the static CGE model can be elaborated to a dynamic one.[3] The flexibility of the employed framework will be demonstrated in terms of analysing policy simulations in the static and dynamic forms of the model. The applications are demonstrated for Indonesia, a country for which elaborate SAMs are now available and for which several CGE models have been applied for more specific uses.[4]

The Indonesian economy is characterised by the availability of rich natural resources, in the form of oil. The mining sector takes in an important place in the industrial structure. The manufacturing sector is rather underdeveloped in comparison with countries at a similar level of development. If put together, as will be done in this chapter, the combined mining and manufacturing sector can be characterised by a very capital intensive technology and is dominated by large private and public firms, of which the revenues are mainly accruing to government and higher income groups. Agriculture is still the largest sector and employs the majority of the rapidly increasing labour force, which is mainly low skilled. The services sector, which includes government services, is the main employer of the high-skilled labour force.

The chapter is organised as follows. The CGE model will be presented in section 2. The derivation of the parameters from the SAM and their calculated values are discussed in section 3. Two demonstrative simulations

---

[2] See Dervis, et al. (1982) for a comparative discussion of CGE models and SAM-based planning models.
[3] A large body of literature is available on SAM-based CGE models. A good description of the way in which a CGE model can be linked to the SAM is given in Robinson (1989).
[4] See Thorbecke (1990) for a discussion of Indonesian CGE models.

will be discussed in section 4. In section 5 several dynamic aspects will be introduced in the model. In section 6 simulations are repeated in the context of the dynamic model. Finally in section 7 some concluding remarks will be made.

2. The Basic Model

In this section we present the core of our general equilibrium model. It is a general purpose model, which contains only a minimal number of equations necessary to describe the economic process. It has the advantage that all parameters needed may be principally derived from the SAM. For more specialized applications the model needs to be elaborated, in which case supplementary data are required to estimate additional parameters. The basic model is presented in table 6.1. Variables are represented by capitals, among which the exogenous ones have overbars. Greek characters represent parameters. The indices i and j are used to represent sectors, g and h stand for institutions and q for types of labour, the index f is used to represent actors abroad.

Every sector is assumed to act as a single representative producer, whose production possibilities are represented by a two-level production function, which is given in eq. (1). At a first level total output is derived from intermediate deliveries and an aggregate of labour and capital, which can be called real value added. Here, we assume Leontiev technology, i.e. no substitution is possible between intermediate deliveries and real value added. At a second level smooth substitution possibilities exist between capital and q categories of labour. The real value added aggregate follows from assuming constant returns to scale Cobb-Douglas function in capital and labour distinguished by skill level. In eq. (1) the function for the real value added is given in the numerator, while the fixed share of real value added is put in the denominator to relate real value added to real gross output. This term is multiplied by the sector price Pj to arrive at gross output in nominal terms. The sectoral capital stock is assumed fixed for the current period, so the volume of sectoral real value added and output can increase only through an increase in sectoral employment.

Total nominal value added[5] by sector can be derived by subtracting the cost of intermediate deliveries including those that are imported, and indirect taxes from the production value, as shown in eq. (2).

---

[5] Nominal value added incorporates besides real value added also a price component which can be called value added price. Because nominal value added can be included in the factor

Producers are assumed to maximise profits under perfect competition in product and labour markets; as a result, in the short run they will hire employees until wages equal the value of their marginal product, as shown in eq. (3).

Equation (4) shows that the remuneration of capital is the remainder of nominal value added after labour is paid its share. Because the volume of capital is fixed, remuneration rates have to adjust to equalise them to the value of the marginal product of capital. Consequently, again in the short run, remuneration rates of capital may differ among sectors.

Equation (5) states that the labour market is characterised by full employment by skill level, while the supply of labour by skill type is fixed in the short run. Wages carry the burden of adjustment.

Factor remunerations are distributed over the institutions in eq. (6). Total institutional income includes besides factor income also income transfers received front other institutions. Income transfers are assumed to be fixed proportions of total institutional income. A variation on equation (6) is included as equation (6a) to allow for the fact that the total income of government comprises also indirect taxes.

In eq. (7) transfers paid are subtracted from total institutional incomes to arrive at disposable income.

Institutions are assumed to be groups of representative consumers, which maximise a Cobb-Douglas utility function given a budget constraint. The first order condition of utility maximisation implies the fixed budget shares in equation (8).[6]

Equation (9) gives the equilibrium condition for the product market. Prices carry the burden of adjustment. Because we are primarily interested in domestic transactions we kept the relations with the rest of the world as simple as possible. Quantities of exports and competitive imports are fixed. Foreign prices are assumed to be equal to domestic prices to keep the model homogeneous in all prices. We assume that investment goods are supplied by one capital goods producing, sector only, as stated in eq. (9a). We assumed a classical closure[7] of the model, so an equation for investment can be omitted because total investment follows as a residual from the other equations.

Because the model can only determine relative prices we have to apply a price normalisation rule. In eq. (10) the price of agriculture is chosen as

---

demand equations (3) and (4), resulting from the Cobb-Douglas technology assumption, there is no need to separate price and quantity components explicitly.

[6] Although it may seem unrealistic to assume the same behaviour for government as for households, in this context government behaviour cornes down to fixed expenditure shares, which is a usual assumption.

[7] See for a discussion on closure Dewatripont and Michel (1987).

numeraire, so all other price and nominal variables are defined relative to agriculture. Therefore, one should be aware that an increase in disposable income does not imply that income has increased in an absolute sense, but only that income has increased relative to the price of agriculture.

Table 6.1. The Static Model

$$X_j = \frac{P_j}{1 - \sum_i \alpha_{ij} - \mu_j - \varphi_j} \vartheta_j \overline{K}_j^{(1-\sum_q \lambda_{qj})} \prod_q L_{qj}^{\lambda_{qj}} \tag{1}$$

$$V_j = (1 - \sum_i \alpha_{ij} P_i/P_j)X_j - \mu_j X_j - \varphi_j X_j \tag{2}$$

$$W_q L_{qj} = \lambda_{qj} V_j \tag{3}$$

$$R_j \overline{K}_j = (1 - \sum_q \lambda_{qj})V_j \tag{4}$$

$$\sum_j L_{qj} = \overline{L}_q \tag{5}$$

$$Z_h = \sum_q \omega_{hq} W_q L_q + \pi_h \sum_j R_j K_j + \sum_g \tau_{hg} Z_g \ ; \tag{6}$$

for h=nongovernment

$$Z_h = \sum_q \omega_{hq} W_q L_q + \pi_h \sum_j R_j K_j + \sum_g \tau_{hg} Z_g + \sum_j \phi_j X_j \ ;$$

for h=government

$$Y_h = Z_h - \sum_g \tau_{gh} Z_h - \tau_{fh} Z_h \tag{7}$$

$$C_{jh} = \gamma_{jh} Y_h \tag{8}$$

$$X_j = \sum_i (\alpha_{ji} P_j/P_i)X_i + \sum_h C_{jh} + P_j(\overline{E}_j - \overline{M}_j) \tag{9}$$

$$X_j = \sum_i (\alpha_{ji} P_j/P_i)X_i + \sum_h C_{jh} + I + P_j(\overline{E}_j - \overline{M}_j) \ ;$$

for j=capital sector

$$P_1 = 1.0 \tag{10}$$

List of notations

Endogenous variables:	Coefficients:
C = consumption expenditure	α = input/output coefficients
I = investment expenditure	φ = indirect tax rates
L = sectoral labour (quantity)	γ = consumption budget shares
P = price index	λ = labour elasticities of
R = remuneration rate of	production
capital	ύ = calibration constant
V = value added	production function
W = wage rate	π = capital income distribution
X = value of gross output	shares
Y = disposable income	τ = transfer rates
A = total income	ω = labour income distribution
	shares
Exogenous variables:	μ = import shares
E = exports (quantity)	
K = capital (quantity)	
L = labour supply (quantity)	
M = competitive imports	
(quantity)	

3. Parameterisation of the Model

A Social Accounting Matrix gives a consistent representation of the money flows which are the nominal counterpart of all real transactions between the agents in an economy. In table 6.2 the SAM for Indonesia for 1975, which serves a the database for our CGE model, is shown. The SAM is an adapted version of the SAM published by Biro Pusat Statistik Indonesia (1982). In table 5.2 we distinguish between three factor of production accounts, eight institutional accounts, i.e. six household groups, corporate business and government, a capital account, four production activities accounts and the rest of the world account, ROW.

Assuming that the SAM represents a benchmark equilibrium, its cells can be viewed as realisations of the variables of the model. To distinguish between quantity and nominal variables prices and wages can be expressed as indices, which are all unity in the benchmark equilibrium. This implies

Table 6.2. Social Accounting Matrix for Indonesia, 1975

	1 LwskN	2 HgskK	3 Prfts	4 Rfo	5 Rfw	6 Rnu	7 Rnl	8 Uui	9 Uli
Factors									
1 low skill earnings									
2.high skill earnings									
3.profits									
Institutions									
4.R farmowners	1627	61	1970						
5.R farmworkers	440	32	131						
6.R nonfarm upper	205	251	84						
7.R nonfarm lower	824	90	354	46	2	14	13	3	2
8.U upper income	322	545	326						
9.U lower income	745	84	652	5	1	2	2	73	47
10.Companies			3810						
11.Government			59	39	2	5	6	40	26
12.Indirect taxes									
13.National capital				332	-39	49	22	229	88
Activities									
14.Agriculture				2422	467	346	882	534	698
15.Industry				351	68	105	196	351	301
16.Trade				268	61	61	160	221	298
17.Services			711	268	53	60	131	233	222
18.Rest world									
Total	4163	1063	8097	3731	615	642	1412	1684	1682

Key: R=rural, U=urban

Table 6.2. (Continued)

	10 Comp-anies	11 Gov	12 I tax	13 Nat cap	14 Agr	15 Ind	16 Trade	17 Serv-ices	18 Rest wrld	Total
Factors										
1. Low skill earnings					1945	694	1248	276		4163
2. high skill earnings					20	81	168	794		1063
3. profits					2503	3218	1637	739		8097
Institutions										
4. R farm owners		73								3731
5. R farm workers		12								615
6. R non farm upper	88	14								642
7. R non farm lower	33	31								1412
8. U upper income	467	24								1684
9. U lower income	43	28								1682
10. Companies										3810
11. Government	1448		277							1902
12. Indirect taxes					87	141	42	7		277
13. National capital	1669	567							493	3410
Activities										
14. Agriculture		2			2571	292	310	21	423	8968
15. Industry		218		3410	204	1348	306	121	907	7886
16. Trade		194			1353	758	77	31	772	4254
17. Services	62	769			56	98	195	37	-26	2096
18. Rest world		-30			229	1256	271	70		2569
Total	3810	1902	277	3410	8968	7886	4254	2096	2569	

Key: R = rural, U = urban

that the quantity variables in the model (factor services, products) are expressed in units which cannot be converted to well-defined physical units as tons or barrels. Product units (units of factor services) are then defined as the amount of a good (factor) that in equilibrium gives a reward of one currency unit in any of its possible uses.

In table 6.3 we expressed the SAM as a set of relations between the variables included in the model presented in table 6.1 as an illustration of the relationship between the SAM and the CGE model. An additional row is included for the (sub) total of sectoral value added. The three factors of production are low-skilled manpower, high-skilled manpower and capital. Agricultural labourers, production workers, clerical, sales and service workers are classified as low-skilled labour, account [1] in table 6.2. The factor high-skilled labour consists of professionals, managers and non-civilians account [2]. Gross operating surplus is assumed to be the remuneration of the factor capital account [3]. Factors receive income payments from production activities, which in table 6.3 are related to the factor demand equations stated in eqs. (3) and (4). In the column factor incomes are distributed in fixed proportions to domestic institutions and the rest of the world. The parameters ωfq and πf represent the share of payments flowing to abroad.

The institutions are distinguished by six household groups, accounts [4 to 9], corporate business [10] and government [11]. For government an additional account is included to record indirect taxes [12]. Households are classified according to the status of the head of the household into landowners [4], farm workers [5], rural non-agricultural lower class households [6], rural non-agricultural upper class households [7], urban lower class households [8] and urban upper class households [9]. Incomings by institution are the institutions' share of factor income and income transfers from other institutions as specified in eq. (6). In the column income transfers are recorded as outgoings of institutions, they are calculated as constant fractions τgh of total income Zh, some institutions also pay a fraction τfh, of their income to institutions abroad. Other outgoings are consumption expenditures, which in rows 14-17 are related to disposable income Yh, using constant budget shares γih, as in eq. (8). Disposable income is defined as total income after payment of income transfers $(1-\Sigma g$ $\tau gh - \tau fh)$ Zh as in eq. (7). Savings can be calculated as a residual.

The capital account [13] has investment expenditure in the column, investment goods are assumed to be supplied by the sector industry and construction only, row 15. The sources of investable funds, savings by institutions, columns 4-11, and net savings from abroad, column 18, are placed in the row. The production activities or sectors are disaggregated by four sectors: agriculture [14], industry and construction [15], trade and transport [16], and government and services [17]. The outgoings of the production activities are payments for intermediate deliveries by other domestic sectors, rows 14-17, and to the rest of the world for non-competitive imports, row 18, payments of indirect taxes to the government, row 12, and factor payments, rows 1-3. It can be seen in table 5.3 that the activity columns incorporate the definition of nominal value added, as in eq. (2). Because price indices are equal to 1 in the benchmark equilibrium, the price ratio Pi / Pj can be omitted in the SAM. Sectoral demand as stated in eq. (9) can be found in the activity rows, which record the incomings of the activities. The incomings comprise receipts for intermediate goods delivered to other sectors, columns 14-17, consumption goods delivered to institutions, columns 4-11, exported goods minus competitive imports, column 18, and investment goods, column 13.

The ROW account [18] records the transactions with the rest of the world. In the row there are payments to the ROW (which are receipts from the point of view of the ROW) and in the column there are the receipts from the ROW. The balance of current transactions with the ROW is given at the intersection of the ROW column with the capital account row. As the capital account of the balance of payments mirrors the current account, this cell also gives the net inflow of foreign capital.

Table 6.3 is also useful in demonstrating how the parameters can be derived from benchmark values of nominal variables. The fact that all price variables are expressed as indices makes it easy to calculate parameters from the SAM for relations between quantity variables as well. The main features of the derived parameters will be discussed briefly, the parameter values can be found in tables 6.4 to 6.8. The input / output parameters aij, μj and φj can be calculated by simply dividing the appropriate rows in the production activities column by their column totals. Agriculture has the largest backward linkages, while the linkages of services are relatively low. The amount of imports and indirect taxes per unit of final product is small, only in industry and construction tile has a significant share of imports: 0.159.

Table 6.3.   Social Accounting Matrix Expressed in CGE Model Variables

	1-3 Factors	4-11 Institutions	12 Indirect taxes	13 Capital	14-17 Sectors	18 Row	Total
Factors Labour capital Value added					$\lambda_{qj}V_j$ $(1-\Sigma_q\lambda_{qi})V_i$ V_j		W_qL_q $\Sigma_jR_jK_j$ Σ_jV_j
Institu-tions	$\omega_{gq}W_qL_q$ $\pi_g\Sigma_iR_iK_i$	$\tau_{gh}Z_g$	$\Sigma_j\varphi_jX_j$				Z_g
Indirect taxes					φ_jX_j		$\Sigma_j\varphi_jX_j$
Capital		residual				residual	I
Sectors		$\gamma_{ih}(1-\Sigma_g\tau_{gh}-\tau_{fh})Z_h$		I_i	$\alpha_{ij}X_j$	$(E_i-M_i)P_i$	X_I
Row	$\omega_{fq}W_qL_q$ $\pi_f\Sigma_iR_iK_i$	$\tau_{fh}Z_h$			μ_jX_j		
Total	W_qL_q $\Sigma_jR_jK_j$	Z_h	$\Sigma_j\varphi_jX_j$	I	X_j		

The labour elasticities λqj can be calculated by dividing the factor payments in the activity columns by the value added subtotal. Elasticities for low-skilled labour are highest in agriculture and trade, services have relatively high high-skilled labour elasticities, while industry and construction is the most capital intensive sector. The calibration constant in the production function μj, is calculated by rewriting eq. (1) as:

$$\vartheta_j = \frac{(1 - \sum_i \alpha_{ij} - \mu_j - \varphi_j).X_j / P_j}{\overline{K}_j^{(1-\sum_q \lambda_{qj})}. \prod_q L_{qj}^{\lambda_{qj}}}$$

By defining prices and the low-skilled wage rate as indices, as described above, X_j / P_j is equal to X_j and L_{1j} is equal to $w_1 L_{1j}$, which are both given in the SAM.[8] For high-skilled labour and capital the same approach could be chosen in the static model, but for reasons of dynamization we used a different method.

In the dynamic model new investment has to be added to the existing capital stock, so capital has to be expressed in the same physical units as investment. The way in which this is done will be treated in detail in section 5, here we will give only the benchmark values of K_j. These are 10,541 for agriculture, 13,552 for mining, industry and construction, 6,894 for trade and transport and 3,112 for services.

In a similar way, in the dynamic model low-skilled and high-skilled labour have to add up to total labour supply. Thus high-skilled labour has to be expressed in the same units as low-skilled labour. To obtain this result, it is assumed that a unit of high-skilled labour earns four times the wage of a low-skilled worker in the benchmark period, which is a reasonable assumption in the Indonesian context. This implies that in the benchmark L_{2j} is equal to $W_2 /4 L_{2j}$. The resulting calibration constants are close to unity for agriculture and trade and transport, nearly three for services and slightly above one half for industry and construction.

The parameters which describe the distribution of factor income over households, ω_{hq} and π_h, can be calculated by dividing the cells in the factor account columns by the column totals. On the basis of the calculated parameters it can be concluded that low-skilled labour income accrues mainly to low income households *and* landowners. High-skilled labour income goes mainly to non-agricultural upper income groups. Recipients of capital income are mainly landowners and firms.

---

[8] Note that according to eq. (3) in the benchmark equilibrium $w_1 L_{1j}$ is equal to $\lambda_{ij} V_j$, which can be found in table 6.3.

The transfer rates τ_{gh} the ratio of income transfers to total income,[9] are calculated by dividing the income transfer matrix $\tau_{gh} Z_h$, by the respective column totals Z_h. Transfers are dominated by flows of funds from firms to households and government, for which transfer rates are 0.122 and 0.377, respectively. Budget shares are calculated by dividing consumption expenditures in the institutions columns by disposable income or $(1-\Sigma_g \tau_{gh} - \tau_{fh}) Z_h$. The largest share of income is spent on agricultural products, on which rural households spend even more than half of their income. The government spends nearly half of its income on services, which include the activities of civil servants.

Table 6.4.   Input-Output Parameters

	agriculture	*industry*	*trade*	*services*
α_{1j}	0.2867	0.0370	0.0729	0.0100
α_{2j}	0.0227	0.1709	0.0719	0.0577
α_{3j}	0.1509	0.0961	0.0181	0.0148
α_{4j}	0.0062	0.0124	0.0458	0.0177
φ_j	0.0097	0.0179	0.0099	0.0033
μ_j	0.0255	0.1593	0.0637	0.0334

Table 6.5.   Production Function Parameters

	agriculture	*industry*	*trade*	*services*
λ_{1j}	0.4353	0.1738	0.4088	0.1526
λ_{2j}	0.0045	0.0203	0.0550	0.4389
$1 - \lambda_{1j} - \lambda_{2j}$	0.5602	0.8059	0.5362	0.4085
ϑ_j	0.9154	0.5635	1.1791	2.8154

---

[9] Total income is defined as primary income plus income transfers received.

Table 6.6.   Factor Income Distribution Parameters

	ω_{h1}	ω_{h2}	π_h
1 LOWN	0.3908	0.0574	0.2433
2 FARM	0.1057	0.0301	0.0162
3 NFUP	0.0492	0.2361	0.0104
4 NFLO	0.1979	0.0847	0.0437
5 URUP	0.0773	0.5127	0.0403
6 URLO	0.1790	0.0790	0.0805
7 COMP	0.0000	0.0000	0.4705
8 GOV	0.0000	0.0000	0.0073

Table 6.7.   Income Transfer Rates

	1. LOWN	2. FARM	3. NFUP	4. NFLO	5. URUP	6. URLO	7. COMP	8.GOV
τ_{1h}	0	0	0	0	0	0	0	0.038
τ_{2h}	0	0	0	0	0	0	0	0.006
τ_{3h}	0	0	0	0	0	0	0.023	0.007
τ_{4h}	0.012	0.003	0.022	0.009	0.002	0.001	0.009	0.016
τ_{5h}	0	0	0	0	0	0	0.122	0.013
τ_{6h}	0.001	0.002	0.003	0.001	0.043	0.028	0.011	0.015
τ_{7h}	0	0	0	0	0	0	0.008	0
τ_{8h}	0.011	0.003	0.008	0.004	0.024	0.016	0.377	0

Table 6.8.   Budget Shares

	1. LOWN	2. FARM	3. NFUP	4. NFLO	5. URUP	6. URLO	7. COMP	8. GOV
γ_{1h}	0.665	0.766	0.557	0.634	0.341	0.434	0.000	0.001
γ_{2h}	0.096	0.112	0.169	0.141	0.224	0.187	0.000	0.125
γ_{3h}	0.074	0.100	0.098	0.115	0.141	0.185	0.000	0.111
γ_{4h}	0.074	0.087	0.097	0.094	0.149	0.138	0.000	0.439

4. Static Experiments

In this section we demonstrate the functioning of the model by simulating two supply impulses to economic growth. The outcomes of these experiments are of a general nature based on the restrictive assumptions of the model. They can give an insight in the implications of the various assumptions and guide future elaborations of the model, but should be cautiously interpreted as being specific to Indonesia, because of the generality of the assumptions and the absence of qualitative structural characteristics of the Indonesian economy in the CGE model. The two experiments are: (1) 10% productivity increase in industry and construction; and (2) 10% productivity increase in services.

Experiment 1: 10% productivity increase in industry and construction.[10] The efficiency parameter in the production function in industry is increased by 10 percent. The result is a 8.78% increase in the volume of output. However, because demand is inelastic,[11] the favourable volume-effect is reversed by a -10.01% price decrease, resulting in a decrease of value added in industry in relation to other sectors. So all factors employed in the sector with the increased productivity undergo a decline in their income. The increased productivity makes more than five percent of the labour employed in industry redundant, while the owners of capital see their remuneration reduced by 5.35%, because of the declined value of the marginal product of capital. Because a relatively large share of the national capital stock is installed in industry, total remuneration of capital falls with value added in industry. The wage rate of high-skilled labour increases slightly relative to the low-skilled wage rate, 0.42% versus 0.21%, because very little high-skilled labour is employed in industry.

The change in factor incomes is not large enough to bring about a large change in income distribution: there is a slight decrease in income for all groups varying from -0.65% for landowners to -0.14% for farm workers. The fall in nominal income does not mean that welfare has decreased, however. Because the consumer price index has decreased by more than the fall in nominal income, purchasing power has increased for all household groups. The welfare increase of the different groups is confirmed by a +2.5% increase in real GDP (average increase in the volume of value added).

---

[10] Only the main results will be shown here, tables containing elaborate simulation output can be obtained from the author.

[11] Aggregate demand consists of demand categories with a (negative) unitary (consumption and investment) and with a zero elasticity of demand (intermediate deliveries, exports, competitive imports). As a consequence, the aggregate demand elasticity lies between -1 and 0.

Experiment 2: 10% productivity increase in services. As in the previous experiment the efficiency parameter of the production function is increased by 10 percent. The resulting production increase in the service sector is +9.17%, which is only slightly higher than the increase in industry production in the previous simulation. However, in this simulation there are hardly any spillover effects to other sectors, in which the increase in production does not exceed 0.2%. This is due partly to the fact that in Indonesia the service sector is rather small and partly to the lack of backward linkages. The resulting increase in real GDP is less than one half of the increase in the industry experiment: +1.19%.

Again, as a result of inelastic demand, the value added of the sector with the productivity increase falls relative to the sectors without productivity increase (-2.52%), although the fall is less than in the previous experiment. Because the majority of high-skilled workers is employed in the service sector, the decrease in value added is detrimental for their relative wage rate, it decreases with -0.21%. The decrease in the remuneration for the high-skilled leads to a worsening of the income position for non-farm upper income groups (both rural and urban: -0.58% and -0.45% respectively). these groups consist for a large part of high-skilled workers. But as the consumer price index has decreased by even more, welfare of these income groups, has increased also, so the increase in real GDP reaches all households.

5. The Dynamic Model

The model can be made dynamic by updating the variables that are exogenous in the current year. The updating can be based on behavioural relationships, historical growth rates or just exogenous fixation. Here the updating will be restricted to the two factors of production: capital and the labour force, to keep the effects of the dynamization on the simulation results traceable. Changes in exports and imports and in parameters are easily introduced.

When we want to update capital stock we encounter two problems that cannot be solved by using the SAM only. First, for investment to be added to capital stock, both variables have to be expressed in the same unit. However the SAM does not give such information. Second, there is a need to know how investment is allocated by destination in the benchmark period. Both problems are solvable by simply assuming that capital stock grows in every sector at the same rate of 5% in the benchmark year. Because it is also assumed that capital depreciates at 5% a year, this implies that national capital stock is defined as ten times benchmark gross investment. If it is also assumed that all rates of return to capital are equal in the benchmark year, investment is then distributed over the sectors in the same proportions as the operating surplus. In later years, sectoral investment shares, and as a result sectoral growth rates, change as a result of differences in sectoral profit rates.

The updating of the capital stock can be described as follows. Investment of the previous period is added at the end of that year to the capital stock of the current period. The investment goods are distributed over using sectors in proportions which are a function of the ratio of sectoral profitability to average profitability *PRj/APR*. Sectors which show high profitability in the current period will increase their share in total investment. Their capital stock and their production should increase faster than for other sectors, their relative prices should decline and so should their profit rates. In this way profits above or below the average will be eliminated in the long term through competitive investment in a competitive market.

The sectoral investment shares ζ_j^t are defined in eq. (11):

$$\varsigma_j^t = \frac{\bar{\varsigma}_j^0 \left(\dfrac{PR_j}{APR} \right)^{\rho}}{\sum_i \bar{\varsigma}_i^0 \left(\dfrac{PR_i}{APR} \right)^{\rho}} \tag{11}$$

The benchmark investment shares which are calculated from the sectoral shares in total operating surplus: $R_j.Kj/\Sigma jR_j.Kj$ are 0.3091 for agriculture, 0.3974 for industry and construction, 0.2022 for trade and 0.0913 for services.

Sectoral profit rates *PRj* are defined in eq. (12) as the return to invested (or financial) capital and has to be distinguished from the value of the marginal product of (physical) capital *Rj*. In the numerator *Rj Kj* is just the operating surplus and the second term is financial depreciation. The denominator gives the replacement value of the capital stock, which is assumed to be equal to the amount of invested capital. Capital is valued at price *Pk*, with *k* being the index of the capital producing sector in the economy, which happens to be the sector of industry and construction.

$$PR_j = \frac{R_j \bar{K}_j - \delta_j K_j \bar{P}_k}{\bar{K}_j P_k} \tag{12}$$

The average profit rate follows from eq. (13):

$$APR = \sum_i \frac{\overline{K}_i P_k}{\sum_j \overline{K}_j P_k} * PR_i \tag{13}$$

In eq. (14) total investment expenditure is distributed over the sectors of destination.

$$I_j^d = \varsigma_j^t I \tag{14}$$

In eq. (15) new investment is added to the capital stock and depreciation is subtracted. Note that the investment outlays have to be divided by the price of investment goods to determine the investment in physical units.

$$K_j = K_{j,t-1}(1-\delta_j) + I_{j,t-1}^d / P_k \tag{15}$$

The second variable in which dynamics are introduced is the supply of labour: both the level of the total labour force and its distribution over the skill types change over time. The total labour force L_{tot}, is defined as the sum of low-skilled and high-skilled labour:

$$L_{tot} = L_1 + L_2 \tag{16}$$

The growth rate of the total labour force is exogenous; the growth rate $\overline{g}_L$ is fixed at 0,025.

$$L_{tot,t} = L_{tot,t-1}(1 + \overline{g}_L) \tag{17}$$

The distribution of labour over both skill types changes endogenously. The workers' choice between low-skilled and high-skilled employment depends on the relative wages and relative education costs. The ratio between the two types can be written for the long term as follows:

$$\left(\frac{L_1}{L_2}\right)^{LT} = \kappa \left(\frac{\dfrac{W_1}{W_2}}{\dfrac{\xi_1}{\xi_2} \cdot \dfrac{D_1}{D_2}}\right)^{\varepsilon} \tag{18}$$

where D_q represents the cost of education of type q and ξ_q the share of costs of education q charged to the user; ε is the supply elasticity and κ is a calibration constant. By introducing the costs of education in the labour supply equation it is possible to analyze the consequences of changes in the costs of education charged to the student on economic welfare. To keep things simple, we assume in this paper that the students cost of higher education is four times the cost of lower education. The substitution elasticity between high-skilled and low-skilled labour is assumed equal to 1, the calibration constant can be calculated from the benchmark as L_1/L_2 = 15.664.

In the short-term the low-skilled/ high skilled ratio is assumed to react with a distributed lag to changes in the wage rate:

$$\left(\frac{L_1}{L_2}\right)_t = (1-\theta)\left(\frac{L_1}{L_2}\right)_{t-1} + \theta\left(\frac{L_1}{L_2}\right)_t^{LT} \qquad (19)$$

The adjustment parameter θ is assumed to be equal to 0.25.

6. Dynamic Experiments

With the dynamic model we simulated the basic time path from 1975 to 1980. The base time path is the sequence of temporary equilibria under unchanged policies. To get an idea of changes that take place over time in the base time path we will first discuss the rates of growth between 1979 and 1980. The growth of GDP is 4.40% per annum. The largest contribution to this growth comes from the sector industry et al., its real value added grows at 5.37%. The good performance of industry is mainly the result of the increased demand for investment goods (+6.73%), of which industry is the only supplier. This leads to higher profit rates for industry and a faster accumulation of capital in this sector (+5.89%). As a result of increased supply the price of industry has already begun to decline by 0.27% in 1980.

The distribution of income changes, although only slightly, in favour of the higher income groups, which can be traced back to the deteriorated position of low-skilled labour in the factor market. The sectors which employ mainly low-skilled workers, such as agriculture and trade. grow at a lower rate than other sectors: 4.12% and 3.78% respectively. With the dynamic model we also repeated the simulations of section 4 starting in 1975. The results of static simulations, which take into account the effects for 1975 only, and of the dynamic simulations are rather similar in the case of the productivity increase in services (experiment 2). The largest difference appears in the decline of the wage rate of the high-skilled. Because potential suppliers of high-skilled labour are discouraged by the lower wage, they quit the education system and start supplying themselves as low-skilled labour. The supply of high-skilled labour drops by -0.83%, which in comparison to the static simulation reduces the wage decrease needed to adjust to the decreased demand with a full percentage point to -0.74%.

In experiment 1 substantial differences are found between the results of dynamic and static simulations. The effect on GDP is more than twice as large in the dynamic simulation: 6.1% as compared to 2.5% in the static simulation. This can be explained by the decline in the price index of the industrial sector by 9.14%, which makes it possible to buy more capital goods at a given level of savings. Therefore, capital is accumulated faster than in the base time path. This effect has been reinforced by the fact that an increased inflow of foreign savings pushes up total investment expenditure by 5.59%.

The performance of the sector industry *et al.* has improved as compared to the static simulation. This can be attributed to both demand and supply factors. Demand for the sector's output has increased resulting from the increase in total investment. On the other hand, the supply of the sector is reduced, because the low profit rate leads to a decrease in investment in this sector. Thus capital accumulation is lower than in other sectors and so is the growth of output. Combined with the inelasticity of demand, the reduced supply has a favourable effect on value added. However, although the decrease in value added is reduced in comparison with the static simulation. value added generated in industry and construction is still lower than in other sectors. So, also in the dynamic simulation the effect of an increase in industrial productivity leads to a reduced importance of industry and construction in the domestic economy.

7. Concluding Remarks

It has been demonstrated how a simple static CGE model can be constructed using a one period SAM as database. We also showed that under a few assumptions this static model can be elaborated to a dynamic one. The dynamic elements in this chapter were restricted to labour supply and capital accumulation only.

The dynamization of labour supply proved to have only a limited effect on the simulation results. To a large extent this can be explained by the fact that labour market adjustment takes place through the education system and thus reacts with a lag. However, adjustment can take place more directly if actors start supplying more hours if their wage rate increases or if non -participants decide to supply their skills on the labour market in reaction to a wage increase. Future analysis would require more flexible specification of labour supply responses to wage changes in the medium term.

The capital accumulation effect can lead to more significant differences between static and dynamic simulations if the price of capital changes substantially. In that case more investment goods can be bought for a given amount of money. Although the results of static and dynamic simulations differ in magnitude the main conclusion remains the same, namely that a productivity increase leaves the innovating sector worse off in comparison with the non-innovating sectors. This phenomenon has been observed for the period 1975-80 by Poot et al. (1984), who found that in traditional industries the replacement of old-fashioned technologies by more efficient techniques led to a substantial decrease in employment due to demand constraints. This outcome can be explained by the low demand elasticities, which resulted from consumption determined by constant budget shares and from fixed quantities of exports and imports. Future analysis would require more flexible demand specifications to be used in combination with elasticities obtained by empirical estimation.

Another reason why more innovating entrepreneurs are worse off than less innovating entrepreneurs is the fact that we assumed that all firms in a sector can be described by one representative firm, which implies that all firms are innovators or none of them are. However if some firms are innovators while others are not, the former can gain at the expense of the latter. In the Indonesian context, where the modern large-scale enterprises are the innovators, this implies that small-scale enterprises will undergo a deterioration in their terms of trade. Modelling the distinction between innovating and non-innovating firms within a specific sector, as well as other differentiations between firms within a sector will be very important refinements. Such type of micro-simulation models, as in Eliasson (1985) and Van Tongeren (1993), would imply a departure from the assumption of the representative firm typical of general equilibrium models.

Chapter 7

Social Accounting and Modelling the Interface Between Population and Development

1. Introduction

Development performance during the seventies and eighties regularly showed that in spite of the reasonable economic growth rates achieved in some developing countries, underemployment and poverty increased, while improvements in living conditions of large groups of the population stagnated or deteriorated in many developing countries. Population and labour participation increased drastically, leading to urban-rural and formal-informal imbalances in many countries. This situation resulted in an increased pressure for initiating and formulating consistent public measures to cope with the mounting problems. Such information and actions have instilled in development planners an interest in the integration of population aspects into development planning.

Many efforts have been made to integrate population issues into development planning, for a review see Horlacher and MacKellar (1988). But there is as yet little agreement as to the relevant variables or type of relationships between these variables that would be considered to assure a logical and operational framework for streamlining development and population activities.

In recent years, however, the possibility of approaching a combined framework for analysing development and population has been greatly enhanced by the appearance of the social accounting matrix (SAM) and the demographic accounting matrix (DAM). They serve as frameworks for organising multidimensional data of the economy and the population. SAM integrates, at one and the same time, disaggregated data on production, income and expenditure by specific population groups, thereby allowing a systematic recording of diversified interactions between the economy and population. DAM accounts for the annual flow of the population from one category to another for a large number of categories. Both SAM and DAM are due to a large extent to Stone (1971).

The objective of this chapter is to present a simplified framework for appraising policy making concerning economic growth and the distribution of incomes received by population groups. Attention is first given to main interactions between development and population variables. Simplifications are introduced to reach an operational framework that considers the main interactions. The SAM framework is used to analyse and reflect on policies of economic growth and income distribution for a large developing country, Indonesia. Refinements are discussed, and final remarks are added on the use of DAM.

2.   Selection of Variables

Getting agreement on the range of relevant population variables in the development context, or for short PD variables, is not feasible. However, the following can be said. Population can be classified according to many criteria outside economics: age, sex, location, education, civil status, etc. Each category allows inclusion of the whole population. Typical for PD variables is a classification of persons per occupation, sector, employment status, income category, etc. These categories are not inclusive of the whole population. One of the few inclusive criteria in PD variables is general activity, which can be defined to fall into:

$$S = \text{engagement in marketable labour;}$$
$$O = \text{engagement in own production;}$$
$$M = \text{home activities; and}$$
$$E = \text{presence at school.}$$

These four activities form the basic preoccupation of population. They appear in relationships to each other in table 7.1. The assignment of a person to a specific activity presupposes that all his/her time is spent at the site of activity. A person may have two joint activities if he/she spends parts of the reference time in the sites of the two activities. A generalised classification of activities for the whole population is to be done with reference to both time and place, therefore.

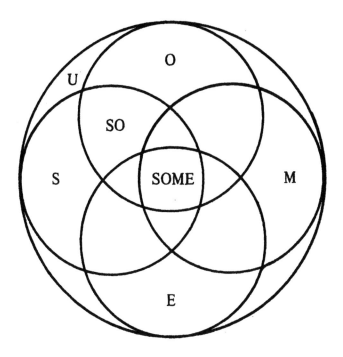

Figure 7.1. Distribution of the Population on General Activities

The distribution of the population on the four general activities and on timesharing joint activities is well demonstrated in the Venn diagram in figure 7.1. For instance, S, with its marketable labour, is typically the modem sector employment, while O, which represents self-employment, is typically the informal sector employment. In between, SO is an intermediate sector, with modern and informal characteristics. The outlaying area between S and O, indicated by U, can be seen to represent unemployment. S, O and U together is the active population while the rest of the circle is the so-called non-active population.

The diagram highlights a major conceptual problem, namely the handling of persons in time-sharing joint activities. For instance, category SOME in the centre of the diagram is very mobile. This category would stand for an "inconclusive" person who may spend the morning in wage employment, is engaged in own production at noon, looks after the children at home in the afternoon, and follows educational courses in the evening. It is apparent that time budget surveys by place of activity are essential tools in gaining insight in relationships between population and development. Research progress in this area is little so that the conceptual integration of the whereabouts of persons in time and place is a major pending issue.

3.   Modeling the Relationship between Population and the Economy

The second obstacle facing incorporating PD variables in policy models is the lack of agreement as to the kind of relationships to be modelled. Some of the main interactions between population and economic variables prevalent in the literature are depicted in table 1, the notations used are part of the same table. Many of the relationships in the table have been empirically investigated in Cohen (1975) and Cohen et al. (1984). A review of the interactions between population and the economy can be found in Horlacher and MacKellar (1988). On the right-hand side of the table it is noted that past tendencies in fertility, death, marriages and divorces result in the present day mix of households by type of household. As examples of types of households one may quote rural and urban and a further disaggregation based on the sex, age, status, occupation, etc., of the head of the household.

Each household is endowed with a diversity of member-days. Within each household four types of decisions regarding the utilization of endowments may be distinguished:

- Decisions on the allocation of household member-days to the *marketable* labour supply, S;
- Decisions on mobilising member-days for *own* production, O;
- Decisions on the extent of inactives at *home,* M; and
- Decisions on keeping children in the *educational* system, E.

The study of these decisions has become the subject matter of new home economics though it is well recognized that the allocation of endowments is multidisciplinary.

Decisions on S and O are directly relevant for the economic variables in the rest of the table. Decisions on M are indirectly relevant while those on E become more relevant at a later stage when students graduate and become eligible for entry in the labour force.

Table 7.1   Structure of a Stylised Model of Population and Development

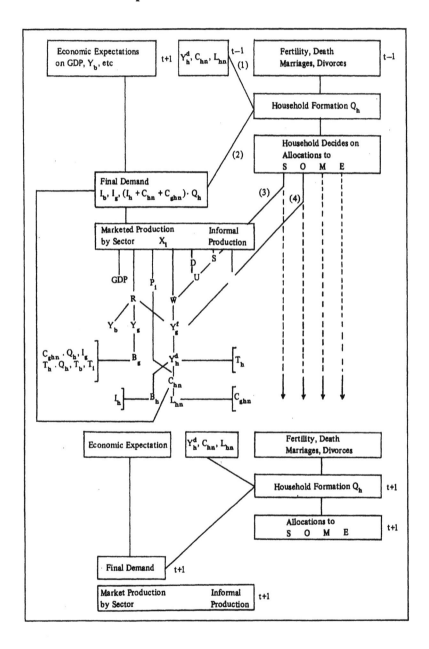

List of Notations

Indices

b	= business
g	= government
h	= household type
i	= sector
n	= need category
t	= time period.

Endogenous Variables

B_g	= budgetary deficit (surplus) of government
B_h	= budgetary deficit (surplus) of household type h
C_{hn}	= consumption expenditure of household type h on good n
D	= demand for labour
GDP	= gross domestic product
I_b	= investment by business
I_h	= investment by household type h
I_g	= investment by government
L_{hn}	= living level attained by household type h of needs category n
P_i	= price index of sector i
Q_h	= number of households by household type h
R	= profits
S,O,M,E	= allocation of member-days of a household to marketable labour supply S, own informal production 0, inactive at home M, and children in education E
U	= unemployment
W	= wages
X_i	= production by sector i
Y_b	= profit income of business
Y_g	= profit income of government
Y_h^d	= disposable income of household type h
Y_h^f	= factor income of household type h

Predetermined Variables

C_{ghn}	= consumption allocations by government to household type h by need category n
T_b	= usiness taxes
T_h	= income tax rate for household type h
T_i	= indirect taxes

lagged variables belonging to t-1; future expectations pertaining to t+1

The PD variables, and their variation over time, which have just been described can be very well integrated in a Demographic Accounting Matrix, DAM. Most of the transition rates in the DAM are usually exogenous, but as more empirical knowledge becomes accumulated it is possible to endogenise more of these transition rates.

Turning now to the economy variables in the left-hand side of table 7.1, most of these are population related, and can be categorised as belonging to either:

- Accounts of the inputs and production by sector;
- Accounts of income and expenditure by household type, firms and government;
- Detailed accounts of attained standards of living per household type; and
- When income, expenditure and living levels per household type are multiplied by the number of households in that type, we obtain aggregate values for the population and the economy.

The factor market in this scheme is modelled as interactions between demand and supply for labour, D and S, and unemployment, U. This results in wages, W, and similarly for capital there is return to capital, R. The product market is also present in the form of sectoral prices which are endogenously determined as a result of demand and supply.

A Social Accounting Matrix, SAM, can approximate the economy variables described above, and their interactions. To be precise, the end results of the factor and product markets at the end of a year can be read from the SAM.

The objective of the remainder of this section is to elaborate on table 7.1 and sketch a compact framework for the modelling of population and development policies based on the SAM and DAM. From table 7.1 it can be observed that there are four direct links between the right- and left-hand sides indicated by (1) to (4):

1.   Income, consumption and living standards attained by a household influence the size and age formation of the household;
2.   In turn, household composition influences the pattern of final demand;
3.   Household decisions on releasing member-days to the marketable labour supply S determine the working of the labour market and affects unemployment U and wages W; and

4. Household decisions on self-employment 0 determine income from
    self-employment.

Furthermore, decisions on M and E can be based on economic
expectations of opportunity costs of mother care and child education,
respectively, but these are not explicited in the table.

The introduction of simplifications regarding the four links mentioned
above produces an operational scheme capable of handling effective
decision-making in a simple planning system. Cutting off lines (1), (2), (3)
and (4) reduces the model into the two independent matrices of DAM and
SAM.

Table 7.2 is the outcome of eliminating the linkages. Via the
introduction of appropriate lags the DAM and SAM can be mapped to each
other in indirect ways at a later stage.

Special mention should be made here of the central role which policy
making for growth and income play in determining the future course of the
remainder of the economy. Given the primary position of final demand in
shaping the development of most variables, and the major role of
household incomes in determining final demand, it follows that the setting
of income targets by household units, whether this occurs voluntarily by
the households or by the means of some directed plan, is very crucial for
the development of the economy, Cohen (1975).

Table 7.2.   Planning Phases in a Stylised Model of Population and Development

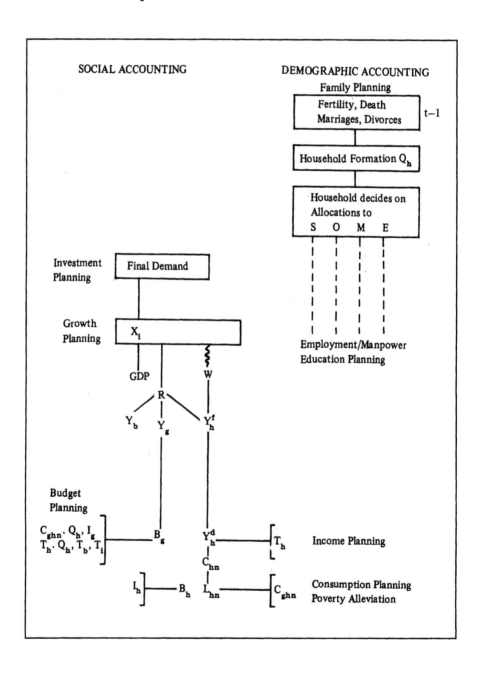

4.   Examples of Modelling Relevant Population-Development Policies

4.1. Introduction

This section examines four policy issues in the development process:
1.   The social efficiency of interventions with fertility;
2.   The social efficiency of resource allocations to human development;
3.   The effective combination between agriculture and industry in promoting income growth and its more equitable distribution among the earning population groups; and
4.   The optimal combination between transfer payments and provisions in kind in guaranteeing minimum consumption needs for poverty groups.

Although these four issues may not seem to be much related yet they share the following characteristics. First, they belong consecutively to the indicated phases of planning in table 7.2 namely (1) family planning, (2) employment, manpower and education planning, (3) income planning and (4) consumption planning. Second, it will be seen that the conventional treatment of these policy issues in a predominantly economic framework renders different policy prescriptions than when a populationist dimension is added to the framework.

4.2. Family Planning

The economically optimal size of the population or its rate of growth are much debated by economists. A report by the US National Research Council (1986) has gone in depth into many of the macro-economic consequences and policy issues involved. The results of the debate are mixed, for it can be always shown that significant economic growth has taken place in several countries characterised by high population growth, while the contrary can also be maintained for many other countries.

A treatment of the implications of a change in the size of population from the point of view of *social welfare* of the concerned population brings the question of the optimal size in quite a new light. M. Nerlove (1987) made such a welfare-populationist treatment. In specifying a social welfare function one may choose between a total and an average formulation. In the classical utilitarian criterion that maximises the sum of individual utilities, we may call W^T in eq. 1 the total social welfare function.

$$W^T(\mu^1,.....,\mu^n) = \sum_{h=1}^{n} \mu^h \tag{1}$$

The alternative is the maximisation of average utility, i.e., per capita, as in eq. (2). We may call W^A the average social welfare function.

$$W^A(\mu^1,....,\mu^n) = \frac{1}{h}\sum_{h=1}^{n}\mu^h \tag{2}$$

Since scaling all utilities up or down by a constant multiplicative factor does not affect any essential property of W, if n *is* known, the two equations do not appear to differ. But in a situation in which different fertility choices by households produce a different population level then the two criteria can lead to different conclusions. For example, if for the population concerned the marginal utility from an additional birth is positive but less than the average, then adding the person will produce a greater total utility W^T but a smaller average utility W^A.

It is evident that the W^T social welfare function leads to a larger population than W^A. What is more significant is that if fertility decisions are taken in accordance with the maximisation of parental satisfaction - which does not mean that the parents prefer too many or too little children but do act rationally - then the situation may yield a population larger than W^T or less than W^A. Thus welfare criteria offer no sure rationale for coercive interference with parental choice.

4.3   Human Resource Development and Utilisation

The second group of policy issues we comment upon is concerned with the unresolved problem of the optimal investment in human resources. This is a debate on the *right* quality of the population as compared to that on the *right* quantity, discussed in the previous section.

It is contended by some analysts that investment in human capital accounts for most of the impressive rising in the real earnings per worker. According to this vision a major part of what we call consumption such as expenditure on education and health, constitutes deliberate investment in human capital whose growth is a decisive factor of economic development. There is indeed mounting evidence to support this contention.

On the other hand, phenomena like the educated unemployment in many countries, mismatches between job requirements and school curriculum, parents spending the same levels on more able and less able children, uneconomic prolongation of written-off lives via expensive medical treatment are abundant. These phenomena tend to throw doubts on whether all the public expenditures on human resources related to these ends are justifiable from the point of view of social efficiency.

These are two opposite positions on this issue that have been worked out empirically in the context of planning for educational and manpower development, cf. Cohen (1994). To start with, conventional methods for estimating returns to education rely on *human capital* theory that equates earnings to the marginal productivity of the worker and explains the latter in terms of the education attained by the worker. In contrast, *job competition* theory, asserts that wages are paid on the basis of the characteristics of a job or an occupation. Occupations differ in their intensities of using capital, handling information, and practising leadership. More demanding occupations are paid higher wages. Productivity is considered to be an attribute of occupations and less so of the education of the person. In the job competition model workers are matched to occupations by certain worker characteristics which may well be identifiable with educational characteristics as well as other background characteristics. Applications made to Pakistan show returns to educational skills following the job competition model to be lower as compared to the human capital model, while the reductions are more pronounced for the higher educational skills. These results suggest that some shift in investment from higher to lower skills would bring about more returns. The results suggest also that a shift of future investment from human capital to physical capital is economically more efficient.

4.4. Income Planning

The third group of policy issues that we consider pertains to the effective allocation of resources between sectors in promoting economic growth and a more equitable income distribution among population groups.

It has been the conventional view of many development economists that a shift of resources from agriculture to industry is a prerequisite of the development process.

An examination of the issue of allocating resources between agriculture and industry from a population's viewpoint can lead to results that differ from those of the conventional view. In the more populous third world countries about seventy percent of the population and the labour force live in rural areas and earn their living from self-employment in agriculture and agriculture-based activities. Many studies have shown that future absorption in the modern modes of employment is limited. The structural ratio of 7:3 may become the new historical trend.

In terms of the population-economy linkages the arguments can be set in favour of agriculture, too. Although, the agriculture-based population is poorer than the industry-based population as far as income per capita is concerned, yet in some countries the total generated income in agriculture is often high enough to surpass that of industry. Besides, a large share of industrial income is spent on food consumption that flows back to agriculture. Furthermore, past investments in agriculture have enhanced productivity significantly leading to an expansion of technological linkages in favour of agriculture.

Development models based on Social Accounting Matrices, SAMs, have been very functional in demonstrating the edge of agriculture on industry in promoting economic growth and its progressive distribution among population groups. In the remainder of this section we show the type of results obtained from applying a SAM model to a large sized country, namely Indonesia.

As was explained in previous chapters, the SAM is nothing more or less than the transformation of the circular flow of economic activity into a matrix of transactions between the various agents. In the rows of such a matrix there are the factors, the institutions consisting of households, firms and government as well as the institutions capital account, the activities and the rest of the world. The columns are ordered similarly. Transactions between these actors take place at the filled cells and in correspondence with the circular flow.

Once an aggregate SAM table is constructed each cell can be extended on the basis of additional data from surveys of the labour force, household income and expenditure, input-output deliveries, finance, government, trade and other statistics to give a disaggregated SAM, which is really what is sought here. Disaggregated SAMs of Indonesia have been assembled in Biro Pusat Statistik (1982) for the calendar years of 1975 and 1980, respectively. The assembled version we shall adhere to is one that falls into an oversized chessboard of 28 rows and 28 columns. The factor incomes and household groups are divided into ten types each. Firms, government capital and rest of the world are taken as they were published. Finally, the activities, which fall into four sectors of production, are taken as they were published.

In the input-output analysis an endogenous vector of sectoral production can be predicted from an inverted matrix of input-output coefficients, and a vector of exogenous final demand. The SAM can be used similarly with the obvious difference that the SAM contains more variables and relationships. To transform the social accounting matrix into an economy-wide model along the lines of input-output analysis requires performing several steps.

First, the accounts of the SAM need to be subdivided into endogenous and exogenous ones, and regrouped accordingly so that the exogenous accounts would fall to the right and bottom of the endogenous accounts. The choice regarding subdivision into x exogenous and y endogenous variables can lead to lengthy discussions on alternative closure rules. Instead, we shall, initially, assume for a typical developing country such variables as expenditure and revenue of government, capital and rest of world as exogenous; the remaining variables are endogenous.

Secondly, each flow in the endogenous matrix is divided by its respective column total to give the matrix of average propensities, denoted by A.

The vector of endogenous variables y can now be solved from eq. (3),

$$y = Ay + x = (I - A)^{-1}x = M_a \ x \tag{3}$$

where Ma is the SAM multiplier matrix. This SAM multipliers can be employed to tell us, among other things:

1. what is the effect of an exogenous additional injection in agriculture or industry (due to government action) on: growth of output and on the generation and distribution of income by population groups; and
2. in a similar way, one can assess the effect of institutional transfers (by government) on growth of output and on the generation and distribution of income.

The multipliers in table 7.4 give an indication of short-term effects of exogenous sectoral injections on output and income.[1] An injection of a million rupiahs in agriculture gives a potential increase in total output of 3.38 and in total income of 1.89, a major share of this income, 50 %, goes to rural households and 24 % to urban households. The impact of a unit injection in industry on total output is only 2.6, and on total income only 1.5, about 45 % of which goes to rural households and 2 4% to urban households.

A higher share of the income multiplier for the poorer groups represents an improvement in income equality when compared to their actual income

---

[1] The difference between the output and income effect is partly due to leakages such as intermediate inputs and imports.

share in the first column of table 7.2. This is not a comprehensive measure of redistribution bias but a sensible and operational one.

The results show that injections in agriculture lead to an overall progressive redistribution of income.[2] Injections in industry shift incomes from all household groups, except the urban rich, to corporate firms.[3]

Note that the narrower input-output framework, laying emphasis on interindustry relationships, has always given higher values of multipliers for industry than for agriculture.[4] The broader SAM framework that considers the whole circular flow gives different policy recommendations. The SAM would recommend expansion of agriculture at the cost of industry on both criteria of growth and equality.

Table 7.5 gives the output and income effects of another type of instrument: transfers to households (for brevity, transfers to only two types of households are shown which happen to be the richest and poorest). Government or rest of the world can make the transfers. It is noted that a transfer to the poorest group of rural farm workers creates more output and income than a transfer to the richest group of urban upper income. As can be expected, the rural transfer lifts up the position of rural farm workers significantly at the cost of other groups.

The share of the poorest in the additionally generated income will increase from 5% to 40%. The urban transfer favours urban upper income households at the cost of the rest of the nation. The share of this rich group in additionally generated income is increased from 12% to 53%.

Subject to limitations that are briefly pointed out at the end of this section, the social accounting framework is useful for calculating plan projections and assessing alternative perspectives.

---

[2] It is noted that rural farm workers would experience a relative increase in incomes of 5.12/4.54 = 1.14, while rural landowners experience a relative gain of 29.0/27.6 = 1.05. Regarding non-farm workers, the group of lower income increases its share by 1.0% while the group of upper income reduces its share by .04%. Also among urban households the better-off see a deterioration and the less-off an improvement.

[3] Share of corporate firms increases from 27.9% to 30.8%.

[4] The issue has been treated at some length in chapters 2 and 3.

Table 7.4. The impact of Sectoral Injections on Output and Incomes by Population Groups. Demonstration of Results for Indonesia

	Actual 1975	*Sectoral Injections*	
		Agriculture	*Industry*
Output multiplier		3.379	2.637
Income multiplier		1.886	1.464
Percentage distribution by income groups			
1. Rural land owners	27.55%	28.97%	27.3%9
2. Rural farm workers	4.54%	5.19%	4.27%
3. Rural non-farm, upper	4.74%	4.32%	4.13%
4. Rural non-farm, lower	10.43%	11.44%	9.86%
5. Urban upper income	12.43%	11.07%	11.51%
6. Urban lower income	12.42%	13.06%	12.09%
7. Firms	27.89%	25.95%	30.75%
Total	100.00%	100.00%	100.00%

Table 7.5. The Impact of Household Transfers on Output and Incomes by Population Groups. Demonstration of Results for Indonesia

	Actual 1975	*Sectoral Injections*	
		Agriculture	*Industry*
Output multiplier			
Income multiplier		2.185	2.734
Percentage distribution by income groups			
1. Rural land owners	27.52%	14.32%	17.94%9
2. Rural farm workers	4.54%	2.58%	39.80%
3. Rural non-farm, upper	4.74%	2.77%	2.98%
4. Rural non-farm, lower	10.43%	5.87%	7.27%
5. Urban upper income	12.43%	52.66%	7.56%
6. Urban lower income	12.42%	8.70%	8.25%
7. Firms	27.89%	13.11%	16.20%
Total	100.00%	100.00%	100.00%

This is done by multiplying a vector of projected targets of sectoral injections and institutional transfers by SAM multiplier matrix.

Table 7.6 demonstrates the distribution of the total output and national income in 1975 and their alternative projections for 1980, as indicated by plans A, B and C. In plan A, it is assumed that each injection and transfer grows annually by 6%. This results in an equivalent growth of output and income of 8% per annum, but the income distribution remains the same. In plan B, injections in agriculture are targeted at 100% higher than those in plan A. Injections in industrial activities are decreased by the same amount of the target. Plan B results in a higher economic growth of 8.13% per annum and a slightly more equitable distribution. Both effects are explainable in terms of the crucial role that agriculture plays in promoting growth and equity. Lastly, plan C goes a step further by doubling income transfers to the less privileged population group of rural, farm workers, while the transfers to the rich group of urban upper incomes are decreased by the same amount of money. The results of plan C show a further improvement in both economic growth and the equitable distribution of national income households, although the magnitudes involved are very slight.

Table 7.6.   Alternative Plan Projections of Output and Income, by Population Group: Results for Indonesia

Sector or Group	Actual, 1975	Projections, 1980		
		Plan A	Plan B	Plan C
Total output billion rupiah	23 204	34 094	34 307	34 313
Percentage distribution:				
Agriculture	38.65	38.65	39.79	39.80
Industry	33.99	33.99	32.82	32.82
Trade/transport	18.33	18.33	18.37	18.37
Services/government	9.03	9.03	9.01	9.01
Total income billion rupiah	13 544	19 901	20 021	20 024
Percentage distribution:				
Rural landowners	27.55	27.55	27.59	27.59
Rural farm workers	4.54	4.54	4.56	4.59
Rural non-farm, upper	4.74	4.74	4.74	4.74
Rural non-farm, lower	10.43	10.43	10.46	10.46
Urban upper income	12.43	12.43	12.42	12.39
Urban lower income	12.42	12.42	12.44	12.44
Firms	27.89	27.89	27.78	27.78

To balance our exposition, we conclude this section by making explicit six limitations of the SAM-multiplier approach. However, it has been demonstrated elsewhere, Cohen (1987), that incorporation of refinements to remedy the six limitations do not change the basic conclusions reached on the advantage of agriculture on industry with respect to growth and equity.

First, like the evaluation of the multipliers of any other economic model, the evaluation of the multipliers of the SAM-model cannot be done in isolation from the closure rules applied. The size of the multipliers depends on the choice of the exogenous and endogenous variables, which in turn depends on the problem studied.

Second, in the multiplier model, supplied amounts are supposed to adjust to demanded amounts. They will, but if the adjustment is not in quantities (whether or not due to restricted capacity) the result is inflation. This may require a revision downward in the realised sizes of multipliers in the future.

Third, the SAM assumes constant shares of factor remuneration in total output, of household incomes in the various factor payments, of commodities in household expenditure, and of sectors in commodity production. However, with more information these shares can be made to vary.

Fourth, the available data on factor accounts stand in the way of linking household earnings to income by sectoral sources in more disaggregated and relevant ways. Here too, the UN System of National Accounts is undergoing revisions that will resolve these shortcomings.

Fifth, income distribution was classified by socio-economic population groups in terms of residence, working status and ownership of human resources and land property. In the context of fiscal policy a classification by income deciles is more practical. The conversion of alternative classifications by population groups to each other is well advanced in the literature.

Sixth, both the input-output and the SAM frameworks are demand-oriented models. The potential effects that they simulate may not be realisable due to the limited scope for significant demand injections or supply constraints.

4.5 Consumption Planning

The fourth group of policy issues we treat belongs to consumption planning, see table 7.2. Poverty groups are a phenomenon that exists in many societies irrespective of the aggregate level of economic development achieved. In the longer run, human resource development measures have proven to have selfsustainable positive effects in eliminating poverty. In the short run, the policy issue faced is the optimal combination between income transfers and provisions of necessity goods in kind. Welfare theory shows that a money transfer would bring the consumers on a higher indifference curve and, talking welfare economics, a money transfer is preferable to a provision in kind. However, incorporation of behavioural aspects of the consuming population may lead to contrary results in terms of social welfare.

In Cohen (1977) we were particularly concerned with the calories consumed per capita per day by the lowest income group, K, as a measure of the incidence of poverty in South Korea. The derivation of calories from a certain amount of food expenditure would require knowledge of the average cost per one calorie. For example,

Calories per capita = (consumption expenditure on food per capita) /
(cost per calorie)

Consumption expenditure on food by this poorest population group consists of a private component which can be expressed as a function of income *Y* (thus $\alpha + \beta Y$) plus public allocations of food directed to this group, denoted by *Z*. Population size of the group is denoted by *P*. The cost per calorie can be assumed to be a rising function of the general level of living of the group, represented by the income per capita of the group (thus $\gamma + \delta Y$). Usually the unit cost tends to increase rapidly as the general level of living approaches higher levels, owing to the gradual shift in the pattern of food composition from cheap food articles to more expensive food articles with the same calorie content. As a result, the above equation can be written as eq. (4)

$$K = \frac{(\alpha + \beta Y) + Z)/P}{\gamma + \delta(Y/P)} \tag{4}$$

A partial analysis can reflect upon the relative effectiveness of using direct transfers (increasing *Y*) versus public allocation in kind (increasing *Z*) in raising the nutritional level. First, in the case of an income transfer part of the income increase will be spent on food and the rest will be spent on other goods and services and as such will be 'redundant' in influencing calorie intake.

Second, equally important is that the cost per unit is a function of income per capita; and increases of income are bound to increase the cost and diminish the purchasable calories. As a result of both effects direct transfers can be shown to be less effective than public allocations in kind in raising calorie intake.

The magnitudes involved can be demonstrated by writing the equation with its estimated parameters, after multiplying by *P*. In passing, it can be mentioned that the consumption and cost functions were tested separately using South Korean data from the sixties and seventies. Both functions fitted very well. The slope coefficients were highly significant and were positive in accordance with *a priori* expectations.

$$K = \frac{.0343 + .3749Y + Z}{.0051P + .0489Y} \tag{5}$$

In the Korean context an increase of one billion Korean won in income *Y* via an income transfer leads to an increase of 4.4 calories p.p.p.d. On the contrary, an increase of one billion won in public provisions of food in kind Z allows the consumption of 14.8 additional calories per person per day, which is more effective, therefore.

5.   Concluding Remarks

In this chapter we discussed a selection of topics dealing with the interface between population economics and development policy. The objective was to review the state of the art and possible avenues for refinement. There are significant obstacles. These are the integration of the time and place dimensions in the classification of people by activity, the operationalisation of population-economy models to meet the practical situations encountered in development planning and adjustment programmes, and the assessment of conflicts and complementarities between alternative policies in the light of alternative theoretical postulates and their empirical testing.

In this chapter, the focus was, among others, on social accounting as a tool for appraising key instruments in the planning of economic growth and the distribution of income among population groups and, consecutively, in making plan projections of growth and income.

Social accounting does not capture the movement of persons from one specific population group to another and is therefore silent on individual changes occurring in their residence, status, education, occupation, income, etc. Demographic accounting is a very helpful tool in capturing these changes.

Chapter 8

Social Accounting and the Modelling of Convergence between Rich and Poor Countries

1. Introduction

The well-known data set of real GDP for 130 countries over 35 years, compiled by Summers and Heston (1988), together with population figures, have been used by many economists in studying income convergence patterns between rich and poor countries. The works include those of: Baumol (1986), followed by Dowrick and Gemmell (1988), Barro (1991), Mankiw, Romer and Weil (1992), Sprout and Weaver (1992), and Theil and Seale (1994). Taking all the rich versus all poor countries together, the statistical material shows that there is a slight catching up tendency. Further disaggregation has highlighted a convergence of income levels within the richer countries but divergence within the poorer countries with some of the latter even falling behind the rest and becoming relatively poorer. These trends can be readily seen from table 8.1.

Two economic models have been invoked to explain the above tendencies: Solow's growth model, which predicts convergence, Solow (1956) and Krugman's divergence model Krugman (1981). The mechanism behind Solow's growth model is diminishing returns to reproducible capital. A poor country characterised by a low capital/labour ratio, has a higher marginal productivity of capital and thereby tends to grow at a higher rate than a rich country with a higher intensity and lower marginal productivity of capital. Furthermore, there is a tendency for capital to move from rich to poor thereby accelerating the convergence process.

Table 8.1.   Income, population and income per capita: values, and growth rates by world regions.

	Values 1987			Average Annual Growth rates 1961-87		
	Income Bill US$	Population Millions	Income per capita	Income	Population	Income per capita
World	24388	4866	5012	4.4	1.8	2.5
Rich countries	13583	1032	13162	3.7	0.8	2.9
OECD	10657	707	15074	3.7	0.8	2.9
Ex-communist	2926	325	9003	3.8	0.9	2.9
Poor countries	10805	3835	2817	5.4	2.2	3.2
S&C America	1782	404	4411	4.8	2.5	2.3
S. Asia	1164	1076	1082	3.9	0.3	1.5
E. Asia	5270	1441	3657	7.0	1.8	5.2
Other Africa	296	448	661	2.8	2.8	0.0

Source: Sprout and Weaver (1992) based on Summers and Heston (1988). Arab region=W. Asia + North Africa

The contrary model of Krugman stresses increasing returns to capital, technological edges and learning in assuring higher levels of more competitive capital and industrial exports in the rich country. Endogenous growth is seen to work to the advantage of the rich country that grows at a higher rate than the poor country. Capital flow tends to reverse from poor to rich, aggravating income gap between rich and poor, fur thermore. Lucas (1993), Barro (1991) and others have elaborated Krugman's model along endogenous growth theory to show basically the same. An increasing income gap between, on the one hand, countries that invest in human resources and are able to capture the public goods character of those investments, and on the other, countries that do not (are unable or unwilling) to invest sufficiently in human resources, learning and innovation.

A synthesis is found in Mankiw, Romer and Weil (1992) who developed a model which combines the mechanical growth theory as represented by Solow and endogenous growth theory as represented by Krugman, Lucas and others. They test their model to the data set of Summers and Heston and find that countries with similar technologies and rates of accumulation and population growth should converge in income per capita. Yet this convergence occurs more slowly than the Solow model suggests. More generally, the results indicate that the Solow model is consistent with the international evidence if one takes account of (dis)advantages of individual countries with respect to human and physical capital endowments.

Another empirical paper, which contributes to a synthesis, is by Barro and Lee (1993). They explain the growth performance of 116 economies from 1965 to 1985. They find a conditional convergence effect, whereby a country grows faster if it begins with lower real GDP per capita in relation to its initial level of human capital; next to other stimulating factors such as high ratio of investment to GDP, small government and political stability.

It is noted that all the models mentioned above emphasise supply factors in determination of economic growth. The debate has so far been unbalanced as it excluded models of economic growth that emphasise demand factors. In this chapter we highlight the insights to be gained from employing a demand-determined growth model. We use here a circular flow model based on the Social Accounting Matrix, SAM. The results of this model, empirically verified for a group of sixteen countries at different stages of economic development, would give general support to the convergence hypothesis. This chapter discusses in section 2 the SAM-based model. In section 3 the SAM multipliers are used to assess the convergence hypothesis. In section 4 empirical results are analysed. In section 5 a numerical demonstration is reviewed, and section 6 concludes.

2. The Demand Model

For the purpose in mind, the fittest framework within the wide range of demand-oriented models is the circular flow model based on the Social Accounting Matrix, SAM. The SAM is a very general database that is well suited for the flexible modelling of the economy, cf. Pyatt (1991). The SAM is nothing more or less than the transformation of the circular flow into a matrix of transactions between the various agents. In the rows of such a matrix there are the products, the factors, the current accounts of institutions consisting of households, firms and government as well as their capital accumulation account, the activities and the rest of the world. The columns are ordered similarly. Transactions between these actors take place at the filled cells and in correspondence with the circular flow. A particular row gives receipts of the account while column-wise we read the expenditure of the actor.

Assuming proportional relationships for the cells in terms of their column totals a SAM coefficient matrix is obtained which can be written as a model of the economy with the endogenous part on the left hand side and exogenous part on the right hand side. The endogenous variables include production, income, consumption, investment, among others. The exogenous variables in such a model are those of government and rest of world. We shall discuss the assumptions of the model in a moment.

A SAM-based model can take the form of eqs. (1) to (6), and the corresponding notations as shown in the boxes overleaf.

Eq. (1) gives the sectoral balance by sector v, consisting of intermediate delivery

$$\sum_{v'} a_{vv'} V_{v'},$$ consumption expenditure $$\sum_z c_{vz} Z_z,$$ capital formation $ev\,K,$

and a variable for the sectoral receipts from both government expenditure and exports $iv\,X$, where iv gives the sectoral share in these receipts.

Eq. (2) defines national income, consisting of factor incomes.

Eq. (3) determines factor incomes by factor w, as being originating from value added coefficients and production by sector $$\sum_v a_{wv} V_v.$$

Eq. (4) determines household receipts by household group z, consisting of portions of factor income $$\sum_w b_{zw} W_w,$$ interhousehold transfers $$\sum_{z'} c_{zz'} Z_{z'},$$

and transfers from government and rest of the world $iz\,T$ where iz gives the household group's share in the transfers.

Eq. (5) determines firm receipts, consisting also from portions of factor income and transfers from government and rest of the world.

Eq. (6) shows the different sources of capital formation to consist of depreviation summed over sectors, savings summed over households, reinvested savings of firms and capital transfer from government and the rest of the world. The coefficients a,b,c are proportions of the total receipts (outlays) for the columns corresponding with V, W, Z respectively, and $\Sigma a = 1.0$, $\Sigma b = 1.0$, $\Sigma c = 1.0$.

The SAM Model of the Circular Flow

$$V_v - \sum_{v'} a_{vv'} V_{v'} \quad - \quad \sum_z c_{vz} Z_z \quad + eK_v = i_v X \quad 1$$

$$Y - \sum_w W_w = 0 \quad 2$$

$$-\sum_v a_{wv} V_v + W_w = 0 \quad 3$$

$$-\sum_w b_{zw} W_w - \sum_{z'} c_{zz'} Z_{z'} + Z_z = i_z T \quad 4$$

$$-\sum_w b_{fw} W_w + F = i_f T \quad 5$$

$$-\sum_v a_{kv} V_v - \sum_z c_{kz} Z_z - d_k F + K = i_k T \quad 6$$

where
V_v = value of production of sector v,
W_w = factor incomes of factor type w which can be wages, profits, etc.,
Z_z = receipts of household group by region z,
F = receipts of firms,
K = capital formation,
Y = national income,
X = purchases of government and/or exports, both of which are assumed exogenous,
T = transfers from government and/or rest of the world, both assumed exogenous.

In the above equations, the endogenous variables appearing on the left-hand side can be denoted by y, and they include national income among other variables. The exogenous variables appear on the right hand side and can be denoted by x. These include outlays of government and rest of the world. While the coefficient matrix which joins them can be denoted by A.

The system can be described in matrix form by $y - Ay = x$, solving gives

$$y = (I - A)^{-1} x = Ma \, x \qquad (7)$$

where *Ma* stands for the matrix of system multipliers. We focus on the national income multiplier of rich and poor countries and examine their growth tendencies to shed light on the convergence hypotheses.

Before proceeding further, we discuss here main assumptions and limitations of the SAM multiplier approach as well as our counterpart arguments in defence of the approach for the purpose in mind.

(1)   The evaluation of the multipliers of the SAM-model cannot be done in isolation from the closure rules applied. The size of the multipliers depends on the choice of the exogenous and endogenous variables, which in turn depends on the problem studied. In the context of the comparative analysis of economic systems there is an established rationale due to Koopmans and Montias (1971) for considering government policy and rest of the world conditions as exogenous and taking the rest of the economy as endogenous. This is also what is postulated in the SAM model.

(2)   The SAM model describes an endogenous economy with fixed relative prices and complementarity-based production and consumption functions. Producers and consumers are assumed to face fixed prices, and in their pursuit of profit and utility maximization, respectively, adjustment takes the form of changes in quantities supplied and demanded. As regards the assumption of producers and consumers facing given relative prices this is common practise in short-run models. Moreover, even in the longer run, having in mind the broad categories of sectors and products in the SAM we can draw on empirical evidence over long periods which supports indefinite shifts in relative prices between such broad categories, cf. Bleaney and Greenaway (1993).

(3)   Cell entries of the SAM are amounts, i.e. products of prices times quantities. However, quantities and prices are not explicitly disentangled. In the SAM model, supplied amounts are supposed to adjust to demanded amounts. They will, but if there is restricted capacity the result is inflation. This may require a revision downward in the real sizes of multipliers. The role of investment in the model is confined to that of enhancing demand, and not of adding to the productive capacity. Whether the potential multiplier effects of impulses will be realized in increased quantities in full or disappear for a part in increased prices depends on the elasticity of supply. If the size of the impulse is relatively small, which is usually the case, these multipliers can still be seen to represent realizable quantity effects with little leakage into price effects. It is also feasible to check in a simple way within the SAM framework whether the capacity limits will be violated or not. The supply side can be simply modelled as a relationship between the investment rate and economic growth via an incremental capital output ratio x as in $K/Y = x \, (\Delta Y/Y)$.

From the SAM we obtain multiplier effects for K and Y. If division of the multiplier effects of K by those of Y gives values equal to or above K/Y for the base period, then this implies that the SAM solves for sufficient investment to meet the projected capacity increase. It is noted that multiplier results show that this condition is fulfilled for the countries studied. In principle, similar checks can be applied to trace whether the base period equilibria in the balance of payments and the government budget are reproduced by multiplier effects, or not.

(4)   The coefficient matrix in the SAM model, A, is a matrix of fixed average proportions. Compared to averages, observed marginal coefficients are better since they incorporate income and scale effects, but they can be disputable as their estimated values may carry other than income effects, which is inconsistent with the SAM framework. While the c set, these are consumption propensities, can be calculated sensibly as marginal instead of average values, the problem is severe for the other sets. These are the a set, the input - output coefficients, as well as the b set, these are sector - factor earnings coefficients; and other coefficients in the model, which do not usually depict stable marginal propensities. Taking a portion of the coefficients as marginal and the other as an average introduces an estimation bias. Moreover, the uniform fixed coefficient assumption in cross-country comparisons is an advantage in contrast with incomparable specifications for individual countries (which, of course, can be suitable for other purposes).

(5)   The size of the multiplier depends to some degree on the level of aggregation. This argument is not relevant in the context of a uniform aggregation for the compared countries. Moreover, the differences in multipliers due to alternative aggregations tested do not go beyond 8% for the individual countries studied here.

(6)   Although it is commonly perceived that a SAM-inverted model belongs more to the prototype of demand-oriented models, yet under general equilibrium conditions it is a representation of the supply side as well, which is why the SAM is directly convertible to the CGE model. Finally, although we use a demand model, this does not mean that we are implying short-run growth rates. By analysing and fitting our hypothesis to the economic growth of countries ranging from developing countries such as India and Pakistan to advanced countries such as Germany and the Netherlands we are clearly emphasising the long range character of economic growth.

3. The Convergence Hypothesis

Recall eq. (7) that gives the endogenous vector as a function of the system multipliers and an exogenous vector, $y = M_a x$. Our concern in this chapter goes to one endogenous variable from the vector y i.e. national income, Y; and one exogenous variable from the vector x, namely government expenditure and exports combined, X, in eqs. (2) and (1). The multiplier elements from the multiplier matrix that interest us here are those giving the sum total effects of equal sectoral injections via X on Y, which we shall call m. We shall thus restrict our interest to the total multiplier effect of the unweighted exogenous injections in government expenditures and exports, X, on the national income, Y, as in eq. (8.1) where m consists of the summed relevant elements[1] from the multiplier matrix Ma.

$$Y = m\,X \tag{8.1}$$

To simplify matters we shall ignore for the moment the less significant multiplier impact of the exogenous variable of transfer payments, T. But we shall comment on the impact of its incorporation in section 4, which will be shown to reinforce our conclusions.

Equation (8.1) can be rewritten as in eq. (8.2)

$$Y = m\,(\,X\,/\,Y\,)\,Y \tag{8.2}$$

and be re-expressed in growth rates using index g as in eq. (8.3)

$$Y^g = m^g + (\,X\,/\,Y\,)^g + Y^g \tag{8.3}$$

If we further denote a hypothesised growth rate by h and a realisable growth rate by o, eq. (8.3) can be rephrased as in (8.3.1).

Note here that we treat the three growth rates on the right hand side as hypothetical values in the sense that these growth rates are either assumed or forecasted and are consistently estimated in relation to each other. The combined effect of the three growth rates result in the realisable growth rate of the national income on the left hand side. We are in a position thus to answer

---

[1] m is a weighted sum of multipliers by sector, i.e.

$y = \sum_v m_v X_v = \sum_v m_v s_v X = m X$, where s_v is sectoral share of the exogenous variable X.

the question how the economy will perform in the longer run based on components derived from the SAM model.

$$Y^{go} \overset{>}{\underset{<}{=}} m^{gh} + (X / Y)^{gh} + Y^{gh} \tag{8.3.1}$$

Eq. (8.3.1) reads more specifically for poor countries, p, and rich countries, r, as follows:

$$Y_p^{go} \overset{>}{\underset{<}{=}} m_p^{gh} + (X / Y)_p^{gh} + Y_p^{gh}$$

$$Y_r^{go} \overset{>}{\underset{<}{=}} m_r^{gh} + (X / Y)_r^{gh} + Y_r^{gh}$$

The hypothetical and realisable values of the growth rate of income, Y^{gh} and Y^{go}, respectively, are generally different due to the independent determinacy of m^{gh} and $(X/Y)^{gh}$.

If it can be shown for the groups of the poor and rich countries for which we have SAMs that starting from the *same* hypothetical growth rates $Y_p^{gh} = Y_r^{gh}$ we can expect

$$m_p^{gh} + (X / Y)_p^{gh} > m_r^{gh} + (X / Y)_r^{gh}.$$

Then, it follows that realisable growth rates will show $Y_p^{go} > Y_r^{go}$, which is an indication of catching up. We may start first with growth of the exogenous share $(X/Y)^{gh}$, and show that this can be expected to be higher for poor than rich countries and take up later the prospects for m^{gh}.

We start first with X/Y. An interesting feature of the accounting system is that the row element of government expenditure and exports X can be divided by the row of total national income Y to give the exogenous share, X/Y. We have defined X to consist of government expenditure and exports. The hypothesis, which we put forward is that the share of these items in the national income, X/Y, tends to grow rapidly during early stages of economic development but ebbs down and stops growing at higher stages of economic development. This hypothesis is put down in figure 1 that shows the relationship between X/Y and income per capita, Y/N, this being the conventional expression for the stage of economic development.

The quasi-logistic curve in figure 1 can be formulated as eq. (9). This is also the form in which the hypothesis will be empirically tested.

$$X / Y = \frac{\beta (Y / N)}{(Y / N) + \alpha} \tag{9}$$

Wagner's law predicts that at higher levels of economic development, that is, as income per capita grows, the relative share of the public sector in national income will grow. Although the basis of the statement of Wagner 's law was the empirics of the nineteenth century, the theoretical foundations behind the phenomenon were developed later by Peacock and Wiseman, Musgrave, Baumol and others using various public choice arguments.

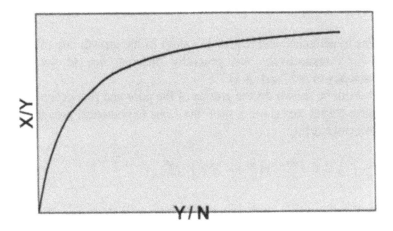

Figure 8.1. Relationship between the Exogenous Share in National Income X/Y and Income per Capita Y/N

More recent experiences in the balancing of budgetary deficits in rich countries directed attention to fiscal, monetary and incentive limits to the further growth of the government share in total expenditure. So the share of the public sector grows as income per capita grows, up to a certain limit. This share has a tendency to stabilise at the higher levels of income per capita.

A similar tendency applies to the share of exports in income, which share is very much dependent on economic development, location and population. As per capita income grows, there is a tendency for the economy to become more open and attain a higher share of exports up to a point where the share levels off as more open economy countries get their portions of world exports. It is also established that the larger the country is in terms of population and economy the lesser the share of exports in income. Among the four rich countries treated in this paper Germany, Italy and Spain will be seen to fall in this class. On the other hand, the small population countries that are also centrally located like the Netherlands tend to have higher shares of foreign transactions with the rest of the world.

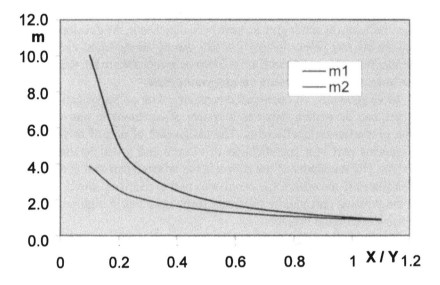

Figure 8.2. Relationship between Multipliers m and the Exogenous Share in National Income X/Y

The conclusion is that as far as the exogenous share is concerned, and this applies to both constituents of government expenditure and exports, the growth of this share for developing countries is higher than for rich countries:

$$(X / Y)_p^{gh} > (X / Y)_r^{gh}$$

We go now to m^{gh}. Recalling equation (8.1) we have: $1/m = X/Y$. Seen as a definition a rise in X/Y should lead to a proportional fall in m.

The relationship between m and X/Y can be put down more generally as equation (10), which will be empirically tested in the next section.

$$m = \gamma \left(X / Y \right)^{-\delta} \tag{10}$$

In figure 2, *curve I* is obtained for values $\gamma = \delta = 1$, while *curve II* corresponds with our empirical estimation, which results in γ having a slightly lower value than *1*, and $\delta < 1$ indicating that the fall in m is somewhat moderated.

The underlying relationship behind empirical *curve II* is that m falls with higher X/Y but increasingly at a lower rate than proportionally. The argument is that the income-expenditure-production linkages in the economy, which have been accumulated throughout the past and which have assured higher circular flow mechanisms and higher *m*, have been enriched in the development process and are not lost proportionally just like that by an increased exogeneity. The circular flow effects fall with a rise in the exogenous share but this fall happens at a lower rate than the rise in the exogenous share.

More generally, an open-ended economy, with no specification of closure as yet, can be written down as a system of equations in one whole matrix with proportionate coefficients. The assignment of part of this matrix as an exogenous part is a specification of closure and gives determinacy to the system. The remainder of the matrix is the inverted part that gives the system multipliers. If the size of the exogenous part is relatively small, then the size of the inverted part will be relatively large, resulting in high multipliers, and hence low external leakage.

The internal leakage, as the term suggests is different, and is determined by the typical pattern of the inverted part. When the transactions of one agent *(A)* with a high multiplier effect flow to agents *(B)* with lower multiplier effects, thus $m(A) > m(B)$, internal leakage tends to be high. The more developed the economy the greater the linkages, the more correspondence between $m(A)$ and $m(B)$, and the smaller is the internal leakage. Once the endogenous linkages are built, their multiplier effects will not be proportionally written off with an increased exogeneity. There is an economic growth advantage here for the rich versus the poor country. Other institutional structures matter also. There should be lesser variation of output multipliers in the free market economy which reacts quickly and competitively in setting up new transactions between agents when the need arises, this in contrast to the case of the centrally planned economy which is characterised by higher internal leakage.

All this means that the relative decline in multiplier m with increased exogeneity can be expected to be higher for the poor than for the rich country, $m_p^{gh} < m_r^{gh}$. This contributes to a widening of the gap between rich and poor, but as will be empirically shown later this is not strong enough to countervail the catching up tendency due to $(X / Y)_p^{gh} > (X / Y)_r^{gh}$, so that in the long run we can expect convergence, nevertheless.

4. Empirical Results

This section will report on selected results from cross-country comparisons of SAM models applied to ten developing countries (India, Pakistan, Sri Lanka, Indonesia, Iran, Kenya, Colombia, Egypt, South Korea, Surinam), two centrally planned economies (Poland and Hungary) and four developed market economies (the Netherlands, Italy, Germany and Spain).

The classification of activities in these SAMs had to be limited to three large groups of sectors: agriculture, industry and services; whereby industry includes mining, manufacturing and energy utilities, and services includes construction and transport among other private and public services. Distinguishing more sectors would reduce the uniformity and comparability of the sixteen SAMs reported here. The disaggregation of households in the SAMs of the developing countries emphasises dualities in the location of population in urban and rural areas, and the differentiation within urban and rural groups by level of income earned. This differentiation is done by a categorical split-up among urban households leading to the distinction between the three groups of employers, employees and self-employed; and a split-up among rural households by size of land ownership leading to three groups of large landowners, medium landowners and small/landless households. As a result, there are six groups of households. For a couple of countries a seventh residual group was incorporated so as to accommodate for classifications which did not fit the standardised six categories. The SAMs of the European countries distinguish household groups by income classes obtainable from personal income distributions.

The testing of eqs. (9) and (10) require data by country on the exogenous share of government and exports in national income, X/Y, and the income multiplier m, which are obtainable from the SAMs and the matrix inversions, respectively. Data on a third variable is needed, this is the GNP per capita, Y/N, expressed in US \$ for the 16 countries and their related years. These are obtainable from published tables of the World Bank Atlas, which are specially suitable in our context as they are based on conversions that smoothen the impact of annual fluctuations in exchange rates. Table 8.2 brings these data together. Note that the value of X/Y varies from a lower value of 0.12 for India (poor country) to a highest value of 0.89 for the Netherlands (rich country).

The income multipliers start from 7.06 for a poor country and fall to 0.85 for a rich country.

Table 8.2.   SAM features and GNP per capita of 16 countries

Country	Year	GNP per cap (1000$)	Exogenous share = X/Y	Average multipliers		
				m	(a)	Highest/ Lowest
Poor countries						
Unweighted		0.55	0.34	2.89	ASI	1.54
India	1968/69	0.09	0.12	7.06	ASI	1.20
Pakistan	1979	0.17	0.24	6.11	ASI	1.24
Sri Lanka	1970	0.17	0.23	2.32	ASI	1.24
Indonesia	1975	0.21	0.37	2.90	ASI	2.15
Iran	1970	0.22	0.13	2.82	ASI	1.40
Kenya	1976	0.24	0.45	1.28	ASI	2.03
Colombia	1970	0.34	0.22	2.47	ASI	1.18
Egypt	1976	0.35	0.43	1.15	ASI	1.86
South Korea	1979	1.51	0.43	1.79	ASI	1.66
Surinam	1979	2.21	0.76	0.95	ASI	1.48
Rich countries						
Unweighted		2.26	0.45	0.85	SAI	1.52
Poland	1987	1.93	0.40	0.92	SAI	1.57
Hungary	1990	2.59	0.49	0.77	SAI	1.46
Rich countries						
Unweighted average		8.70	0.54	1.30	SAI	1.32
Spain	1980	5.40	0.29	1.53	ASI	1.26
Italy	1984	6.42	0.43	1.50	SAI	1.42
Germany	1984	11.13	0.57	1.32	SAI	1.47
The Netherlands	1987	11.86	0.89	0.85	SAI	1.13

(a)ASI = Agriculture-Services-Industry; SAI = Services-Agriculture-Industry
(b)For example in the case of India dividing the average income multiplier of agriculture by that of industry gives 1.20

The regression results of eqs. (9) and (10) are found in table 3. Eq. (9) describes a quasi-logistic function that makes the level of the exogenous share dependent on the income per capita. To account for a particularly lower share in case of a large size rich country, e.g. Germany, Italy and Spain, and too high a share of exports for a few particularly foreign trade oriented small countries e.g. the Netherlands, Surinam and Kenya, a dummy variable is included that takes the value of 1.0 for the first group and -1.0 for the second group. The equation is estimated by non-linear least squares. The regression performs very well, in terms of the signs of the coefficients, their t-values and goodness of fit as indicated by R^2 (above 0.8). The predicted highest value of the exogenous share in the observed sample, disregarding the dummy, can be calculated at 61 per cent for the richest country. The predicted and observed lowest values of the exogenous share are the same, at 12 per cent for the poorest country.

Because Y is determined by the whole system including eq. (9), the question is raised on possible correlation between the explanatory variable, per capita income Y/N, and the disturbance term, yielding a biased non-linear least square estimator. Note that the explanatory variable is expressed as Y/N and not in terms of Y only. Furthermore, the residuals in eq. 9 were found not to correlate with the explaining variable of national income per capita ($r = 0.34$), giving no ground for applying more sophisticated regression methods than the followed non-linear least squares method.

Eq. (10) describes a convex function between the income multiplier and the exogenous share. For estimation purposes the equation is formulated as *ln m = ln γ + δ ln (X/Y)* and tested by ordinary least squares. One dummy needs to be introduced to account for a high income multiplier bias in the SAMs of both India and Pakistan: the available SAMs of India and Pakistan do not register complementary imports to the full extent or at all, and hence underestimate the leakage and overestimate the multipliers.

Another dummy is required to account for the differential impacts of economic systems, e.g. Poland and Hungary. Although one should expect higher multipliers for the less rich Eastern Europe (Poland and Hungary) as compared to the richer Western Europe; instead, they have about the same levels, as table 8.2 shows. This under-performance of Poland and Hungary is due to the presence of institutions that do not make full use of the potential internal leakage effects within the system. The variation of income multipliers among the West European countries as represented by the ratio of the highest/lowest sectoral multiplier can be calculated as 1.44. For Eastern European countries the variation is higher. It is noted too that Poland has a wider variation (1.57) than Hungary (1.46), which reflects a more balanced and well-knitted economy in this respect.

Eq. (10) was tested with two separate dummies as well as with one dummy carrying the value of -1.0 for India and Pakistan and 1.0 for Poland and Hungary. The results are very similar so that we can work as well with the simpler case of one dummy, which is reported in table 8.3. The regression performs very well in terms of all prerequisites.

Table 8.3. Regression Results of Equations (9) and (10)

Item	Explained, explanatory variables and coefficient estimates			R^2
Eq. (9)	$X/Y =$	$\beta\,(Y/N)\,/$	$[\alpha + (Y/N)]$	$+ E_9\,D_9$	
Coefficient		0.632	0.369	-0.201	0.813
t-value		(12.95)	(3.25)	(-4.84)	
Eq. (10)	$\ln m =$	$\ln \gamma +$	$\delta \ln (X/Y)$	$+ E_{10}\,D_{10}$	
Coefficient		-0.077	-0.619	-0.799	0.890
t-value		(-0.58)	(5.41)	(-6.39)	

The focus of the chapter is not the relationship $Y = mX$ for a specific country but searching for a valid relationship between the three variables over a range of poor and rich countries. This has led us to use two equations: one for explaining m in terms of X/Y (eq. 10) and one for explaining X/Y in terms of national income per capita (eq. 9).

If the mean of *m* over the 16 countries in eq. 10 was anything meaningful, we would have obtained values of 1 for γ and for δ in eq. 10 (*curve I* in figure 8.2), but we do obtain *curve II* in figure 8.2 with values $\ln(\gamma) = -0.077$ and $\delta = 0.619$. These results are not due to whether the values of *m* are calculated as weighted or unweighted sectoral impact multipliers, but they are due to the shapes and significance of linkages changing with economic development which were stated under figure 8.2.

We calculate *m* as an unweighted sectoral average. It can be readily seen from table 8.2 that if *m* was calculated as a weighted sectoral average the curve of eq. 10 would fall more steeply and flatten earlier with values of $\ln(\gamma)$ and δ even further away from $\gamma = \delta = 1$. Note that in table 8.2 agricultural multipliers score highest and have the highest share in poor countries. Weighting sectoral multipliers by sectoral shares would result in higher aggregate values of *m* for the poor countries as compared to rich countries causing the curve to shift further away from *curve I*.

5.   Demonstration

With the estimates of α, β, γ and δ we are now in a position to predict for a poor and a rich country respectively, such growth rates as $(X/Y)^{gh}$ and m^{gh} for assumed values of Y^{gh}, insert them in eq. (8.3) for the poor and rich country separately, and solve for realised growth rates of income of the poor and rich countries $Y_p^{g\,o}$ and $Y_r^{g\,o}$. Recall eq. (8.3.1) for the poor and rich country:

$$Y_p^{g\,o} \underset{<}{\overset{>}{-}} m_p^{g\,h} + (\,X\,/\,Y\,)_p^{g\,h} + Y_p^{g\,h}, \, and$$

$$Y_r^{g\,o} \underset{<}{\overset{>}{-}} m_r^{g\,h} + (\,X\,/\,Y\,)_r^{g\,h} + Y_r^{g\,h}$$

In tables 8.4 and 8.5, giving respectively values and growth rates, we start from initial income, population and income per capita for a poor and a rich country (poor and rich as was indicated by the averages in table 8.2). We assume for both types of countries the same annual rates of growth of 2% per income, 1% for population and 1% for income per capita. Using the estimates of α, β, γ and δ we obtain the predicted values of growth rates of X/Y, of X, and of m in columns 8, 10, and 12 respectively. These are used in solving for the realised growth rates of income of the poor and rich country in the last column. The calculations show that the realised growth rate of income of the poor country will exceed that of the rich country. The poor country would achieve an annual growth rate of 2.17% while the rich country would grow annually at 2.02%. Another scenario is run with assumed growth rates of income per capita for the poor and rich at 3%, this scenario results also with a higher rate of realised growth for the poor than the rich, 3.19% compared to 3.05%.

In a more general way, table 8.6 simulates the annual growth rate of income for rising levels of income per capita. The table shows higher growth rates of income at lower levels of income per capita, the growth rates diminishing slowly and practically stabilising at a high level of income per capita of around US$ 20,000.

Table 8.4.   Selected simulations: Initial runs for rich and poor countries, values of selected variables

	Assumed			Predicted		
	Income per capita Y/P	Population P	Income Y	Exogenous share X/Y	Exogenous value X	Multiplier m
Rich						
0	8703	220.0	191466	0.606	11609	1.2612
1	8790	222.2	195314	0.607	11847	1.2609
1	8877	222.2	197248	0.607	11969	1.2606
Poor						
0	551.0	880.0	484880	0.379	1835	1.6879
1	556.5	888.8	494626	0.380	1880	1.6838
1	556.5	897.6	499523	0.380	1898	1.6838
1	562.0	897.6	504469	0.382	1925	1.6797
1	567.5	897.6	509415	0.383	1951	1.6757
1	573.0	897.6	514361	0.384	1978	1.6718

Table 8.5.   Selected simulations: Initial runs for rich and poor countries, growth rates of selected variables

	Assumed			Predicted			Solution
	Income per capita Y/P	Population P	Income Y	Exogenous share X/Y	Exogenous value X	Multiplier m	Income growth rate
Rich							
1	0.01	0.01	0.020	0.00040	0.02051	-0.00025	0.02026
1	0.02	0.01	0.030	0.00080	0.03102	-0.00049	0.03053
Poor							
1	0.01	0.01	0.020	0.00399	0.02417	-0.00246	0.02171
1	0.01	0.02	0.030	0.00399	0.03431	-0.00246	0.03185
1	0.02	0.02	0.040	0.00793	0.04865	-0.00487	0.04377
1	0.03	0.02	0.050	0.01182	0.06302	-0.00724	0.05578
1	0.04	0.02	0.060	0.01567	0.07742	-0.00957	

The convergence tendency, $Y_p^{go} > Y_r^{go}$, is decomposable into a part due to X^g and a part due to m^g, eq. (8.1). The positive but diminishing contribution of X^g standing for a growth potential at a lower level of economic development and an exhaustion of possibilities for exogenous growth at higher levels of economic development dominates the negative effect of m^g, standing for the diminishing multiplier effects but at a reduced rate.

The analysis concentrated so far on the endogenous effects of exogenous injections in sectoral allocations originating from government and the rest of the world, X. How significant are the endogenous effects of exogenous changes in transfers originating from government and rest of world, say T for transfer multipliers, and in which direction do they act?

In principle, the above analysis as in tables 8.2, 8.3 and 8.4 can be repeated but with focus on T. It is also possible to demonstrate the effects via short-cuts. Recalling eq. 7 that gives the vector of endogenous variables y as function of multiplier matrix M and vector of exogenous variables x.

$$y = M_a x$$

This can be specified for variables of interest: endogenous income Y, exogenous allocations X and exogenous transfers T.

$$Y = m X + m T$$

Dividing throughout by Y gives

$$1 = m \ X/Y + m \ T/Y$$

This equation can be specified for poor and rich countries as

$$1 = (m)_p (X/Y)_p + (m)_p (T/Y)_p \tag{11.1}$$

$$1 = (m)_r (X/Y)_r + (m)_r (T/Y)_r \tag{11.2}$$

Inserting the average values of the above parameters for the two groups of countries - see appendix table 2 - gives the following results:[2]

$$1 \approx (2.545)(0.356) + (2.423)(0.078) \approx 0.83 + 0.17 \tag{11.1}$$

$$1 \approx (1.3)(0.543) + (1.648)(0.242) \approx 0.63 + 0.27 \tag{11.2}$$

These results show the effect of X to be about 2.5 to 5.0 times that of T in determining economic growth. At higher levels of economic development the relative strength of X and T effects shifts from X to T. This happens via an increase in the share of T/Y (and a lower share of X/Y) as well as less reductions in m' (as compared to m).

---

[2] The sum of eq. (11.1) does not tally to one because of unweighted values over sectors and countries. The same applies for eq. (11.2).

**Table 8.6.   Selected Simulations: Alternative Runs Assuming
Different Income Levels, Values and Growth Rates; the
Assumptions**

Year	Income per capita Y/P		Population P		Income Y	
		Assumed levels				
	($)	$ growth rate	mln. $	growth rate	mln. $	growth rate
0	100.0		220.0		22000	
1	101.0	0.01	222.2	0.01	22442	0.0201
0	551.0		220.0		121220	
1	556.5	0.01	222.2	0.01	123657	0.0201
0	1000		220.0		220000	
1	1010	0.01	222.2	0.01	224422	0.0201
0	2000		220.0		440000	
1	2020	0.01	222.2	0.01	448844	0.0201
0	4000		220.0		880000	
1	4040	0.01	222.2	0.01	897688	0.0201
0	6000		220.0		1320000	
1	6060	0.01	222.2	0.01	1346532	0.0201
0	8000		220.0		1760000	
1	8080	0.01	222.2	0.01	1795376	0.0201
0	8703		220.0		1914660	
1	8790	0.01	222.2	0.01	1953145	0.0201
0	10000		220.0		2200000	
1	10100	0.01	222.2	0.01	2244220	0.0201
0	12000		220.0		2640000	
1	12120	0.01	222.2	0.01	2693064	0.0201
0	20000		220.0		4400000	
1	20200	0.01	222.2	0.01	4488440	0.0201

Table 8.6. (Continued) Selected Simulations: Alternative Runs Assuming Different Income Levels, Values and Growth Rates; the Predicted Levels and the Solution for the Growth Rate of Income

Year	Predicted						Solution
	Exogenous share X/Y		Exogenous value X		Multiplier m		Income growth rate
	(%)	growth rate	(mln. $)	growth rate	value	growth rate	
0	0.135		30		3.1977		
1	0.136	0.00785	30	0.02811	3.1822	−0.00483	0.02328
0	0.379		459		1.6879		
1	0.380	0.00399	470	0.02417	1.6838	−0.00246	0.02171
0	0.462		1016		1.4928		
1	0.463	0.00268	1039	0.02283	1.4903	−0.00165	0.02118
0	0.534		2348		1.3649		
1	0.534	0.00154	2399	0.02168	1.3636	−0.00095	0.02072
0	0.579		5092		1.2982		
1	0.579	0.00084	5199	0.02095	1.2975	−0.00052	0.02044
0	0.595		7860		1.2754		
1	0.596	0.00057	8022	0.02069	1.2750	−0.00035	0.02033
0	0.604		10633		1.2640		
1	0.604	0.00044	10852	0.02055	1.2636	−0.00027	0.02028
0	0.606		11609		1.2612		
1	0.607	0.00040	11847	0.02051	1.2609	−0.00025	0.02026
0	0.610		13410		1.2571		
1	0.610	0.00035	13684	0.02046	1.2568	−0.00022	0.02024
0	0.613		16188		1.2524		
1	0.613	0.00030	16518	0.02040	1.2522	−0.00018	0.02022
0	0.621		27306		1.2432		
1	0.621	0.00018	27860	0.02028	1.2430	−0.00011	0.02017

At still higher levels of economic development the increases T/Y are restricted by the same constraints which apply to X/Y. First, the T/Y share for individual rich countries has reached its ceiling in the late-eighties/ early-nineties and is falling in others, c.f. Cohen and Bayens (1994). Second, the growth effect of transfers in rich countries, m'_r, forms 68 % of that for poor countries, m'_p. Therefore the conclusions reached on converging tendencies due to the X effects apply to the T effects as well.

6.   Conclusions

Investigation of whether the gap in the income per capita between rich and poor countries is widening or diminishing has relied mainly on supply side models of economic growth appropriately adapted to include elements of endogenous growth.

In this chapter a demand side model, based on the social accounting matrix is estimated for 16 countries. The SAM models predict higher economic growth at lower levels of income per capita, and indicate, therefore, the presence of a convergent tendency. The main cause behind this convergent tendency is the ability of a poor country to increase significantly exogenous injections of exports and government. This in contrast to the exhaustion of possibilities for exogenous growth - of both exports and government - at higher levels of income per capita; while the positive effects from linkage economies at higher levels of income per capita are too low to compensate for the loss in the exogenous growth potential.

Can one, with the SAM based demand side approach, speak of conditional convergence as has become common place in supply side explanatory approaches? In principle, this can be said to apply here too. The SAM analysis was supplemented by dummy variables to account for particularly low/high exogenous shares, these tend to associate with large/small sizes of the economy in relation to the rest of the world and the openness of an economy. Furthermore, the type of the economic system as to whether it is predominantly centrally planned or market oriented was found to influence the size of the multiplier effects. The inherent long-run tendencies towards convergence can be interpreted as conditional to the extent that the above stated particular features of individual countries - expressed as intervening dummies - enjoy a permanent presence. *Ceteris paribus*, the SAM analysis supports the convergence hypothesis.

Appendices

Appendix 1. SAM Statistics

The tables below give basic variables from the SAM's used in the analysis.

Table A1.   Selected SAM Features for 16 Countries

Country	(1) Final demand consumption	(2) Investment	(3) Government	(4) Export	(5) Intermediate delivery	(6) Output	(7) Import	(8) GDP
India	27.471	5.103	0.000	1.450	18.744	52.768	1.868	32.156
Pakistan	0.199	0.042	0.022	0.034	0.168	0.465	0.059	0.238
Sri Lanka	7.601	1.962	0.302	2.113	4.358	16.336	1.389	10.589
Indonesia	8.201	2.227	1.062	3.253	5.797	21.223	3.009	11.734
Iran	0.450	0.146	0.050	0.021	0.327	0.993	0.111	0.556
Kenya	0.951	0.199	0.120	0.472	0.932	2.673	0.431	1.310
Colombia	93.863	28.66	9.962	18.51	108.06	259.066	20.64	130.362
Egypt	3.927	1.198	1.893	0.800	3.482	11.300	1.604	6.214
Korea	6.729	2.078	0.990	2.748	8.383	20.928	3.878	8.667
Surinam	1.026	0.181	0.000	0.917	0.507	2.631	0.921	1.203
Poland	8.371	4.425	2.937	3.516	19.373	38.622	3.218	16.031
Hungary	1.094	0.409	0.166	0.685	1.953	4.360	0.605	1.749
Spain	9.791	3.548	1.929	2.400	14.071	31.739	2.664	15.004
Italy	414.754	121.710	136.677	149.717	588.080	1410.938	162.013	660.845
Germany	823.300	310.642	350.230	476.852	1508.506	3469.530	499.370	1461.654
Netherlands	196.071	52.902	70.590	203.354	222.793	745.710	213.312	309.605

Note: All values are in billion of own currency unit. The years and currency units of the SAMs for the individual countries are indicated in Appendix table 2.

Table A2.   Selected Structural Features and Injection Multipliers from SAMs, and GNP per capita

Country	Year	Currency unit	X/O	O/Y	X/Y	Average income multiplier from injections in X	GNP cap (1000$)
India	1969	rupee	0.027	1.641	0.045	7.06	0.09
Pakistan	1979	rupee	0.121	1.953	0.237	6.11	0.17
Sri Lanka	1970	rupee	0.148	1.543	0.228	2.32	0.17
Indonesia	1975	rupiah	0.203	1.809	0.368	2.90	0.21
Iran	1970	rial	0.071	1.786	0.128	2.82	0.22
Kenya	1976	shilling	0.221	2.041	0.452	1.28	0.24
Colombia	1970	peso	0.110	1.987	0.218	2.47	0.34
Egypt	1976	pound	0.238	1.818	0.433	1.15	0.35
Korea	1979	won	0.179	2.415	0.431	1.79	1.51
Surinam	1979	guilder	0.349	2.187	0.762	0.95	2.21
Poland	1987	zloty	0.167	2.409	0.403	0.92	2.59
Hungary	1990	forint	0.195	2.493	0.487	0.77	0.84
Spain	1980	peseta	0.136	2.115	0.289	1.53	5.40
Italy	1984	lira	0.203	2.135	0.433	1.50	6.42
Germany	1984	mark	0.238	2.374	0.566	1.32	11.13
Netherlands	1987	guilder	0.367	2.409	0.885	0.85	11.86

Note: For definitions of symbols refer to appendix table 1, whereby X = Government (col. 3) + exports (col. 4). O = Output (col. 6). Y = GDP (col. 8).

Table A3. **Selected Structural Features and Transfer Multipliers from SAMs, and GNP per capita**

Country	Year	Currency unit	T/O	O/Y	T/Y	Average income multiplier from transfers in T	GNP cap (1000$)
India	1969	rupee	0.058	1.641	0.095	4.34	0.09
Pakistan	1979	rupee	0.036	1.953	0.070	4.28	0.17
Sri Lanka	1970	rupee	0.105	1.543	0.163	2.28	0.17
Indonesia	1975	rupiah	0.009	1.809	0.017	2.64	0.21
Iran	1970	rial	0.080	1.786	0.142	2.78	0.22
Kenya	1976	shilling	0.063	2.041	0.129	1.98	0.24
Colombia	1970	peso	0.016	1.987	0.032	2.17	0.34
Egypt	1976	pound	0.027	1.818	0.050	1.87	0.35
South Korea	1979	won	0.013	2.415	0.032	2.13	1.51
Suriname	1979	guilder	0.008	2.187	0.018	1.67	2.21
Poland	1987	zloty	0.019	2.409	0.047	1.54	1.93
Hungary	1990	forint	0.055	2.493	0.138	1.40	2.59
Average poor countries					0.078	2.42	0.84
Spain	1980	peseta	0.079	2.115	0.167	1.87	5.40
Italy	1984	lira	0.107	2.135	0.228	1.73	6.42
Germany	1984	mark	0.083	2.374	0.196	1.57	11.13
Netherlands	1987	guilder	0.157	2.409	0.377	1.42	11.86
Average rich countries					0.242	1.65	8.70

Note: T= transfer multiplier. O=output. Y=GDP.

Appendix 2. SAM Sources

The SAMS for the developing countries have been adapted from the following sources.

Egypt: Eckhaus, R.S., McCarthy. F.D. and Mohie-Eldin, A. (1981) A Social Accounting Matrix for Egypt (1976) in Journal of Development Economics Oct. 1981.

India: Cole, S. and Meagher, G.A. (1984) Growth and Income Distribution in India, a General Equilibrium Analysis in Cohen, S.I., Cornelisse, P.A., Teekens, R.. and Thorbecke, E. (eds.) The Modelling of Socio-Economic Planning Processes, Gower Publishing, Aldershot.

Indonesia: Biro Pusat Statistik Indonesia (1982) Social Accounting Matrix Indonesia 1975, BPS, Jakarta.

Iran: Pyatt G. and Round, J.I. (1985) Social Accounting Matrixes, Symposium Series, The World Bank Publications Department, Washington D.C.

Kenya: Vander Hoeven, R.E. (1987), Planning for Basic Needs, A Basic Needs Simulation Model Applied to Kenya, Free University Press, Amsterdam.

Sri Lanka: Pyatt, G. and Roe, A. (1977) Social Accounting for Development Planning, Cambridge University Press.

The SAMs for Columbia, Surinam, Korea and Pakistan were constructed by the author and several associates, They are reported upon in detail in Cohen S.I. (1989): Multiplier Analysis in Social Accounting and Input-Output Frameworks, evidence for several countries; in Miller, R.E., Polenske, K.R., and Rose, A.Z. Frontiers in Input-Output Analysis, Oxford University Press.

The SAMS for the European countries have been adapted from the following sources. See also the earlier volume, *Social Accounting for Industrial and Transition Economies*, Cohen, August (2002).

Italy: Civardi M.C.B. and Lenti, R.T. (1990). A SAM for Italy. Paper presented at the conference A SAM for Europe, Universidad Internacional Mendez Pelayo, Valencia, September 1990.

Spain: Kehoe T. et al. (1985) A Social Accounting Matrix for Spain 1980. Working paper 6386, Universidad Autonoma de Barcelona.

Several associates under supervision of the author have constructed the SAMs for the Netherlands, Germany, Hungary and Poland. The SAMs for Hungary were done in collaboration with Revesz, T. and Zalai, E. of Budapest University of Economic Sciences and SAMs for Poland were done in collaboration with Czyzewski, A., Zienkowki, L. and Zolkiewski, Z. of the Research Centre for Economic and Social Studies, Central Statistical Office, Warsaw. More details on the SAMs for Italy, Germany, Netherlands, Spain, Hungary and Poland are found also in Cohen (1993).

Appendix 3. Multiplier Decomposition

Specifically, the SAM can be written as a partitioned coefficient matrix. The A Matrix takes the form of eq. (1).

$$A = \begin{matrix} 0 & 0 & A_{13} & 0 \\ 0 & 0 & 0 & A_{24} \\ 0 & A_{32} & A_{33} & 0 \\ A_{41} & 0 & 0 & A_{44} \end{matrix} \tag{1}$$

A_{13} represents the intersection between wants and households and firms, A_{24} for those between factors and activities, etc. From A separate $\tilde{A}$ and invert to obtain M_1, as in eq. (2).

$$\tilde{A} = \begin{matrix} 0 & 0 & 0 & 0 \\ 0 & 0 & 0 & 0 \\ 0 & 0 & A_{33} & 0 \\ 0 & 0 & 0 & A_{44} \end{matrix} \; , \; M_1 = (I - \tilde{A})^{-1} = \begin{matrix} I & 0 & 0 & 0 \\ 0 & I & 0 & 0 \\ 0 & 0 & (I - \tilde{A}33)^{-1} & 0 \\ 0 & 0 & 0 & (I - \tilde{A}_{44})^{-1} \end{matrix} \tag{2}$$

It is noted that $(I - \tilde{A}_{44})^{-1}$ is nothing more than the Leontief-inverse from the simple sectoral models. It translates original exogenous impulses in final demand into sectoral output. It does not take into account the impact of the composition of endogenous final demand. $(I - \tilde{A}_{33})^{-1}$ fulfills the same role with regard to institutions. It calculates the first round efect of an exogenous increase in institutional income through the transfer mechanisms between the different institutions.

As a result of the separation in eq. (2), we have A^* in eq. (3).

$$A^* = \begin{matrix} 0 & 0 & A_{13}^* & 0 \\ 0 & 0 & 0 & A_{24}^* \\ 0 & A_{32}^* & 0 & 0 \\ A_{41}^* & 0 & 0 & 0 \end{matrix} \tag{3}$$

where:

$$A_{13}^* = A_{13}$$
$$A_{24}^* = A_{24}$$
$$A_{32}^* = (I - \tilde{A}_{33})^{-1} A_{32}$$
$$A_{41}^* = (I - \tilde{A}_{44})^{-1} A_{41}$$

A^* shares some of the properties of a permutation matrix: (1) It contains only one block of non-zero entries within each set of rows and each set of columns. (2) Raising such a matrix to the k-th power does not alter this property, it only shifts the position of each block. All blocks shift at the same time, so there are only four permutations showing different positions of the blocks.

Given $k = 4$ in the SAMs we deal with, one obtains M_2 and M_3 as specified in eqs. (4) and (5), respectively.

$$M_2 = \begin{matrix} I & A_{13}{}^*A_{32}{}^* & A_{13}{}^* & A_{13}{}^*A_{32}{}^*A_{24}{}^* \\[2mm] A_{24}A_{41} & I & A_{24}{}^*A_{41}{}^*A_{13}{}^* & A_{24}{}^* \\[2mm] A_{32}{}^*A_{24}{}^*A_{42}{}^* & A_{32}{}^* & I & A_{32}{}^*A_{24}{}^* \\[2mm] A_{41}{}^* & A_{41}{}^*A_{13}{}^*A_{32}{}^* & A_{41}{}^*A_{13}{}^* & I \end{matrix} \qquad (4)$$

$$M_3 = \begin{matrix} (I-A_{13}{}^*A_{32}{}^*A_{24}{}^*A_{41}{}^*)^{-1} & 0 & 0 & 0 \\[2mm] 0 & (I-A_{24}{}^*A_{41}{}^*A_{13}{}^*A_{32}{}^*)^{-1} & 0 & 0 \\[2mm] 0 & 0 & (I-A_{32}{}^*A_{24}{}^*A_{41}{}^*A_{13}{}^*)^{-1} & 0 \\[2mm] 0 & 0 & 0 & (I-A_{41}{}^*A_{13}{}^*A_{32}{}^*A_{24}{}^*)^{-1} \end{matrix} \qquad (5)$$

Bibliography

Barro, R. J. (1991): Economic Growth in a Cross Section of Countries, in *Quarterly Journal of Economics*, pp. 407-443.

Barro, R. J. and Lee, J. W. (1993): Losers and Winners in Economic Growth, in *Proceedings of the World Bank Annual Conference on Development Economics*, pp. 267-298.

Baumol, W. J. (1986): Productivity Growth, Convergence, and Welfare: What the Long-Run Data Show, in *American Economic Review*, pp. 1072-1185.

Biro Pusat Statistik Indonesia (1982): *Social Accounting Matrix Indonesia 1975*, Vol. I & II, Indonesian Central Bureau of Statistics, Jakarta.

Bleaney, M. and Greenaway, D. (1993): Long-run trends in the Relative Price of Primary Commodities and in the Terms of Trade of Developing Countries, in *Oxford Economic Papers*, Vol. 45, pp. 349-363.

Bojo, J., Maler, K. G. and Unemo, L. (1992): Environment and Development: an economic approach, Kluwer Academic Publishers, Boston.

Bulmer-Thomas, V. (1982): *Input-Output Analysis in Developing Countries*, New York, John Wiley.

Chenery, H. B. and Watanabe, T. (1958): International Comparisons of the Structure of Production, in *Econometrica*, Vol. 26, pp. 487-521.

Cohen, S. I. (1975): *Production Manpower and Social Planning, Korean Applications*. Rotterdam University Press, Rotterdam.

Cohen, S. I. (1977): A Social-Economic Development Model, Korean Applications, in *The Seoul National University Economic Review*, No. II : 1.

Cohen, S. I. (1985): The Labour Force Matrix of Pakistan, Selected Applications, in *Pakistan Development Review*. Vol. XXIV, Nos. 3 & 4. pp. 565-584.

Cohen, S. I. (1987a): Input-output versus Social Accounting in the Macro Analysis of Development, in *Industry and Development*, No. 22.

Cohen, S. I. (1987b): Modelling the Prospects of Economic Growth and Social Development, in *Pakistan Development Review*, Vol. XXVI, 4.

Cohen, S. I. (1988): A Social Accounting Matrix Analysis for the Netherlands, in *De Economist*, Summer 1988, pp. 253-272.

Cohen, S. I. (1989): Multiplier Analysis in Social Accounting and Input-Output Frameworks: Evidence for Several Countries in Miller R. E., Polenske, K. R. and Rose, A. Z.: *Frontiers in Input-Output Analysis*, Oxford University Press.

Cohen, S. I. (ed.) (1993): *Patterns of Economic Restructuring for Eastern Europe*, Avebury, Aldershot.

Cohen, S. I. (1994): *Human Resource Development and Utilization*, Avebury, Aldershot.

Cohen, S. I., Cornelisse, P.A., Thorbecke, E. and Teekens, R., eds. (1984): *The Modelling of Socio-Economic Planning Processes*, Gower Publishing Company, Aldershot.

Cohen, S. I., Havinga, I. and Saleem, M. (1985): A Simple Inter-industry Model of Pakistan, in *Pakistan Development Review.* Vol. XXIV, Nos. 3 & 4. pp. 531-545.

Cohen, S. I. and Jellema, T. (1987): Construction and Analysis of Social Accounting Matrices, an Application to Colombia, in *Kwantitatieve Methoden,* No. 24.

Cole, S. and Meagher, G. A. (1984) Growth and Income Distribution in India, a General Equilibrium Analysis in Cohen S. I., Cornelisse, Teekens, P. A. R. and Thorbecke E., eds.: *The Modelling of Socio-Economic Planning Processes,* Gower Publishing, Aldershot.

Decaluwe, B. and Martens, A. (1988): CGE Modelling and Developing Economies: A Concise Empirical Survey of 73 Applications to 26 Countries, in *Journal of Policy Modelling,* Winter 1988, pp. 529-568.

Defourny, J. and Thorbecke, E. (1984): Structural Path Analysis and MultiplierDecomposition within a Social Accounting Matrix Framework, in *Economic Journal,* Vol. 94, pp. 111-136. See also section on SAM of Korea.

Dervis, K., de Melo, J. and Robinson, S. (1982): *General Equilibrium Models for Development Policy,* Cambridge University Press, New York.

Dewatripont, M. and Michel, G. (1987): On closure rules, homogeneity and dynamics in applied general equilibrium models, in *Journal of Development Economics,* June 1987, 65-76.

Dhanani, S. (1988): A SAM-based General Equilibrium Model of the Pakistan Economy 1983-84, in *The Pakistan Development Review,* Vol. XXVII, No. 4.

Dowrick, S. and Gemmell, N. (1988): Industrialisation, Catching Up a and Economic Growth: A Comparative Study Across The World's Capitalist Economies, in *Economic Journal,* Vol. 101, pp. 263-275.

Eckhaus, R. S., McCarthy, F. D. and Mohie-Eldin, A. (1981): A Social Accounting Matrix for Egypt (1976) in *Journal of Development Economics,* October issue.

Eliasson, G. (1985): *The Firm and Financial Markets in the Swedish Micro-to-Macro Model,* Almqvist & Wicksell International, Stockholm.

Fox, K. A. and Miles, D. G. (1987): Systems economics: concepts, models and multi-disciplinary perspectives, Ames, Iowa: Iowa Satte University Press.

Hayden, C. and Round, J. I. (1980): *Developments in Social Accounting Methods as Applied to the Analysis of Income Distribution and Employment Issues,* Discussion Paper 2, University of Warwick, Warwick.

Hoeven, R. E. van der (1987): *Planning for Basic Needs, A Basic Needs Simulation Model Applied to Kenya,* Free University Press, Amsterdam.

Horlacher, D. E. and MacKellar, F. L. (1988): Population Growth versus Economic Growth, in Salvatore, D. (ed.): *World Population trends and Their Impact on Economic Development:* Greenwood Press, West Port.

King, B. B. (1981): What is SAM? A layman's guide to social accounting matrices, World Bank Staff Working Papers No. 463. The World Bank, Washington D.C.

Koopmans, T. and Montias, J. M. (1971): On the Description and Comparison of Economic Systems, in Eckstein, A. (ed) *Comparison of Economic Systems,* pp. 27-28.

Krugman, P. R. (1981): Trade, Accumulation and Uneven Development, in *Journal of Development Economics*, Vol. 8, pp. 149-161.

Lucas, R. E. (1993), Making a Miracle, in *Econometrica*, Vol. 61, No. 2, pp. 251-272.

Lysy, F. J., and Taylor, L. (1979): Vanishing income redistributions: Keynesian clues about model surprises in the short run, in *Journal of Development Economics*, Vol. 6, No. 1.

Mankiw, N. G., Romer, D. and Weil, D. N. (1992): A Contribution to the Empirics of Economic Growth, in *Quarterly Journal of Economics*, pp. 407-437.

Naqvi, Syed Nawab Haider, *et al.* (1983): *The PIDE Macro-econometric Model of Pakistan's Economy.* Pakistan Institute of Development Economics, Islamabad.

Nerlove, M. (1987): *Population Policy and Individual Choice,* Invited Lecture at The First Annual Conference of the European Society for Population Economics, Erasmus University, Rotterdam.

Pakistan Institute of Development Economics, PIDE (1985): A Social Matrix of *Pakistan, 1979-80.* Volumes I & II. Research reports prepared in the framework of collaborative research between PIDE and Erasmus University Rotterdam, Netherlands.

Pakistan Institute of Development Economics, PIDE (1986): *Socio-economic Development Simulations, A SAM-corresponding Model of Pakistan.* Vols I & II. Research reports prepared in the framework of collaborative research between PIDE and Erasmus University Rotterdam, Netherlands.

Pleskovic, B., and Treviño, G. (1985): *The Use of a Social Accounting Framework for Public Sector Analysis: The Case Study of Mexico,* International Centre for Public Enterprises in Developing Countries, Ljubljana.

Poot, H., Kuyvenhoven, A. and Jansen, J. (1990): *Industrialisation and trade in Indonesia,* Gadjah Mada University Press, Yogyakarta.

Pyatt, G. (1991): Fundamentals of Social Accounting, in: *Economic System Research* 3, pp. 315-341

Pyatt, G. and Roe, A. (1977): Social Accounting for Development Planning, Cambridge University Press. See also chapter on SAM for Sri Lanka.

Pyatt, G. and Round, J. I. (1985): *Social Accounting Matrices,* Symposium Series, World Bank Publications Department, Washington D.C. See also chapter on SAM of Iran.

Robinson, S. (1989): Multisectoral Models, in Chenery, H.B. and Srinivasan, T. N. eds., *Handbook of Development Economics,* North-Holland, Amsterdam.

Robinson, S. and Tyson, L. (1984): Modelling Structural Adjustment: micro and macro elements in a general equilibrium framework, in Scarf, H.E. and Shoven, J. B., *Applied General Equilibrium Analysis*, Cambridge University Press, pp. 243-271.

Salamons, E. (1983): A Social Accounting Matrix of Suriname, Master thesis, Centre for Development Planning, Erasmus University Rotterdam, Rotterdam.

Shoven, J. B. and Whalley, J. (1992): Applying general equilibrium New York, NY, Cambridge University Press

Solow, R. M. (1956): A Contribution to the Theory of Economic Growth, in *Quarterly Journal of Economics*, Vol. 70, pp. 65-94.

Sprout, R. V. A. and Weaver, J. H. (1992): International Distribution of Income: 1960-1987, in *Kyklos*, Vol. 45, pp. 237-258.

Stone, R. (1971*): Demographic Accounting and Model Building* Organisation for Economic Cooperation and Development, Paris.

Stone, J. R. N. (1978): The disaggregation of the household sector in the national accounts, paper presented at the *World Bank Conference on Social Accounting Methods in Development Planning*, Cambridge.

Summers, R. and Heston, A. (1988): A New Set of International Comparisons of Real Product and Price Levels, estimates for 130 countries, in *Review of Income and Wealth*, Vol. 34, pp. 1-25.

Theil, H. and Seale, J. L. (1994): The Geographic Distribution of World Income, 1950-1990, in *De Economist*, Vol. 142, No. 4, pp. 387-419.

Thorbecke, E. (1984): Overview and conclusions, in Cohen, S. I. *et al*: *The Modelling of Socio-Economic Planning Processes*, Gower Publishing, Brookfield, pp. 445-460.

Thorbecke, E. (1990): *Adjustment, Growth and Income Distribution in Indonesia*: OECD Development Center, Paris.

US National Research Council (1986): *Population Growth and Economic Development Policy Questions* National Academy Press, Washington, D.C.

Van Tongeren, F. W. (1993): *Corporates in an Economy-wide Model, a Microsimulation Approach,* Ph.D. Thesis, Erasmus University, Rotterdam.

Wassennan, S. and Faust, K. (1998): Social network analysis: methods and applications New York, NY: Cambridge University Press.

Index

For Product Safety Concerns and Information please contact our EU
representative GPSR@taylorandfrancis.com
Taylor & Francis Verlag GmbH, Kaufingerstraße 24, 80331 München, Germany